Who Decides, and How?

Who Decides, and How?

Preferences, Uncertainty, and Policy Choice in the European Parliament

Nils Ringe

OXFORD
UNIVERSITY PRESS

OXFORD
UNIVERSITY PRESS

Great Clarendon Street, Oxford OX2 6DP

Oxford University Press is a department of the University of Oxford.
It furthers the University's objective of excellence in research, scholarship,
and education by publishing worldwide in

Oxford New York

Auckland Cape Town Dar es Salaam Hong Kong Karachi
Kuala Lumpur Madrid Melbourne Mexico City Nairobi
New Delhi Shanghai Taipei Toronto

With offices in

Argentina Austria Brazil Chile Czech Republic France Greece
Guatemala Hungary Italy Japan Poland Portugal Singapore
South Korea Switzerland Thailand Turkey Ukraine Vietnam

Oxford is a registered trade mark of Oxford University Press
in the UK and in certain other countries

Published in the United States
by Oxford University Press Inc., New York

© Nils Ringe 2010

British Library Cataloguing in Publication Data
Data available

Library of Congress Cataloging in Publication Data
Data available

Typeset by SPI Publisher Services, Pondicherry, India
Printed in Great Britain
on acid-free paper by the
MPG Biddles Group, Bodmin and King's Lynn

ISBN 978–0–19–957255–7

1 3 5 7 9 10 8 6 4 2

Für meinen alten Freund und Lehrer
Klaus Bergmann

Contents

Contents

Acknowledgments

I am indebted to all those who have contributed to the successful realization of this book by providing encouragement and direction, raising concerns, and helping resolve questions along the way. I want to thank Thomas Bräuninger, David Canon, Chris Carman, Mark Copelovitch, Holger Döring, Matthew Gabel, Steffen Ganghof, Michael Goodhart, Justin Gross, Lisbeth Hooghe, Simon Hug, Joseph Jupille, Michael Kaeding, Helen Kinsella, Jimmy Klausen, Jason Koepke, Lothar Krempel, Amie Kreppel, German Lodola, Melanie Manion, B. Guy Peters, Juan Carlos Rodriguez-Raga, George Ross, Sebastian Saiegh, Nadav Shelef, Daniel Thomas, Daniel Treisman, Timo Weishaupt, Jennifer Victor, and Antoine Yoshinaka.

Alberta Sbragia and Mark Hallerberg, in particular, have provided guidance throughout all stages of this project, for which I am deeply grateful. Michael Shackleton has been my "reality check" since I first started my research on the European Parliament as an undergraduate at Brandeis University. I would have to buy him too many lunches in Brussels to ever repay him for his help and support. Dominic Byatt at Oxford University Press has been supportive of this project early on and ensured that I was able to see it through. His confidence and help are greatly appreciated.

I would like to especially thank my respondents (and their staff) in the European Parliament, the European Commission, the Council of Ministers, and a number of Permanent Representations to the European Union (EU). I appreciate their time and generosity in meeting with me and providing captivating opinions and insights into the inner workings of the legislative process of the EU.

This study would not have been possible without funding and research support from the European Union Centers of Excellence at the University of Pittsburgh and the University of Wisconsin, the Max Planck Institute for the Study of Societies in Cologne (Germany), the National Science Foundation, the Andrew Mellon Foundation, and the Graduate School at the University of Wisconsin. I would also like to thank the *American Journal of Political Science* for giving me permission to use previously published materials.

Peter Truby provided research support for which I am grateful, and I thank Mary Stafsholt for her help in preparing my tables and figures.

I want to express deep gratitude to my parents, who have always backed my endeavors unconditionally. Their generosity and support cannot be overestimated. Finally, Sarah Halpern-Meekin is not only my partner in love and life, she is also a colleague whose insights, critiques, and suggestions have been vital in the process of completing this book.

List of Figures

List of Tables

List of Abbreviations

ALDE	Alliance of Liberals and Democrats for Europe
ELDR	European Liberal Democrat and Reform Party
EP	European Parliament
EPP-ED	European People's Party and European Democrats
EU	European Union
EUR	Euro
Greens/EFA	Greens/European Free Alliance
GUE/NGL	European United Left/Nordic Green Left
IND/DEM	Independence/Democracy Group
MEP	Member of the European Parliament
NP	New policy
PES	Party of European Socialists
PPC	Perceived preference coherence
SQ	Status quo
UEN	Union for Europe of the Nations

Chapter 1

Who Decides, and How? Preferences, Uncertainty, and Policy Choice in the European Parliament

What makes the European Parliament (EP) different from other parliaments? The list of answers to this question is long. The EP is the first ever directly elected international parliament in history. It is a genuine law-making assembly, yet part of the institutional structure of what is formally a treaty-based international organization, the European Union (EU). It meets in two cities, Brussels and Strasbourg, in two countries, Belgium and France. No government is drawn from the EP's ranks or fully accountable to it. Members of the EP (MEPs) come from 27 countries; they represent 175 national party delegations comprising seven transnational party groups. The EP conducts its business in the 23 official languages of the EU. The laws it enacts are binding on all 27 member states of the EU, with no national ratification process confirming or challenging these decisions. EP elections take place simultaneously across the EU, but according to national electoral rules and procedures.

Despite these unique features, the literature on the EP and EP politics has provided some striking insights that undermine the notion that the EP is truly a *sui generis* legislature. While the proposition of singularity may be intuitively appealing, it is difficult to sustain in light of what we know about the institution, most importantly that:

- Political conflict in the EP takes place primarily along traditional left-right lines.
- MEPs overwhelmingly vote in accordance with their party affiliations, rather than their national affiliations.
- The party system in the EP has become more consolidated and more competitive as the powers of the EP have increased over time.

- Party group cohesion in the EP is (strikingly) high; that is, EP parties display considerable levels of unity when voting on the EP floor. In fact, while party cohesion in the EP is lower than in national European parliamentary systems, it is actually higher than in the U.S. Congress (Attinà 1990; Raunio 1997; Hix, Noury, and Roland 2007).

These realities indicate that the EP is, indeed, a "normal" legislature in many important ways. This is perhaps the primary contribution that the quantitative analyses of large numbers of votes taken on the EP floor have made over the course of the past decade (see, especially, Hix, Noury, and Roland [2007]). It is also a proposition that this book takes as a starting point, in that it acknowledges the inherent value of treating the EP not as a "one-of-a-kind" legislature, but as an institution that can usefully be compared to traditional national law-making bodies. It does not, however, accept the proposition of normality as its final conclusion. Instead, it considers how this basic insight can be fine-tuned by more in-depth investigations of EU politics. In fact, this analysis of EP politics is grounded in the suspicion that important elements of EP politics are ignored when painting a picture of the institution with too broad a brush. In particular, the primary focus of the existing literature has been on voting patterns in the EP, and thus on political *outcomes*, while we know surprisingly little about the *processes* that precede voting on the EP floor. As McElroy (2007: 439) puts it in a recent review article, we face many questions that can only be answered "by closer examination of the activities of MEPs both within their political groups and within the committee system." In an effort to extend our understanding of EP politics, this book:

- explicitly investigates policy-making processes, not just decision-making outcomes;
- avoids drawing conclusions about individual-level behavior on the basis of aggregate level observations, such as voting patterns on the EP floor; and
- builds on an eclectic methodological approach that combines quantitative and qualitative data and analysis.

The basic question this book seeks to address is "how do individual legislators make decisions in the EP?" It thus examines the micro-foundations of EP politics. Rather than make assumptions about the preferences, behavioral patterns, and political choices of individual legislators, it looks at how legislators adopt the positions they take toward policy proposals, and how these individual positions are aggregated into collective choices. It does not assume exogenous preferences and deduce individual or collective positions, but acknowledges that preferences and policy positions are uncertain and inconsistent, and therefore open to both persuasion and manipulation. This allows for the possibility of discovering nuances that would remain concealed otherwise, and of identifying important particularities that should not be ignored. In other words, this book aims to provide an accurate description and analysis of EP politics while generating generalizable insights into legislative politics beyond the EU arena. It seeks to build theory without neglecting the "real world" of EP politics. Today this is more important than ever, as the EP is no longer the consultative "talking shop" it once was, but an institution with extensive authority that plays a critical role in EU politics.

The focus on the individual legislator does not, however, mean that the structural and institutional framework within which legislative decisions are made is neglected. In fact, a primary contribution of the micro-level approach is that it takes the "politics" in "EP politics" seriously while explicitly conceptualizing it as a *dynamic process* based on the *interplay* of institutions and individuals. By considering how individual legislators make policy decisions, and how their positions are aggregated into collective choices, I seek to shed light not only on how policies are agreed on in the EP, but also on the institutional context that structures, supports, and constrains decision-making, including the roles of EP parties and committees.

The micro-level analysis provides for new insights into EP politics beyond those based on large-N analyses of voting patterns. What is more, it casts doubt on some of the key conclusions derived from these studies, in particular those related to the role of legislative parties. Most importantly, it challenges prevailing conceptualizations of EP politics that emphasize the ability of legislative parties to control the behavior of their members through successfully enforced party discipline. Instead, the book shows that policy-making in the EP is a more dynamic process than the existing literature suggests and provides a new answer to one of the most intriguing empirical questions about EP politics, namely what accounts for the surprisingly high levels of party unity we observe in the voting behavior of EP party groups. The answer undermines the notions that either party discipline or legislators' shared policy preferences can account for party cohesion in the EP, and highlights a dynamic decision-making process based on the exchange of political and policy information between legislative experts and nonexperts.

The degree of cohesion of EP party groups is striking given the great degree of ideological, partisan, and national heterogeneity of the legislature. The extant literature has explained this phenomenon largely in reference to successfully executed party control (e.g., Hix [2002]; Hix, Noury, and Roland [2005]; Hix, Noury, and Roland 2007; Bowler [2002]). The basic argument of this research is that party groups are, in one way or another, capable of disciplining their members and coercing them into following the party line. This conclusion is intuitively appealing and attractive due to its parsimony, but it is problematic on both theoretical and empirical grounds. Theoretically, the party control argument is informed by a functionalist, backward reasoning, where the observation of high levels of party cohesion has led commentators to argue that it must be due to party discipline. Thus, problematic inferences are drawn about how individuals make decisions on the EP floor, based on the aggregate-level finding of party cohesion, when in fact evidence for party groups disciplining their members is sparse. Simply put, the causal relationship between party control and party cohesion has not been fully interrogated.

In empirical terms, it is difficult not to recognize the structural weakness of EP party groups, who do not possess the traditional tools of party control and the capacity to satisfy their members' vote- or office-seeking ambitions. For example, EP party groups do not have the power to exclude individual members from electoral lists and thus threaten their reelection, because it is the national parties that draw up the party lists for elections to the EP. Moreover, while EP party groups have the ability to provide some positive incentives for cooperation in the form of office perks, these incentives do not seem to be a sufficient condition for party cohesion on the EP floor. This is because the great majority of MEPs is unlikely to have a long-enough time horizon, due to substantial turnover in EP elections, to trade payoffs in the present for uncertain office benefits in the future. Moreover, party groups are bound by internal rules of proportionality in the distribution of official positions within the EP and the party structure, where national party delegations are allocated a certain number of positions based on their sizes (Kreppel 2002). As a result, party groups are quite constrained in their ability to credibly promise office perks to individual legislators most loyal to the party line.

We thus have reason to believe, *a priori*, that factors other than party discipline may account for the high levels of EP party unity. The legislative studies literature provides an obvious alternative explanation for party cohesion, which focuses on legislators' shared preferences. This logic suggests that parties are cohesive because their members are not part of random groups of individuals, but of collectives of politicians who join together to promote a set of core ideas and values in the creation of public policy. Accordingly, they share each other's preferences with regard to the policies they enact, which explains high levels of party unity. The assumption that shared preferences drive party cohesion in EP politics is also problematic, however, because it implies that legislators are actually capable of identifying or defining their own policy preferences across a great range of issue areas. Yet, we should not assume that legislators have well-defined preferences with regard to a multitude of decisions on the very broad range of policy areas with which they are confronted. While legislators should, in principle, be generalists who can make equally informed decisions regarding border security, antitrust legislation, trade policy, emission standards, intellectual property rights, work safety regulation, international affairs, and a multitude of other issues, in reality all legislators face high opportunity costs in reaching the levels of expertise necessary to make well-grounded choices in even a limited number of policy areas. Hence, when seeking to establish how legislators make decisions, we should recognize that it may be quite difficult, if not impossible, for them to determine their policy positions with regard to every single legislative proposal they have to consider and vote on. Given limited time and resources, how a policy choice relates to a legislator's most preferred policy outcome is often highly uncertain in a context of competing interests, substantive uncertainty, and asymmetrically distributed information.

Despite the uncertain relationship between political intentions and consequences, however, much of the existing literature on policy choice in legislative politics assumes that the conversion of ideological and constituency interests into policy preferences and positions is direct and automatic, that is, that preferences are fixed and exogenous and simply constitute an "input" into the legislative decision-making process. This approach assumes, implicitly or explicitly, that some kind of "objective interest" underlies the choices of political decision-makers. I question this proposition from the start and, as I will argue in more detail in the next chapter and illustrate throughout the book, it is indeed a reality in EP politics that its members suffer from a distinct "informational deficit": MEPs are severely constrained in terms of the time and resources that they can allocate toward evaluating the great number of often highly technical pieces of EU legislation. Under these circumstances, how do MEPs make decisions on issues outside their particular areas of specialization, while remaining confident that their policy choices approximate their most preferred policy outcomes?

This question constitutes the starting point for the argument proposed in this book. Its core thesis maintains that when MEPs have to make decisions on issues outside their areas of expertise, they adopt the positions of their EP colleagues who possess genuine expertise in the policy area under consideration. In the EP, this expertise is grounded in the responsible EP committees, which suggests that EP committees are, in the language of the U.S. Congress literature, informational committees that help the legislature and its members reap the benefit of specialization (Krehbiel 1991; McElroy 2006). As repositories of policy expertise, committees provide information about the content and likely consequences of a policy proposal to the chamber and thereby help legislators make informed choices when voting on the floor.

Nonexpert MEPs do not just follow any policy specialist, however, since they have to be concerned with the consequences of the legislation they enact. Therefore, they adopt the positions of their expert colleagues in the responsible committee whose preferences they believe most closely match their own. This is based on the assumption that these positions resemble what they *would* favor *if* they possessed the resources and expertise required to truly judge the content and likely implications of a specific policy proposal. The critical mechanism explaining the policy choice of MEPs is thus what I label *perceived preference coherence* (PPC) between expert and nonexpert legislators.

This argument does not imply that preferences alone, based on *objective* preference coherence, drive policy choice. After all, this would suggest that legislators not only know their own preferences, but also that they have the capacity to objectively compare their preferences to those of their expert colleagues. For this to be true, we would have to assume full content expertise (i.e., technical knowledge of the issues under negotiation) and preference information (i.e., knowledge of other actors' preferences and political constraints) (Wall and Lynn 1993; Beach 2005). This assumption is highly problematic in any political setting, never mind a legislative institution suffering from an informational deficit. Moreover, if legislators could actually identify their own preferences on every policy issue, they would not have to rely on their expert colleagues for information in the first place. For these reasons, I maintain that nonexpert legislators make decisions on the basis of perceived preference coherence: They adopt the positions of those expert colleagues with whom they *believe* to share general preferences regarding the expected consequences of a policy once it has been enacted and implemented. This provides for the possibility of errors in perception and, as a result, a divergence between perceived preference coherence and actual preference coherence. The best that legislators can do in the absence of full information about the policy preferences and positions of their expert colleagues, however, is to rely on those with whom they share a common set of preferences about the most desired political outcomes.

Who are these colleagues with whom MEPs perceive to share these outcome preferences? In a parliament in which political contestation takes place principally along the socioeconomic left-right divide, we should expect the outcome preferences of nonexpert legislators to be primarily ideology-based. This suggests that legislators Perceive to share a common set of outcome preferences with colleagues with the same partisan affiliation. Hence, we would expect perceived preference coherence to be highest among legislators from the same party, and that nonexpert legislators use shared party affiliation as an indicator of common preferences concerning the likely implications of a policy choice. Yet, EP politics are not completely de-territorialized; while members of transnational party groups, MEPs are also representatives of national constituencies who have to be concerned about the consequences of their policy decisions for their member states. If we assume that MEP outcome preferences are both ideology- and constituency-based, we would expect that members of the EP perceive the greatest degree of outcome preference coherence with members of their national party delegations, which together comprise the EP's transnational party groups. For example, a German Social Democrat would perceive her preference ideal points to most closely match those of other German Social Democrats in the responsible committee. This is because as members of the same national party, their ideological preferences most likely approximate each other, while their common national affiliation helps ensure that particular national interests will be accounted for.

This logic only provides for cohesive national party delegations in the EP, however, not for cohesive positions of the transnational EP party groups they collectively comprise. It is quite likely though that committee specialists from different national party delegations within the same party group assume a common policy position most of the time, for two reasons. First, in order to see their most preferred outcomes approximated, policy specialists from individual national party delegations have to coordinate and compromise with their party group colleagues in committee. They can only hope to shape legislation if they are able to arrive at a party group line that is broadly acceptable across national party delegations—and they know it. Second, committee deliberation involves only a relatively small number of members from the same party group, among whom it is much easier to coordinate collective action than in the party plenary. If this coordination is successful, the common position they propose toward a given policy proposal is likely adopted as the formal line of their EP party group.

In fact, party positions are not imposed from above by the party group leadership, as my empirical analyses will show, but they constitute the endogenous products of deliberation and cooperation among party group colleagues in the responsible committee. This common party position, which is successfully established among the party group's policy experts in the committee, is then adopted by the party's nonexpert rank and file on the basis of perceived preference coherence, which means that the party will be cohesive when voting on the EP floor. In other words, the foundation for cohesive policy positions of EP party groups lies in the perceived preference coherence between members of the same EP party group, as long as the party group policy experts in the responsible committee present a united position to their nonexpert colleagues. This, I argue, is the "normal" decision-making procedure in the EP, which accounts for most of its policy decisions.

The PPC dynamic facilitates legislative decision-making in that it allows the great majority of legislators, who do not possess specialized knowledge about the content and consequences of the majority of policies they enact, to make relatively informed decisions across a great range of policy issues. Moreover, the consequences of these decisions are likely to approximate their most preferred outcomes, since the party label—as a proxy for common preferences concerning the consequences of legislation upon its implementation—serves as an efficient and reliable decision-making shortcut.

One of the key premises of the model presented here is that policy experts in the EP's informational committees provide the input into the PPC dynamic, which suggests that the EP's standing committees and its members, rather than the party groups, are at the heart of EP decision-making. Politics in the EP thus appears to be an example of (informational) committee government, where committees are the primary actors setting the agenda and determining the policy content of legislation. The PPC model, however, assigns a critically important role to parties in the EP, because it is joint party affiliation that provides the basis for perceived preference coherence. This is a first important party effect in EP politics. A second one comes into play in the pre-floor stage of the legislative process, when members of the same EP party group coordinate and compromise among themselves to establish a common position in committee that forms the basis of their party group's formal party line.

For these reasons, there is no inherent conflict between the delegation of policy-making authority to informational committees and the realization of partisan policy objectives. The PPC dynamic effectively provides legislative parties and their leaderships with the ultimate asset in realizing their policy objectives, namely informed policy choice and high levels of voting cohesion among party members. We should, therefore, expect high levels of party cohesion even in the absence of successfully enforced party discipline.

This suggests that parties in the EP play a different role in the policy-making process than national parties. Rather than acting as top-down enforcers of party discipline like their hierarchically structured counter-parts at the national level, EP party groups serve as an umbrella for MEPs with similar preferences concerning the expected consequences of a law (Eldersveld 1964; Sorauf 1964). Policy positions in the EP are party-based only in the sense that joint partisanship promotes and facilitates the creation of policy agreement through information provision from experts to nonexperts. This crucial observation is built on the examination of EP decision-making from the perspective of the individual MEP. Rather than make assumptions about individual behavior on the basis of aggregate-level voting trends, I explain how individual legislators make decisions, and how their aggregated behavior then accounts for the final policy decisions taken collectively on the EP floor.

Outline of the book

This introductory chapter presents descriptive information on members, parties, and committees in the EP, including a brief review of the relevant literature. Subsequently, Chapter 2 elaborates on the concept of perceived preference coherence as the primary factor explaining policy choice in the EP. It concludes with a series of explicit hypotheses derived from the PPC model and juxtaposes these expectations with the propositions of the party control model, which explains party cohesion by emphasizing the ability of legislative parties to coerce their members into voting the party line, and the shared preferences model, which maintains that party unity on the EP floor is due to *actual* (not perceived) preference coherence between legislators from the same party group.

Chapter 3 is structured around these hypotheses and provides a first set of empirical results based on both qualitative interview data and the quantitative analysis of legislative votes. The first part of the chapter presents general lessons about the flow of information from committees to the EP plenary. Drawing on 90 in-depth interviews with members of the EP and EU officials, the analysis casts doubt on the shared preferences and party control arguments, while supporting the propositions of the PPC model. First, it shows that MEPs do not have well-defined preferences with regard to most legislative proposals with which they are confronted, not because they are too lazy or apathetic to derive these preferences, but because the EP's informational deficit constrains their ability to make fully informed choices across the great range of policy issues they deal with on a daily basis. This suggests that shared preferences concerning policy proposals cannot explain cohesive EP party positions, because with regard to most issues most MEPs do not know what their positions ought to be independent of input from their expert colleagues. Second, it demonstrates that the formal positions that EP party groups assume toward specific policy proposals are formulated endogenously in the responsible EP committee. In other words, these positions are not put forward by the party group leaderships, but rather develop out of internal committee coordination by transnational party group representatives from different national party delegations. Moreover, the qualitative data shows that party groups are even more constrained in their ability to discipline their rank and file than is commonly assumed, because the ability of party group leaderships to provide access to positions of power within the legislative and party structures is even more limited than often suggested. As the chapter demonstrates, the EP party groups' formal authority to serve as gatekeepers to positions of legislative influence is constrained by a norm of proportionality that distributes such positions across national party delegations.

While disconfirming the propositions of the party control and shared preferences models, Chapter 3 provides support for the hypotheses derived from the PPC logic. Aside from showing that party positions are endogenous to the political process in committee, it stresses the importance of coordination among committee colleagues when formulating these positions. It is coordination, rather than coercion, that ensures party unity. Finally, it tests the proposition that the positions of members of the responsible committee constitute potent predictors of voting patterns on the EP floor, that is, that MEPs in plenary follow those representatives in committee with whom they perceive to share a common set of outcome preferences. The analysis confirms this proposition in a multinomial regression analysis involving 122 parliamentary votes and 52,363 individual-level observations.

Chapter 4 returns to some key theoretical considerations. Most importantly, it problematizes a core assumption of the PPC model as presented up until that point, namely that nonexpert MEPs blindly adopt the policy positions of "their" expert colleagues when making choices on legislation with often important consequences for EU citizens. Recognizing that this assumption is questionable, the chapter introduces the distinction between *indifferent* and *invested* legislators. The former are legislators who do not care enough about a particular policy proposal to demand information about how it relates to their most preferred outcome. These legislators act as the unrefined PPC model suggests: They simply adopt the positions of their expert colleagues with whom they perceive to share common outcome preferences. Invested legislators, however, care enough about a particular policy proposal to seek reassurance that their outcome preferences have been accounted for by their expert colleagues. They are not indifferent, and therefore they do not just want to know what position to take with regard to a particular legislative dossier, but also *why* they ought to take this position. In other words, they want to know how the proposal relates to their most preferred outcomes. Chapter 4 introduces a second core theoretical concept into the discussion to account for this reality and argues that the supply mechanism for such information comes in the form of *focal points* (Ringe 2005). These focal points are simplified images about the expected implications of the legislation upon its implementation. They are provided by specialist legislators in the responsible EP committees, who condense the minutiae of a given legislative proposal into concise evaluations that indicate to their nonexpert colleagues why they should support or oppose the legislation. Hence, expert legislators use focal points to link the normative and ideological preferences of their nonexpert colleagues to positions on specific policy proposals.

From the point of view of the receiver, these focal points are shorthand devices for communicating information: They shift attention toward particular aspects of a legislative proposal, thus helping to classify and evaluate its perceived content and consequences. By shaping the process of deliberation, focal points serve as a means to establish mutually acceptable general positions toward a policy proposal, thus providing a common theme around which policy coalitions can form. However, just like nonexpert MEPs would not adopt the positions of just any policy expert, they are also not equally receptive to all focal points. Only if they perceive to share a common set of preferences concerning desirable policy outcomes with the provider of focal points will they accept and act upon their input. In other words, perceived preference coherence is again key to understanding policy choice.

Chapter 5 examines the role of focal points as mechanisms of information provision by analyzing a series of legislative proposals as case studies. It draws on the interview data and the statistical analysis of individual final votes on the EP floor. This chapter confirms the core insights of the PPC model, while illustrating how focal points shape EP policy-making processes and outcomes. That is, while Chapter 3 demonstrates that the policy positions of expert legislators determine the positions of their nonexpert colleagues on the EP floor, Chapter 5 shows how this process takes place for invested nonexpert legislators. The legislative proposals analyzed concern EU takeover legislation; the statute and financing of EU-level political parties; proposals on fuel quality and motor vehicle emissions; liability for environmental damage; the liberalization of port services in the EU; and EU citizenship and the free movement of people.

Finally, Chapter 6 synthesizes the findings and outlines the book's contributions. Primarily, the book enhances our understanding of the behavioral patterns of individual members of the EP and, in the process, sheds new light on the inner workings of one of the primary institutions of the EU. In particular, it provides new insights into EP politics by going beyond the analysis of EP voting records and looking at the processes of policy creation and policy choice. This allows us to better understand how individual MEPs make decisions and what role legislative institutions, such as parties and (informational) committees, play in this process. One of the most important parts of the story told in this book is its unique explanation for the high levels of party cohesion in the EP, which suggests that party cohesion in the EP would be high even in the absence of party discipline. In other words, party unity is the result of a dynamic decision-making process in which coercion plays a residual role, since EP party groups neither formulate formal, endogenous policy positions toward most legislative proposals, nor do they have the capacity to enforce them.

The theory of legislative decision-making presented in this book takes the powers that political actors lack as a starting point. It is based on the recognition that political actors face important constraints, and explicitly theorizes the behavior of legislative actors in light of their structural weaknesses. For example, EP party groups do not have the ability to control their rank and file through party discipline, while individual legislators do not have the expertise and resources to independently determine their positions with regard to most legislative proposals. These constraints are not assumed away, but rather incorporated into the explanatory model.

This model also makes a general contribution to our understanding of legislative politics by providing a generalizable explanation of how legislators make decisions under conditions of uncertainty, while maintaining a semblance of democratic accountability. The concepts of perceived preference coherence and focal points, while conceived of in the context of EP politics, could be applied in other legislative contexts. In fact, their applicability might well go beyond the legislative sphere and help explain dynamics of delegation and decision-making in contexts of uncertainty and asymmetrically distributed information across a variety of political arenas.

The mixed method approach used is critical to the story told in this book, as it allows us to analyze both political processes and political outcomes. This prevents us from deriving conclusions about the behavior of individual legislators on the basis of aggregate-level observations. Using mixed methods to examine EP politics also enables us to critically assess alternative theoretical explanations for MEP policy choice that predict observationally equivalent policy outcomes. This novel account of EP politics is thus the result of combining the respective strengths of qualitative and quantitative research, and it draws a picture of legislative politics that is about much more than sanctions and rewards, as the party control argument suggests. It is also, and crucially, about shared and contradictory preferences, constraining and facilitating institutions, political information, deliberation and contestation, persuasion, and at times about manipulation. It is, in other words, about politics.

The EP: members, parties, and committees

The legislative role of the EP

Over the course of the last three decades, the EP has become an equal partner of the Council of Ministers, where the EU member states are directly represented by ministers of the national governments, in most important areas of legislation. While the right to initiate legislation lies with the European Commission, a collegial EU executive appointed by the member states but charged with acting in the general European interests, most proposals for EU law must receive the approval of both EP and Council. In fact, a "draft directive" introduced by the Commission is truly only a draft version (Corbett, Jacobs, and Shackleton 2007: 3, 9), with MEPs and members of the Council in turn going through the proposal sentence by sentence. After much rewriting and amending, the positions of the two institutions must be reconciled. In practice, this means that a large number—more than 80 percent—of amendments tabled by MEPs ultimately become law (Kreppel 2002, 2006).

The extent of the EP's legislative powers depends on the decision-making procedure applicable to particular pieces of legislation. It is only with the recent introduction of the "codecision procedure" through the Treaties of Maastricht (1993), Amsterdam (1997), and Nice (2001), that the EP became a genuine co-legislator. Codecision now covers the majority of policy areas and has become the *de facto* "normal" decision-making procedure. It is only one of four decision-making procedures governing the EP's legislative role, however, which apply depending on the policy area of the proposal in question. The other three are the consultation procedure, the cooperation procedure, and the assent procedure. The *consultation procedure* was the EU's main legislative procedure historically. It is used much less today, but remains applicable to important institutional and budgetary matters, as well as certain aspects of citizens' rights and justice and home affairs.[1] Under this procedure the EP gives its consultative opinion on a Commission proposal, but the Council is not bound by the EP's position.

While the EP provides its opinion only once under the consultation procedure, the *cooperation procedure* provides for two parliamentary readings. After consideration by the Council the text is referred back to the EP for a second reading at which time the EP may approve the text, reject the text, or propose amendments. The Commission may incorporate any additional amendments into the text, which can then only be modified by unanimity in the Council. Amendments not supported by the Commission also require unanimous support to be adopted in the Council. Hence, under the cooperation procedure the EP's role is no longer merely consultative. The scope of the procedure is quite limited, however, as it only applies to some narrow aspects of Economic and Monetary Union.[2]

Under the *assent procedure*, the Council must attain the EP's assent before certain important decisions can be taken. While the EP thus has the power to accept or reject a proposal, with a rejection being final, it does not have the power of amendment. The assent procedure applies today to very few issue areas, including decisions with regard to sanctions against EU member states in the case of "serious and persistent breach of fundamental rights" (Article 7), aspects of EU central banking, structural funds,[3] and international agreements.

Finally, the *codecision procedure* is the primary legislative procedure by which European laws are created today. Codecision provides the EP with the power to adopt legislation jointly with the Council of Ministers. It makes the two institutions equal partners in the legislative process by requiring them to agree on an identical text before a proposal becomes law. A conciliation committee featuring an equal number of members from the EP and the Council is set up when the two bodies cannot reach agreement after two parliamentary readings. This committee seeks to negotiate a compromise text subject to approval by both institutions.[4] Under codecision, the EP and the Council have the power to reject a proposal either at second reading or following conciliation, causing the entire procedure to lapse and the proposal to fail. Codecision was introduced in the Maastricht Treaty on European Union, but its scope was expanded considerably by the Treaties of Amsterdam and Nice. Today, about 80 percent of legislation is decided under the codecision procedure.[5] The volume of codecision dossiers has increased dramatically just during the last few years. While only 165 codecision acts were adopted during the 1994–9 legislative term, this number increased to 403 during the 1999–2004 term, after the Treaty of Amsterdam increased the number of areas covered by the procedure from 15 to 32 (Corbett, Jacobs, and Shackleton 2007: 226).

This study focuses on EP decision-making under the codecision procedure, which warrants a more detailed description of this process. It begins with a legislative proposal being drafted and introduced by the Commission and considered independently by both EP and Council. The EP appoints a member of the EP committee responsible for the proposal as the "rapporteur," who is usually an MEP with expert knowledge in the issue area in question.[6] The rapporteur has three primary responsibilities:

- incorporating the EP's amendments into the draft proposal (containing suggested amendments as well as statements of reasons behind these amendments),
- steering the proposal through the different stages of the legislative process, and
- negotiating compromise both within the EP and with the other two institutions: Council of Minister and Commission.

Rapporteurs are chosen by a system whereby each party group receives a quota of points according to its size. Reports to be allocated are discussed by the group coordinators who decide on the number of points an individual report is "worth." They then make bids on different reports on behalf of their party group until they have used up their quota. Existing research concerning the distribution of rapporteurships has produced contradictory results. While Mamadouh and Raunio (2002) and Benedetto (2005) argue that the division of rapporteurships between party groups is largely representative of their size, other research indicates that the distribution is hardly proportional among party groups and national party delegations within the committee (Kaeding 2004, 2005). Hoyland (2006) maintains that MEPs from national parties represented in the Council of Ministers are more active on codecision dossiers than those not represented, while Kaeding (2004) points to differences related to background, expertise, and constituency interests as factors accounting for the active involvement of MEPs in the legislative decision-making process as rapporteurs.

The rapporteur's report is discussed and voted on in the responsible committee. Any MEP may table amendments at the committee stage, but most amendments are tabled by members of the responsible committee. If parts of the proposal fall into their given jurisdictions, other committees may also be asked for an opinion report, but their amendments are subject to a vote in the responsible committee before the report is submitted to the plenary. After this, the report is referred to the EP plenary for debate and a vote during the first parliamentary reading. The finished report is voted on in full plenary, where further amendments may be introduced to the existing text by the responsible committee, EP party groups or at least 40 MEPs. The report must be adopted by a simple majority, that is, the majority of MEPs taking part in the vote. There is no formal time limit on the first parliamentary reading.

Before the proposal is forwarded to the Council of Ministers, the Commission may alter its initial legislative proposal to incorporate EP amendments that, in its view, improve the initial proposal and/or are likely to facilitate an agreement. The Council can do one of two things in its first reading. First, it may accept the text as adopted in Parliament, which ends the legislative process with the proposal coming into effect as amended by the EP. Alternatively, the Council may reject the text as it is and formulate a *common position* among the member state governments. This common position usually accepts some of the amendments of the EP in order to facilitate a compromise with Parliament in subsequent stages of the decision-making process, but may reject all EP amendments.

Within three months of the Council's common position Parliament must conduct its second reading or formally extend the timetable by one month; otherwise, the common position enters into force. In second reading, the EP can either adopt changes to the common position or reject it entirely, which would end the codecision procedure at this point in time. For both options, an absolute majority of MEPs is needed, that is, more than 50 percent of the total number of members, and strict rules govern the introduction of amendments in second reading.[7] Most importantly, amendments adopted in first reading may be retabled if they were not accepted by the Council; amendments may be concerned with a part of the common position which did not appear in, or is substantially different from, the Commission's initial proposal; amendments may be introduced as a compromise between the positions of the EP and the Council.

In second reading, the text is first discussed in the responsible committee, following the same rules and practices as in first reading. The only difference is that the text to be amended is the Council's common position and not the Commission's initial proposal. Also, the parliamentary committees which were asked for an opinion in first reading are not consulted again. While the lead committee adopts the report in second reading by simple majority, the text must be approved by an absolute majority of MEPs. The EP may also reject the common position in second reading, which ends the legislative procedure, but has rarely exercised this prerogative to this date. Usually, the text is amended and referred back to the Council. At this point, one of three things will happen. First, Council may adopt the proposal including the changes proposed by the EP. Second, it may reject the text completely, causing the proposal to fail. Third, the two institutions may enter conciliation.

The conciliation committee is composed of an equal number of MEPs and representatives from the Council and tries to forge a compromise text acceptable to both institutions. Negotiations are conducted during informal trialogue meetings involving small teams of negotiators from each institution, with the Commission playing a mediating role (hence the name "trialogue"). The participants in these trialogues report to their respective institutions, which must approve the results of their negotiations. In the end, conciliation has two possible outcomes. If the committee fails to come up with an agreement, the proposal is withdrawn and the procedure lapses. If the conciliation committee does succeed in agreeing on a compromise text, however, this text goes into third reading, in which either the EP or the Council may reject the proposal. In this case, the text is withdrawn and the proposal fails. If, on the other hand, the text is adopted by both institutions, the proposal enters into force.

In sum, the EP is truly a co-legislator with the Council under codecision. This conclusion is clear both in terms of the number of successful amendments and the substantive impact on proposed legislation (Judge and Earnshaw 2003: 291). Accordingly, it is increasingly inappropriate to view the EP, as once was the norm and remains popular, as a "powerless, money-wasting 'talking shop'" (Peterson and Bomberg 1999: 43).

Members and parties

MEPs have been elected every five years since 1979. A large number of MEPs have extensive political experience. For example, 28 percent of MEPs in the 1999–2004 parliamentary term (the fifth term) had national parliamentary experience, a number that increased to 36.6 percent in the 2004–9 legislature (the sixth term). Often, these MEPs held important posts, such as Speaker or Deputy Speaker. 10.2 percent in the fifth term and 16 percent in the sixth term have national ministerial experience, and many MEPs hold leadership positions in their national parties. Six MEPs in the fifth term and 11 in the sixth term are former heads of state or prime ministers, and numerous members have previously served as regional presidents, state or regional prime ministers, members of the European Commission, or held other posts in regional and municipal governments (Corbett, Jacobs, and Shackleton 2007: 48–54).

MEPs sit in transnational party groups. Currently, there are seven such party groups comprised of 175 national party delegations. The two largest party groups are the center-right group of the European People's Party and European Democrats (EPP-ED, consisting of Conservatives and Christian-Democrats) and the center-left Socialist group in the EP (comprised of Europe's Social Democrats from the Party of European Socialists, PES). Smaller groups are the group of the Alliance of Liberals and Democrats for Europe (ALDE, previously the group of the European Liberal Democrat and Reform Party, ELDR),[8] the group of the Greens/European Free Alliance (Greens/EFA), the group of the European United Left/Nordic Green Left (GUE/NGL), the Independence/Democracy group (IND/DEM), and the group of the Union for Europe of the Nations (UEN).

The leadership of EP party groups is composed of a chair, vice-chairs, treasurer, and others. Leaderships vary in size and influence, but they do constitute influential players within the party structure. Group chairs, for example, speak on behalf of the party group and represent the group in official parliamentary forums. The party group leadership is supported by a staff whose size is based on its number of members and working languages.

Most members tend to follow the collective position, or "party line," of their party groups. Recent analyses of EP voting patterns highlight the continuous increase over time of both party group cohesion and ideology-based party competition. While earlier research already suggested that MEPs are more likely to vote along transnational party lines than national lines (Attinà 1990; Brzinski 1995; Hix and Lord 1997; Raunio 1997), more comprehensive roll-call vote analyses confirm that MEPs vote in accordance with their party affiliations, rather than their national affiliations. In fact, roll-call vote analyses confirm that EP party groups are "remarkably cohesive party organizations" (Hix, Noury, and Roland 2005: 216; see also Hix [2001]; Noury [2002]; Thomassen, Noury, and Voeten [2004]). Moreover, these recent roll-call vote studies demonstrate that policy contestation in the EP takes place along two substantively important dimensions, namely the traditional left-right ideological divide and a pro-/anti-EU dimension ranging from more to less support for the European integration process (see also Han [2007]; McElroy and Benoit [2007]), and that the distance between parties on the left-right dimension is the strongest predictor of interparty group coalition patterns (Hix, Noury, and Roland 2005, 2007). Such findings indicate that the party system in the EP has become more consolidated and more competitive as the powers of the EP have increased over time (Hix, Kreppel, and Noury 2003).

National party delegations play an important part in the structure of the EP party group, and most of them even have their own officers and staff (which tend to be quite small, however). National party delegations constitute the direct link between national parties and EP party groups, meet collectively as subsets of the party group, and often assume a common position and act as a cohesive bloc in party group discussions. Moreover, positions within the party groups are distributed on the basis of the sizes of the national party delegations that comprise them. As a result, larger national party delegations are in a very potent bargaining position within their EP party groups (Raunio 1996: 72). Finally, it is the national parties that draw up electoral lists in EP elections. In rare instances, national party delegations receive specific voting instructions from their national leadership, but most of the time they act as their own principals while engaging in a continuous exchange of views and information with their national party leaderships. In general, however, there is no single leadership group that fully controls the activities and vote choices of individual MEPs (Kreppel 2006: 260).

While the literature on the development of the EP and its party groups has generally found their authority to be increasing, party groups in the EP remain structurally and organizationally weak compared to their counterparts in national parliamentary systems. Most importantly, EP groups are themselves made up of full, sovereign political parties, making it more difficult for the party groups to "bind the parts" (Lord 1998: 205). This makes them different from the internally hierarchical, strong parties in West European parliamentary systems.

The committee system of the EP

The EP's permanent committee structure has been described as its "legislative backbone" (Westlake 1994: 191). In effect, "the work of the EP is the work of committees" (Kreppel and Gungor 2006: 7) as most of the detailed parliamentary work is conducted in and by committees, the majority of substantive changes and compromises are constructed inside the committee, and committee work is the most time-consuming activity for parliamentarians and defines the focus of their work. As the powers of the EP have increased over time, so has the role of its committees in shaping legislation. EP committees today are more active and influential than their counterparts in national European parliaments.[9]

The number, sizes, and responsibilities of the committees are decided in the early days of a newly elected Parliament. They are confirmed after two and a half years, at the mid-point of the parliamentary term. The 2004–9 EP has a total of 20 committees. This number is up from 17 during the 1999–2004 parliamentary term.[10] Committees vary substantially in size; during the 1999–2004 parliamentary term, for example, the Environment Committee had 56 members and the Legal Affairs Committee only 30. Membership is effectively decided by the EP party groups through the use of proportional representation of both party groups and nationalities, in such a way that the composition of each committee reflects the balance between the party groups in plenary. As a result, their composition broadly reflects that of the EP as a whole (McElroy 2006). The majority of MEPs serve on one committee each as a full member and a substitute.

Committees act as largely autonomous entities within the EP. All legislative proposals are referred directly and without debate to the responsible committee, which examines and deliberates the proposed legislation before returning it to the plenary in the form of a draft report. Committees are not only the main repositories of policy expertise in the EP, they also have important gatekeeping powers within their areas of jurisdiction (Kreppel 2006: 250). In fact, one could very well make a reasonable case that EP committees are more powerful than EP party groups. EP committees are more active and powerful than their counterparts in other national parliaments; they are more like committees in the U.S. Congress. EP committees propose amendments to legislation in the form of a report and a draft resolution, and although amendments can be initiated on the EP floor, they usually come out of the responsible committee. Legislative reports are submitted to the EP plenary in an almost "take-it-or-leave-it" form (Hix 1999: 78).

The EP's committee system provides members with the opportunity to acquire and make use of existing expertise in specific policy areas. As a result, committees in the EP can fulfill their role as formal mechanisms of establishing a division of labor among legislators of (nominally) equal status (Judge and Earnshaw 2003) and facilitate legislative decision-making by providing "economies of operation" (Mattson and Strøm 1995). This leads to efficiency gains, as legislation is processed more quickly than if the plenary as a whole were involved collectively, and promotes specialization and expertise to deal with "problems of complexity, technicality and information overload" (Judge and Earnshaw 2003, see also Bowler and Farrell [1995]; Kasack [2004]; Selck and Steunenberg [2004]). Much like the permanent committees with fixed jurisdictions in the U.S. Congress, the jurisdictional organization of EP committees is based on the need to specialize, and its committees have considerable influence on the legislative agenda.

Each committee has one chair and four vice-chairs, who are elected by the committee members. In practice, however, these positions are carefully distributed by agreement among the party groups based on their number of members. The chairs preside over the meetings of the committee, speak on its behalf at plenary sessions, and represent it at the regular meetings of committee chairs. Yet, the rapporteur system means that individual members, and not committee chairs, are the key actors negotiating individual pieces of legislation.

Another important role on a committee is that of the group coordinator, who is the main spokesperson of his or her party group in each committee. In fact, previous research suggests that MEPs generally view coordinators as the most dominant force in EP committees, but that the degree of their influence is determined by their personalities (Whitaker 2001: 78–80). The coordinator also distributes tasks among the committee members of her party group. Most importantly, once a report has been allocated to a party group in a committee, it is usually the coordinator who chooses the rapporteur from among her party colleagues. The coordinators also convene the meetings of committee members from their party group and work to achieve coherent party positions in committee (Whitaker 2001: 68; Corbett, Jacobs, and Shackleton 2007: 133). Jointly, the coordinators of the party groups set the committee's future agenda, discuss forthcoming votes, and distribute rapporteurships.

The EP party groups that do not receive the rapporteurship for a specific report appoint a "shadow rapporteur" responsible for preparing the group's position and monitoring the work of the rapporteur. This position has become increasingly important in the recent past. Shadow rapporteurs (often referred to simply as "shadows") inform the other members of their party groups of the progress of the deliberation and negotiation process, give them recommendations, draw up amendments, lead the discussion, and rally the troops when "their" issue is discussed in committee or plenary. This position has become necessary because many dossiers discussed in the EP today are highly technical, making an "in-house" expert a necessity. It is also increasingly common for rapporteurs dealing with important reports to have separate meetings with the shadows, who may even be invited to participate in meetings with Commission and Council.[11]

Committees have a small staff, especially compared to the U.S. Congress, for example. They usually have only between two and eight administrators, one or two committee assistants, and a number of secretaries. Committees are also assisted by the EP's Legal Service. Finally, the transnational party groups have up to three people in charge of following a specific committee who, together with the personal assistants of individual members, assist the committee and its members.

The existing scholarship on EP committees remains sparse, despite some recent research on committee assignment and party control of EP committees (e.g., Mamadouh and Raunio [2002, 2003]; McElroy [2002, 2006]; Whitaker [2001]; Hausemer [2006]). Therefore, our understanding of committees, along with other key aspects of the internal operation of the EU's only directly elected institution, remains strikingly limited.

Conclusion

The EP plays a critical role in EU politics today and has evolved from a mere consultative institution into an assertive and powerful actor in the Union's political and institutional framework, particularly over the past two decades. Throughout this time period, our understanding of the behavioral patterns of individual legislators, the EP's institutional setup, and its policy-making process has improved substantially.

The account of politics and policy-making in the EP presented here forces us to reconsider some of the basic assumptions that have been made in the past, however, especially concerning party politics. Specifically, the view of parties as umbrellas for like-minded individuals conflicts with existing conceptualizations of party politics in the EP that emphasize the importance of party control and discipline. Previous interpretations seem to be driven by assumptions about what EP party control of its members ought to look like, rather than observable realities. Yet, the nature of internal party politics in the EP is not based on conventional forms of party control and discipline that build on party members' vote- or office-seeking ambitions. Instead, intra-party dynamics revolve around an exchange of information from expert legislators in the EP's informational committees to nonexpert MEPs not directly involved in the deliberation and negotiation of a given policy proposal.

Still, EP party groups are more than mere coalitions of individual members who vote together when it suits them. Because perceived preference coherence is most likely between members of the same party, who share a common set of core preferences regarding the outcomes of the policies they enact, party affiliation serves as a decision-making shortcut allowing nonexpert legislators to make decisions concerning legislative proposals they may know very little about. In sum, politics in the EP revolves around information, informational limitations, and expertise as the critical variables linking the preferences of individual legislators to their policy choices.

Notes

1. For more details on all four procedures, refer to Corbett, Jacobs, and Shackleton (2007: 196–247).
2. Economic and Monetary Union refers to the harmonization of economic and monetary policies of the EU member states; its most visible component is the common currency, the Euro.
3. These funds are allocated by the EU to support the poorer regions of Europe and to integrate European infrastructure, especially in the transport sector.
4. For a recent analysis of the conciliation process, see König et al. (2007).
5. Further details on the codecision procedure can be accessed at: http://ec.europa.eu/codecision/index_en.htm.
6. Corbett, Jacobs, and Shackleton (2007: 140) maintain that "if the suggested rapporteur is recognised as a specialist on the issue it is easier to get agreement on his or her nomination. Certain technical issues on which there is little political controversy but on which a committee member is a specialist are again and again referred to the same specialist."
7. Rule 152, European Parliament Rules of Procedure. Key negotiators in the EP are well aware of the implications of the absolute majority requirement in second reading and plan their strategy accordingly (Rasmussen and Shackleton 2005: 17).
8. The ELDR group in the EP became the ALDE group in 2004.
9. For a comparison between EP committees and those in other European national legislatures, see Mamadouh and Raunio (2003). For a comparison between the EP and the U.S. Congress, see Kreppel (2006).

10. Subsequent analyses are based on data from the fifth parliamentary term (1999–2004), when the EP had the following 17 standing committees: Committee on Agriculture and Rural Development; Committee on Budgetary Control; Committee on Budgets; Committee on Citizens' Freedoms and Rights, Justice and Home Affairs; Committee on Constitutional Affairs; Committee on Culture, Youth, Education, the Media and Sport; Committee on Development and Cooperation; Committee on Economic and Monetary Affairs; Committee on Employment and Social Affairs; Committee on Fisheries; Committee on Foreign Affairs, Human Rights, Common Security and Defence Policy; Committee on Industry, External Trade, Research and Energy; Committee on Legal Affairs and the Internal Market; Committee on Petitions; Committee on Regional Policy, Transport, and Tourism; Committee on the Environment, Public Health, and Consumer Policy; and Committee on Women's Rights and Equal Opportunities.

11. Different studies have shown that the Council is quite interested in informal contacts and negotiations with rapporteurs and shadow rapporteurs from big political groups to ensure that deals are backed by a large range of opinion in the Parliament and are therefore more likely to be acceptable (Farrell and Héritier 2003*b*: 592; Shackleton and Raunio 2003: 178; Rasmussen and Shackleton 2005: 10).

Chapter 2

Perceived Preference Coherence in Legislative Politics

This book approaches the analysis of European Parliament (EP) decision-making from a micro-perspective that explicitly focuses on the individual legislator as the primary unit of analysis. It poses a most basic question: How do individual legislators make decisions regarding specific policy proposals? That is, how do they come to define their policy positions, legislative actions, and parliamentary votes? In considering these questions, this chapter theorizes EP politics not just on the basis of political *outcomes*, but also by explicitly examining the political *processes* that precede these outcomes.

The micro-level approach allows us to address some of the key questions about legislative politics in the EP that the existing literature has not fully answered. Most importantly, how exactly do individual legislators, parties, and committees interact in shaping decision-making processes and outcomes? Since this book conceptualizes politics as a dynamic process based on the interaction between individuals and institutions, it is important to examine the interplay between individual legislators on the one hand, and parties and committees—the two primary elements in the institutional structure of most legislatures—on the other. This chapter considers how individual legislators' preferences concerning particular policy proposals are shaped by their preferences over political outcomes, and how committees and parties help structure their policy positions.

Moreover, by explaining how individual legislators make policy choices, this chapter provides an explanation for the high levels of party cohesion in the EP that challenges existing accounts emphasizing party control. It introduces in more detail the concept of perceived preference coherence (PPC) and lays out how the PPC dynamic provides the basis of EP decision-making and party cohesion. The model suggests that members of the EP

(MEPs) adopt the positions of those expert colleagues in the responsible EP committees with whom they perceive to share a common set of preferences over political outcomes. Common party affiliation serves as a proxy for shared preferences, and therefore party positions are cohesive as long as a unified party line is achieved among party policy experts in committee. Decision-making on the basis of perceived preference coherence thus provides for an efficient policy-making process in which nonexpert MEPs are able to make informed decisions that approximate their most preferred outcomes, expert legislators in EP committees can shape policies in their areas of expertise, and party groups can act cohesively to advance their policy agendas despite their structural weaknesses.

Party cohesion in the EP

While the literature on the EP, including its evolution (e.g., Williams [1995]; Rittberger [2007]), its institutional setup (e.g., Corbett, Jacobs, and Shackleton [2007]), its powers (e.g., Tsebelis et al. [2001]; Thomson et al. [2006]), and its internal politics (e.g., Kreppel [2002]; Hix, Noury, and Roland [2007]) has grown tremendously in the recent past, little attention has been paid to the way in which individual legislators actually make decisions on the increasing volume of legislation passed by the EP. In effect, most of what we think we know about policy choices by individual MEPs has been derived from large-N data sets of roll-call votes taken on the EP floor. This data has been invaluable in enhancing our understanding of EP politics, and it deservedly serves as the foundation of the field of EP studies. However, the analyses of large numbers of roll-call votes has also distracted us from asking some basic questions about the behavior of individual legislators, because the voting data seems to provide answers to these questions. I maintain that the answers we have may not suffice, and in fact may be misleading in terms of our understanding of who decides, and how, in the EP.

The most important example of a possible misinterpretation of EP politics concerns conclusions about the factors driving EP party group cohesion, which is largely explained in reference to the ability of EP parties to discipline their members. For some, this conclusion seems self-evident: Parties are cohesive, therefore party leaderships must be able to discipline their rank and file. Bowler (2002: 175) provides an example for this logic: "By standard roll call measures, party groups inside the EP cohere even when electoral incentives are weak to nonexisting. *Therefore* incentives

provided within the chamber *must* comprise a large part of any understanding of party group discipline." (*Emphasis added*)

Since no alternative mechanism is offered, the implication of this argument is that individual legislators make decisions by simply adopting the
formal party lines of their party groups, and that they would face sanctions
if they did not. Hence, the decisions of individual MEPs on European
Union (EU) legislation are a function of successfully enforced party discipline. The functionalist logic behind this reasoning, however, is problematic from both a theoretical and empirical point of view. Theoretically, it
makes assumptions about the powers party groups and their leaderships
ought to possess given what we observe empirically. That is, rather than
taking the empirical observation of party cohesion as a starting point for
investigating the underlying reasons for party unity, it tends to equate
party cohesion with party discipline. Empirically, it is problematic because
evidence showing that EP party groups actually discipline their members is
too sparse to support these strong conclusions. In fact, the existing literature has not conclusively demonstrated the link between party group
discipline and party group cohesion.

Nonetheless, the party control argument has been, explicitly or implicitly, accepted as a key aspect of EP politics. This is striking for several
reasons. First, EP politics does not feature a stable government-opposition dynamic, since there is no European-level government based on the
partisan majorities in the EP. Hence, there is no traditional executive
reliant on the support of a cohesive parliamentary majority, which
means that one strong incentive for legislative party cohesion is absent
(see Diermeier and Feddersen [1998]; Huber [1996]). Second, EP party
groups are comprised of unusually heterogeneous groups of national
party delegations and individuals representing a wide range of national,
regional, or sectoral interests, which impedes the realization of party
cohesion. Third, and finally, EP party groups are structurally quite weak
and possess neither the means to sanction defection from the party line
by barring members from reelection nor to sufficiently reward loyalty by
providing access to desirable positions within the EP's institutional structure. Perhaps most importantly, the power of nomination through party
lists lies not with the EP party group leadership but with the national
party delegations that comprise the group. EP party groups are thus
unable to threaten their members with the possibility of precluding
their reelection. This prevents the party group leaderships from manip-
ulating their rank and file into sacrificing their preferred policy positions
for the sake of securing a place on the party list come election time. As

a result of these constraints, party groups are unable to satisfy or undermine their members' vote-seeking ambitions, whereby politicians are driven by their desire to be reelected to their position and act opportunistically in their policy decisions to maximize the likelihood of winning elections.

Given that the ultimate carrot-and-stick of barring members from reelection is unavailable to party groups, the high levels of party cohesion in the EP have been explained with the ability of EP party groups to grant or refuse intra-parliamentary positions of legislative influence, such as committee membership or the responsibility for drafting legislative reports (McElroy 2003). According to this logic, party groups effectively overcome their lack of sanctioning power by fulfilling their members' office-seeking objectives: party groups provide positive incentives that make adhering to the party line worthwhile. This suggestion is intuitively appealing and empirical evidence indicates a correlation between party loyalty and the likelihood of office assignments (McElroy 2003; Yoshinaka, McElroy, and Bowler 2006). It is questionable, however, that the ability of EP party groups to satisfy its members' office-seeking ambitions is a *sufficient* condition to explain the high levels of party cohesion observed in the EP. This is because an individual MEP's chance of gaining a prestigious and influential position simply by adhering to the party line is limited, and thus unlikely to provide a sufficient incentive to override strong personal convictions or constituency concerns. There are two key reasons for this. First, the EP exhibits high levels of turnover. In the 1994 EP election, 57.5 percent of elected MEPs had not been members during the prior parliamentary term. In 1999, this number was 54.3 percent. In 2004, 58 percent of the incoming MEPs were entirely new to the institution, although comparisons of turnover are complicated by the large number of members from the ten new members states following the 2004 enlargement (Corbett, Jacobs, and Shackleton 2007: 48). These high levels of turnover, however, make it less likely that any given member will have a long enough time horizon to sacrifice present-day policy positions for highly uncertain office perks in the future. Second, and as will be discussed in more detail in the next chapter, party group leaderships are quite constrained by intra-party norms of proportionality between national party delegations when distributing their share of positions. Since national party delegations put forward their candidates for the positions they are eligible for, party groups cannot simply threaten to withhold office perks from individual members as they see fit.

Parties and shared preferences

We thus have reason to ask if party discipline can, in fact, account for the high levels of party cohesion we observe in the EP and explain the policy choices of individual MEPs. Specifically, we must address the counterfactual situation satisfactorily: Would we observe similarly high levels of party group cohesion in the absence of party discipline? This counterfactual lies at the heart of the parties versus preferences dichotomy that is of central importance in the literature on legislative parties (Ozbudun 1970; Norpoth 1976; Krehbiel 1993).[1] The former maintains that if parties are cohesive, it is because party leaderships are capable of coercing their rank and file into following their voting instructions. In this view, party cohesion would be lower in the absence of party discipline, which is what the existing literature on the EP implicitly assumes or explicitly argues. This logic is captured in Figure 2.1, where two legislators from the same party have differential preferences. They are, however, "whipped" into deviating from their own preference ideal points through either sanctions (e.g., the threat of being barred from reelection) or rewards (e.g, being granted access to desirable positions either within the legislature or even, for government parties in parliamentary systems, in the national executive). As a result, they take a common policy position, which results in party cohesion. In the absence of party discipline, however, they would take different policy positions, and party cohesion would break down.

In contrast, the shared preferences logic suggests that parties are cohesive because members of the party share the same policy preferences, which will lead them to cast like-votes on the floor. This is illustrated in Figure 2.2, where shared preferences between two legislators from the same party entail shared policy positions, and thus a cohesive party. Party cohesion is assured through common preferences among party members and would remain high even in the absence of party discipline.

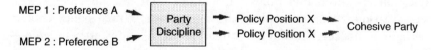

Figure 2.1 Party cohesion through party control

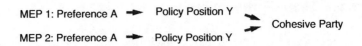

Figure 2.2 Party cohesion through shared preferences

The preference-based explanation of party cohesion thus suggests, quite rightly, that factors other than party discipline may account for party cohesion. I consider the dichotomy of party versus preference effects to be problematic, however, for one because it distracts from alternative "pathways to party unity" (Andeweg and Thomassen 2008, see also Skjæveland [2001]). Gabel and Hix (2007), for example, make an attempt to address the party versus preferences question through the use of MEP surveys as measures of legislators' true preferences. They argue, quite rightly, that even though the survey data may not be the best measure of exogenous preferences, including a separate indicator for MEP preferences is an improvement over previous research that only takes into account the preferences of MEPs as revealed in their voting behavior. However, the study does not actually go beyond the assumption that any "party effect" found in EP politics must be due to successfully enforced party discipline. While finding a substantial EP party effect, the authors do not consider the possibility that the effect they observe may be due to something other than coercive action by EP party groups.

Even more problematic is that both the party discipline and the shared preferences theses assume that legislators actually know their true policy preferences: the party control argument suggests that in the absence of party discipline, members would follow their true preferences and regularly deviate from the party line (see the differentiated preferences between MEPs 1 and 2 in Figure 2.1), while the shared preferences argument is built on the proposition that party unity is the result of party colleagues sharing preferences with regard to the great majority of the legislative proposals they pass (see the common preferences of MEPs 1 and 2 in Figure 2.2). I question, however, that MEPs can identify their true preferences with regard to most legislative proposals before making final policy choices because, in the absence of full information, the relationship between preferences and consequences is quite uncertain. Hence, while the suggestion that EP party group cohesion would be high even in the absence of party discipline is a reasonable one, it is questionable that we can simply ascribe party cohesion to shared preferences.

Problematic preferences and informational uncertainty

Preferences are not simply a fixed and exogenous "input" into the legislative decision-making process based on some kind of "objective interest." Political actors may have multiple objective interests and, as a result, might perceive different and potentially competing policy alternatives as desirable. The translation process of objective interests into actual policy choices may be complicated at two levels. First, a legislator can pursue several objectives simultaneously, which may be at odds with one another. For example, a policy-seeking pro-environmentalist might have genuine concerns about the economic and social impact of environmental legislation in addition to his interest in conservation. Additionally, the legislator may lack "cause-and-effect knowledge" regarding the effects of a legislative proposal (Cooper 1977: 148; Austen-Smith and Riker 1987: 897; Gilligan and Krehbiel 1990: 533): she might not have sufficient information to judge if her policy objectives would be realized once the policy was implemented. The translation of objective interests into actual policy choice may thus be anything but a straightforward process, as it often involves complex decisions under conditions of competing interests, substantive uncertainty, and asymmetric information.

Under these circumstances, legislators require a great amount of expertise or informational resources to make informed choices. This is particularly important in a legislature with powers to influence the shape of legislation, which makes the EP more comparable to a legislature in a separation of powers system such as that of the United States than to a classic parliamentary assembly (Shackleton 2005). In this system, the EP assumes policy positions independent of those pursued by the executive body, be it the Commission or the Council of Ministers. Its influence remains separate from other sources of power in the EU system and the EP uses its formal powers to amend and even reject legislation proposed by the Commission "to the fullest possible extent" and "much more effectively than national legislatures in other parliamentary systems" (Rittberger 2007: 3). The EP's policy influence is thus "greater than that of most national chambers in the EU," which means that the EP "deserves to be ranked at least toward the upper end of the category of 'policy influencer'" (Scully 2000: 238–9). In other words, the EP engages in real policy-making; it creates legislation, "a classical parliamentary function almost forgotten by some national parliaments" (Corbett, Jacobs, and Shackleton 2007: 9).

31

One implication of this reality is that MEPs do not rely on the EU's executive bodies as their principal sources of policy information, as this would undermine the EP's status as a strong and independent "policy influencer." Hence, unlike their colleagues in national parliaments, MEPs do not have the equivalents of government ministries that serve as the political system's primary repositories of expertise and loci of policy creation. Moreover, policy decisions in the EP are not predetermined by an existing government-opposition cleavage, where policy outputs match the positions of the legislative majority, as defined by the executive; instead, they are the endogenous results of genuine deliberation and negotiation processes inside the legislature. This means that MEPs have to determine their policy positions toward particular policy proposals to maintain the institution's status as an autonomous policy-maker. Yet, given the small personal staff available to MEPs (with an average of two assistants per MEP) and the great volume of legislation they must handle, one should not assume or expect that MEPs are fully informed about every piece of legislation they vote on. This is especially the case because EP legislation tends to be highly complex and technical, and because early agreements under the codecision procedure—where proposals are adopted in first reading and following a series of informal meetings between the main negotiators from EP, Council, and Commission—are becoming increasingly common (Farrell and Heretier 2004; Häge and Kaeding 2007). These early agreements result in an increasingly rapid legislative pace, which augments the "informational deficit" MEPs face when making policy decisions. This informational deficit can take two forms. First, MEPs may simply lack sufficient information or information-gathering resources to properly determine what positions they ought to be taking in order to fulfill their own preferences or those of their constituents. They do not have *enough* information. Second, they may be faced with an informational overload, in the sense that MEP offices are often barraged with position papers, policy evaluations, and other pieces of information provided by corporate and interest group lobbyists seeking to influence EP policy decisions. Under these circumstances, a lack of time and resources means that MEPs cannot efficiently process the great deal of information they receive. In other words, they have *too much* information. In either case, MEPs cannot make fully informed decisions as they lack adequate resources to collect or evaluate relevant information.

The implication of this observation is not that MEPs do not have exogenous preferences, but merely that they do not have well-defined preferences concerning the majority of legislative proposals they have to make decisions on. In other words, while MEPs have exogenous *outcome preferences*, their *policy preferences* are uncertain and endogenous to the decision-making process. Outcome preferences are the general preferences of legislators regarding the expected consequences of a given policy proposal once implemented; they are preferences concerning policy outcomes and are generally stable and largely exogenous to a particular decision-making process. Policy preferences, in contrast, are the particular positions decision-makers assume toward specific policy issues or proposals, based on their beliefs about how a given policy action relates to their most preferred outcome (Krehbiel 1991). Policy preferences are thus derived from outcome preferences, but they are potentially changeable and inconsistent, because the link between policies and outcomes is often uncertain (Krehbiel 1991: 66–7). Therefore, policy preferences are sensitive to the information decision-makers acquire about the relationship between a policy proposal and its consequences.

Differentiating between exogenous, stable outcome preferences and endogenous, problematic policy preferences means that we have to consider how political processes within particular institutional structures shape the policy preferences of individual legislators. We have to ask how individual legislators, in an environment of informational uncertainty, make policy choices that maximize the probability of their most preferred outcomes being realized.

Minimizing uncertainty: perceived preference coherence in legislative politics

The answer to this question is that legislators rely on an external input when taking policy positions that are in line with their exogenous outcome preferences. Specifically, they follow the lead of the generally small number of legislators who possess the necessary expertise and/or have invested their limited resources in more fully understanding the issue at hand. This forms the basis of what I call *perceived preference coherence*. This concept stipulates that when legislators lack adequate information concerning the content and expected consequences of a policy proposal and when they do not possess the necessary expertise, resources, and time to collect and properly evaluate the proposed legislation, they adopt the positions of those expert colleagues with whom they perceive to share a common set of preferences concerning the likely implications of the policy upon its implementation.[2] This informal institution serves as a solution to the dilemma associated with squaring the quest for good policy with a lack of resources necessary to make fully informed decisions under conditions of uncertainty.[3]

Building on the differentiation between outcome and policy preferences, the concept of perceived preference coherence suggests that legislators hope to enact policies that approximate their outcome preferences by adopting the policy positions of those expert colleagues whose outcome preferences they perceive to most closely match their own. They assume that the policy preferences of these expert colleagues with similar outcome preferences most closely resemble the positions they *would* choose *if* they possessed the expertise and resources to make their own fully informed decisions.

Perceived preference coherence and individual MEPs

The process of linking outcome preferences with policy preferences is very different for expert and nonexpert MEPs. Members who possess expertise in the policy area under consideration can determine what their positions should be regarding a policy proposal. They can translate their outcome preferences into policy preferences without outside assistance, as they possess information about the likely consequences of a legislative proposal upon its implementation. Nonexpert legislators, on the other hand, do not possess the specialized knowledge necessary to determine how a proposal relates to their outcome preferences and thus what their policy preferences and positions should be. They have to rely on policy experts to provide the information necessary to establish the link between outcome and policy preferences. Legislators can thus be placed on a continuum ranging from high to low levels of expertise and information about the likely consequences of a policy decision.

When actors possess high levels of expertise, and by extension a significant amount of private information, they can meaningfully connect their policy preferences with their outcome preferences. Under these conditions, decision-making corresponds to the *committee voting model* (Hinich and Munger 1997), which presupposes a decision-making context in which a relatively small number of political actors has full information and well-defined preferences regarding the policy alternatives on the table and can properly evaluate their content and likely consequences upon implementation. The assumptions of full information and well-defined preferences underlying the committee voting model is problematic with regard to nonexpert legislators, however. In fact, for these actors the process of making a decision on a given policy proposal more closely resembles a *mass elections model* (Hinich and Munger 1997), where many voters are assumed to possess only a limited amount of information on the choices they face and do not have well-defined preferences concerning the available policy alternatives. The critical difference, of course, is that the element of choice for legislators is not a candidate (as in mass elections), but a policy being decided under conditions of uncertainty. I argue that just as in mass elections, preferences drive policy choice in legislative politics, but shared party affiliation serves as a decision-making "shortcut" that helps legislators choose among complex alternatives (see Dalton and Wattenberg [2002]). This is why it is *perceived* preference coherence between experts and nonexperts that drives EP decision-making, rather than *actual* preference coherence. Like voters in mass elections who use the "party label" to decide what candidate is most likely to pursue policies reflective of their outcome preferences, legislators use the party label to decide whose expert colleagues' policy positions are most likely to approximate their own outcome preferences.[4] This provides for the possibility of errors in perception, but in the absence of full information about the link between their own outcome preferences and the policy positions of their expert colleagues, relying on the party label allows MEPs to make their best educated guess.

The party label facilitates legislative policy choice by reducing nonexpert legislators' costs of gathering information in two ways. First, it allows them to make decisions concerning a specific policy proposal without detailed knowledge of its content and expected consequences, meaning they do not have to invest in accumulating significant amounts of substantive expertise for every single policy proposal.[5] Second, a common party label provides legislators with considerable confidence that their preference ideal points are approximated because they are most likely to share outcome preferences with their party colleagues. Party affiliation thus provides the basis for perceived preference coherence in that shared party group membership serves as a proxy, or stand-in, for common preferences concerning the likely implications of a policy choice.

The operation of the PPC logic solves key problems associated with policy-making, for both nonexpert legislators and policy specialists. It allows the great number of legislators who do not possess the expertise to meaningfully link outcome preferences to policy preferences to take positions on legislation with which they are largely unfamiliar, without having to expend valuable resources. Critically, from their perspective, these positions are not arbitrary or random, but actually yield a substantial probability of approximating their outcome preferences. Policy experts, in turn, are served by the PPC dynamic as it allows them relative autonomy in the policy-making process. However, they have to retain a basic level of trust among their colleagues, who would no longer follow their lead if they perceived a mismatch of preferences. Hence, perceived preference coherence, in an iterative context, allows expert legislators to shape legislation and make what they consider to be good policy in a relatively unencumbered fashion, while allowing their colleagues to rely on their policy expertise to make decisions largely congruent with their outcome preferences.

Perceived preference coherence and EP committees

The PPC model attaches a great deal of significance to the role of specialized legislators with high levels of expertise in "their" policy areas, who can provide nonexperts with information about the relationship between the policy proposal under consideration and their outcome preferences. In the EP, policy expertise is principally rooted in standing committees, which have a "relative monopoly on information and expertise" (Kreppel 2006: 251). This is of critical importance for a strong policy-influencing legislature like the EP. Unlike in a parliamentary system, where legislature and executive are fused, having committees as repositories of information and expertise that are largely autonomous from outside influence is of particular importance. While legislators in a parliamentary system rely on their party organizations and, if in government, on their ministries for expertise and policy information, this is not an option in a system like the EP, for two reasons: first, there are no ministries that are tied to a legislative majority in the EP and, second, this information would not be reliable for a legislature that actually makes policy, compared to one that leaves this responsibility to the executive.

The suggestion that nonexpert MEPs rely on members of the EP's standing committees when forming positions toward policy proposals implies that EP committees are informational rather than mere distributional devices. This differentiation is at the heart of one of the key debates in the U.S. Congress literature that views committees as either distributive or informational. The *distributive perspective* (Shepsle 1979; Shepsle and Weingast 1981) focuses on members' gains from trade and is based on the premise that it is the role of legislatures to allocate policy benefits. Consequently, the primary role of legislators in the distributive model is to secure a favorable distribution of direct benefits to their constituents. Committees serve as instruments to fulfill this goal and are composed of high-demanders, that is, members who are preference outliers in their policy areas. Legislative rules and procedures give such committees control over policy-making within their domain, and the committee system serves as a mechanism for an intra-institutional logroll: members gain influence in the policy areas they care most about, while sacrificing the ability to determine policy in areas less salient to them (Weingast and Marshall 1988). In effect, they trade influence with one another.

This conceptualization of legislative politics is challenged by the *informational perspective* (Gilligan and Krehbiel 1987, 1989, 1990; Krehbiel 1991). In this view, institutional arrangements reflect the need to acquire and disseminate information for policy-making, and committees provide the necessary incentives for legislators to specialize in order to achieve their political goals. Legislators can reap the gains of specialization, as a potential collective good, through institutional organization (Krehbiel 1991: 5). This perspective highlights the importance of expertise and information, both with regard to the actual substance of a given legislative proposal and the political process of making a collective decision on the matter. Unlike the distributional model, the informational perspective suggests that individual committees reflect the heterogeneity of the whole house rather than consisting of high-demanders, so that legislators can secure the gains from specialization while ensuring that the policy outcome does not deviate from the majority preference. Hence, information and expertise play a more important role in the legislative process than the desire to distribute legislative pork.

The proposition that EP committees are informational rather than distributive is intuitively attractive. After all, MEPs do not actually have any pork to distribute, since the number of distributive policy proposals in the EP is, in fact, very limited and MEPs cannot dispense tangible benefits directly to their constituents. Confirming the propositions of the informational model in the case of the EP, McElroy (2006) demonstrates that committees are representative of the EP as a whole, in two ways. First, the composition of EP committees is proportional with regard to the total seat shares of the EP party groups and the national party delegations. Second, committee members are not significantly different from the chamber as a whole in terms of their policy views, either on a general left-right dimension or with regard to specific policy domains.

In the present theoretical context, the EP's informational committees provide the "input" into the PPC dynamic: the policy preferences of MEPs are derived, on the basis of perceived preference coherence, from the information and policy positions of expert legislators in the committee responsible for a given piece of legislation. In other words, policy positions are endogenous to the decision-making process in the EP's informational committees, rather

37

than formulated prior to committee deliberation by the party group or national party delegation leadership.

Perceived preference coherence and EP parties

In a sense, the PPC logic describes a simple supply and demand situation, where policy experts provide policy positions that are demanded, and ultimately adopted, by nonexpert MEPs. It thus benefits both groups of legislators. However, even the party groups benefit from the PPC dynamic. This proposition may seem counter-intuitive at first. After all, one of the key premises of the model presented here is that policy experts in the EP's informational committees provide the input into the PPC dynamic, which suggests that the EP's standing committees and their members, rather than the party groups, are at the heart of EP decision-making. Politics in the EP thus appears to be an example of (informational) committee government, where committees are the primary actors setting the agenda and determining the policy content of legislation. The PPC model, however, assigns a critically important role to parties in the EP, because it is joint party affiliation—as a proxy for perceived common preferences concerning the likely implications of a policy choice—that provides the basis for this decision-making dynamic.

It is unclear, however, what exactly shared party affiliation means in the case of the EP, as its transnational party groups are comprised of numerous national party delegations. To address this question one might conceive of outcome preferences as *policy-based* (or *ideology-based*) on the one hand and *constituency-based* on the other. Following the proposition that parties are collectives of individuals who share a basic set of values, the policy-based outcome preferences are directly linked to party affiliation. Hence, we would expect MEPs to perceive a high degree of outcome preference coherence with policy experts from their own party. Constituency-based preferences, meanwhile, capture the reality that legislators necessarily have to be concerned with more than just their most preferred policies, but also with the impact of their choices on the people they represent back at home.

McElroy rightly emphasizes that the notion of constituency in the EP is quite vague (2007: 438); in the context of the PPC model constituency in the EP is most reasonably conceived as shared nationality, however. This is for four reasons. First, the majority of member states feature a single national electoral district for EP elections and the majority of MEPs (about 60%) are elected from national party lists.[6] Hence, most MEPs do not have subnational constituencies that they formally represent. Second, even for those MEPs who do represent a particular subnational constituency, the link between legislators and their electoral districts is much less developed than in other district-based electoral arenas (Kreppel 2002: 23). In fact, research shows that "European" considerations hardly impact voters' decisions in EP elections (Reif and Schmitt 1980; van der Brug and van der Eijk 2007) and that public awareness of the EP and its policy-making process, and the salience EU citizens attach to it, is low compared to national European arenas (Blondel, Sinnott, and Svensson 1998). Accordingly, conceptualizing "constituency" as literally those people who elect the MEP at the district-level appears problematic. Third, MEPs do not seem to differentiate much between the importance of representing citizens of their member states and citizens in their regional constituency. As a 2006 MEP survey shows (Farrell and Scully 2007: 105), 57.7 percent of MEPs indicate that representation of "all people in my member state" is "of great importance," while 63.5 percent say the same about "all people in my constituency/region." This represents the maximum on a five point scale ranging from one ("of little importance") to five ("of great importance"). If we include respondents in this comparison who give a score of four out of five, the already modest difference becomes even less pronounced, at 78.9 percent for national constituents and 80.7 percent for regional constituents. Finally, the PPC logic suggests that MEPs follow policy specialists in the responsible EP committee when making policy choices. Most of the time, however, MEPs do not have a policy specialist from their regional constituency sitting in the responsible committee whom they can follow when casting votes on the EP floor.

The implication of all this is that, except perhaps in exceptional cases where an MEP has reason to believe that a particular policy proposal would disproportionately affect what she perceives to be her core constituency, MEPs likely perceive the greatest degree of preference coherence with those expert colleagues with whom they share both a partisan and a national affiliation. Accordingly, we ought to expect that MEPs share the greatest degree of perceived preference coherence with policy experts from their national party delegation, at least if they are represented by a member of their own national party in the responsible committee. If this is not the case, however, which is fairly frequent (especially for members of the small party groups), we should expect them to follow their EP party group colleagues, because ideology trumps nationality in the EP.

Nonetheless, the PPC dynamic does not automatically translate into cohesive party group positions. In fact, it has been shown that party cohesion breaks down when national party delegations in the same EP party group take opposing policy positions (Hix 2002; Faas 2003; Hix, Noury, and Roland 2007). In other words, perceived preference coherence translates into cohesive party group positions only if party group members from different national party delegations share a common position on a given piece of legislation. For this reason, there is a second necessary step toward cohesive party group positions in the EP plenary, namely successful coordination among legislative specialists from the same party group in the responsible committee. Only if members of a party group achieve consensus amongst themselves in the responsible committee will the PPC dynamic translate into party group unity. Such a coherent position is quite likely, however, as it provides all actors involved with important advantages. From the perspective of nonexpert legislators, a common position among committee experts from their party group is a strong signal that the party line is unlikely to deviate too far from their outcome preferences, because those colleagues in the responsible committee who most likely share their outcome preferences—including members of their national party delegation who may sit in the responsible committee—agree on what constitutes the best policy choice. Perceived preference coherence is thus "maximized." For expert legislators in the responsible committee, a coherent position is also desirable (as long as it does not actually deviate too far from their policy preferences), because it maximizes their influence over the collective policy choice of their party colleagues. This is because once the policy experts in an informational committee agree on a common position, it is likely perceived as representative of the party median and unlikely to be overturned by the nonexpert rank and file, the national party delegation leaderships, or the EP group leadership. A coherent party group position in committee is beneficial for individual national party delegations as well, because it is only through successful coordination across national party delegation lines that EP parties can hope to shape policy processes and outcomes; after all, national party delegations alone do not have sufficient numbers of members and organizational strength to influence legislative outcomes. Finally, a common policy position in committee is of value to the party group as a whole, and its leadership, as it maximizes the probability that the PPC dynamic will lead to party group cohesion on the EP floor.

This part of the PPC argument seems strangely circular at first sight: the positions of individual MEPs are aggregated into cohesive party positions as a result of a decision-making dynamic that seems to be built on the premise of party cohesion. This circularity disappears, however, once we make two important distinctions. First, we have to differentiate between general levels of party cohesion across all issues and party cohesion with regard to specific policy items, and we must recognize that the former by itself does not provide a reliable basis for perceived preference coherence. Second, we have to distinguish between two levels of analysis, namely the plenary and committee levels, and emphasize that what matters for the PPC dynamic are the policy positions that are endogenously created in the responsible EP committees, not the final votes taken on the EP floor (as a measure of general party cohesion). In other words, there is a critical difference between general levels of party cohesion *across all issues on the EP floor,* and cohesive positions among legislators from the same party group *with regard to one specific policy item in the responsible EP committee.* From the perspective of the individual nonexpert legislator, the former is a poor indicator of preference coherence, as the following example shows. Consider legislator A, faced with a decision on policy X, which lies outside her area of expertise. Legislator A is a member of Party M, which votes cohesively on the floor 90 percent of the time. Policy X is discussed in Committee N before being sent to the floor, and two members of Party M (legislators B and C) sit on this committee. Following the PPC logic, it is these two members that A relies on when deciding what position to take on the floor. However, B and C cannot agree on a common position with regard to policy X in committee: while B is in favor, C is opposed. In this situation, it is of little help to A that all members of Party M vote cohesively on the floor nine out of ten times. What matters is the position of B and C *in Committee N with regard to issue X.* Hence, to the extent that perceived preference coherence between legislators depends on any kind of party cohesion, it is on the cohesion of party group representatives in the responsible committee, not the overall cohesion of the entire party group in the EP plenary. This is why coordination among members of the same party group in the responsible committee is so important to the realization of party unity on the EP floor. It is party cohesion in committee that leads to party cohesion in plenary, and it is the iteration of this process that creates an overall record of party cohesion.

In sum, the foundation for cohesive policy positions within EP party groups lies in the perceived preference coherence between members of the same EP party group, as long as the party group policy experts in the responsible committee present a united position to their nonexpert colleagues. This reality is of great value to party group leaderships in the EP, given that they do not possess the powers and resources to satisfy their members' vote-seeking and office-seeking ambitions available to their national counterparts. The PPC dynamic, however, provides a low-cost way of securing party unity even in the absence of active party control.

Through the PPC dynamic, there is no inherent conflict between the delegation of policy-making authority to informational committees and the realization of partisan policy objectives. In fact, the PPC dynamic effectively provides the legislative parties and their leaderships with high levels of party cohesion, and thus the ultimate asset in realizing their policy objectives. Moreover, the dynamic solves a second problem for party groups leaderships, and thus kills two birds with one stone, as it allows for the delegation of policy-making power to a subset of legislators with genuine expertise in the policy area in question. This latter element is quite critical in the context of EP politics because party leaderships in the EP are dependent on the policy expertise of their committee representatives. Like every other legislative actor, party leaderships have to evaluate the content and expected consequences of a legislative proposal. In the absence of a strong party organization with autonomous sources of policy expertise backing the legislative party group,[7] the party group leaderships need genuine policy specialists to guide decision-making. Hence, EP party groups select policy specialist as both committee delegates (McElroy 2006) and rapporteurs (Yoshinaka, McElroy, and Bowler 2006). This is exemplified by the comments of one MEP (as cited in McElroy [2006: 14]) who noted in a personal interview that "I was convinced by the party leadership to take a position on the Industry Committee *because of my background*. I was really not so inclined myself but they felt it would strengthen the bargaining position of the party as we have only got five members on this particular committee." (*Emphasis added*)

Without experts, party groups and their leaderships would be quite limited in their ability to determine a party position concerning every single legislative proposal that makes its way through the EP. Party groups not only lack the capacities to successfully engage in coercion of their members, they also lack the resource gathering and evaluating capacities necessary to establish policy positions independent of their policy specialists in committee. The PPC dynamic, however, provides solutions to the problems of limited resources for both party leaderships and individual MEPs, and for the party leaderships' incapacity to enforce party discipline.

Hypotheses

One of the challenges in differentiating between a party effect and the impact of shared preferences on party unity is that their relative influence is very difficult to disentangle empirically (Krehbiel 1993). After all, the two factors are assumed to be highly correlated, since parties are collectives of individuals who band together to advance a common set of policy objectives. The same would apply to attempts to determine the relative impact of party control, common preferences, and the PPC dynamic, because all three factors predict the same outcome: cohesive parties. We can differentiate between these alternative explanations, however, by examining political processes as well as political outcomes, which is why the hypotheses below relate to both. The next chapter, which provides a first set of empirical analyses, will allow us to evaluate the following competing propositions.

If the PPC model were correct, we should find that MEPs do not have the capacity to independently form policy preferences with regard to the majority of legislative proposals they make decisions on. Therefore, in the search for policy-relevant information, they should rely on their party colleagues in the responsible EP committee as their primary sources of information. The EP's informational committees, in turn, ought to have significant influence on the policy agenda of the chamber as a whole, as well as within the individual party groups that have delegated agenda power to their expert members. This is because party group positions should not be exogenously supplied by the party leadership, but should constitute the endogenous outcome of the pre-floor legislative process; they ought to be formulated by the committee delegates of the respective party groups. Finally, if MEPs perceive a common set of shared outcome preferences with the committee experts, they will adopt their positions when voting in the plenary. As pointed out earlier, MEPs perceive the greatest degree of preference coherence with those colleagues with whom they share both a partisan and a national affiliation. Accordingly, we should expect to find that MEPs are most likely to adopt the positions of those expert members in the responsible committee from their national party delegation. However, since MEPs are not always represented by a member from their national party, and since we should expect ideology-based outcome preferences to trump constituency-based outcome preferences in the EP, we should also expect MEPs to consider the positions of their EP party group colleagues in the committee in charge of a given piece of legislation. Finally, the national affiliation of committee members alone should have the least impact on the variance in voting patterns on the EP floor.

The applicability of the PPC argument would be in doubt if these propositions did not hold. In particular, there would be little need for perceived preference coherence as a decision-making aid if MEPs were capable of independently forming policy preferences with regard to most legislative proposals. This finding would indicate that shared preferences explain behavioral patterns in the EP, including cohesive voting on the EP floor. The PPC argument would also be disconfirmed if party positions were not the endogenous outcome of intra-committee deliberation and negotiation, but imposed and propagated exogenously by the party group leaderships. Finally, any evidence for systematic exertion of party discipline would suggest that it is indeed party control, rather than the PPC process, that accounts for individual-level policy choice.

Conclusion

The PPC dynamic assumes that nonexpert MEPs seek policy alternatives closest to their preference ideal points, but that they have to make policy choices under conditions of significant substantive uncertainty about the content and consequences of legislation due to a lack of informational resources in EP politics. Under these circumstances, MEPs cannot be sure about the location of a policy proposal in relation to their most preferred policy outcomes. They have to rely on their expert colleagues in the responsible committee to provide both substantive and political information to help them translate their outcome preferences into policy preferences and, ultimately, into policy decisions. However, in the absence of good ways of measuring actual preference coherence with each of their colleagues in the responsible committee, nonexpert legislators rely on common national and transnational party affiliation as a proxy for shared outcome preferences. This dynamic results in cohesive parties, as Figure 2.3 illustrates. Here, the two MEPs from the same party group have neither shared nor preferential policy preferences, but uncertain policy preferences. They arrive at a common policy position due to the PPC dynamic, which results in a cohesive party line.

This account of EP politics does not make assumptions about the powers that political actors ought to possess, but takes the limitations they face seriously. It asks, how do individual MEPs make decisions given the

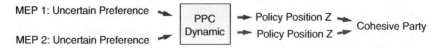

Figure 2.3 Party cohesion through perceived preference coherence

constraints imposed by the EP's informational deficit, and how is party cohesion achieved given that EP party groups are structurally weak? It also avoids drawing conclusions about individual-level behavior on the basis of observations at the aggregate level and making *a priori* assumptions about how parties or committees *should* function in EP politics. Instead, the micro-level focus of the analysis distills how the policy positions assumed by individual MEPs are conditioned by personal convictions (in the form of outcome preferences) as well as the EP's principal institutional structures, in the form of both parties and committees. These institutional structures allow MEPs to develop policy positions that approximate their outcome preferences without having to form independent policy preferences on issues outside of their realms of expertise. They can make the "right" decisions in a resource-restricted environment because the committee structure identifies groups of MEPs with policy expertise, while partisanship—as a proxy for shared preferences—specifies who among these policy experts ought to be the "trusted colleagues" nonexpert legislators follow.

The EP's standing committees are informational committees in two important ways. On the one hand, committees are informational from the perspective of the chamber as a whole; they are repositories of expertise that help realize the potential of specialization as a collective good (Krehbiel 1991). At the same time, delegates of a particular party group are informational to their party groups. They help capture the gains from specialization by negotiating and proposing the policy positions, and formal party lines, of their party groups. These positions are thus the endogenous product of the committee stage of the legislative process, rather than exogenously provided by the party leadership. EP parties remain critical to the policy-making dynamic in the EP, however. They "matter" in two important ways. First, party affiliation serves as a proxy for perceived outcome preference coherence, as nonexpert members rely on shared party affiliation with their expert colleagues in the responsible committee as a stand-in for common preferences concerning the likely implications of their policy choice. Second, committee deliberation is structured along party lines, with the objective of achieving consensus among policy experts from the same party group. If a common position is achieved, it will be adopted by the party rank and file on the basis of perceived preference coherence.

Hence, committees and parties are not at odds because political dynamics in the EP are influenced in important ways by the institution's standing committees as well as partisan-based policy preferences. Powerful committees and party politics *together* (and endogenously) produce high levels of party cohesion. EP votes are highly cohesive within party groups not because of a top-down effect, where party leaderships impose discipline upon their rank and file, but because of a bottom-up effect where the majority of members seek guidance from their expert colleagues in the responsible committees. In fact, there is little need for party discipline in the EP because the default action for the majority of MEPs is to adopt the party line without having been "whipped." For this reason, I do not see the ability of EP party groups to punish their members or satisfy their office-seeking ambitions as a sufficient condition to explain the high levels of party cohesion observed in the EP. We should expect to observe high levels of party cohesion in the EP even in a counterfactual scenario in which parties lacked even these rewards and punishments. MEPs within each party group would generally vote cohesively *as they lack alternative means of decision-making. Most* of the time, *most* MEPs will vote the party line that comes out of the responsible committee. They do this not because they are being disciplined, but because they adopt their policy positions on the basis of perceived preference coherence with their expert colleagues.

It is also critical to note that my argument does not suggest that joint preferences *alone* drive party cohesion and policy choice in the EP. This perspective would imply that there is no party effect in EP politics at all, and that individual legislators vote with fellow party members simply because of their agreement on a given policy. Voting outcomes would thus be the same regardless of the presence of a "party effect." However, most MEPs simply do not know what their policy preferences regarding a particular piece of legislation *should* be, meaning that preferences cannot drive policy choice independent of joint party affiliation as a decision-making shortcut for nonexpert legislators. Hence, it is not preferences or party, or preferences *plus* party (i.e., party cohesion = shared preferences + party effect) that explains policy choice and cohesive party positions. Instead, joint preferences and party affiliation have a mutually contingent effect on party cohesion.

The PPC logic suggests that both preferences and parties matter, while specifying how the two factors interact in driving high levels of party cohesion: nonexpert MEPs assume that they share outcome preferences with their party groups' legislative experts, and that the policy positions assumed by these experts will approximate their own outcome prefer-ences. Joint party affiliation thus constitutes a critical intervening factor in the translation of MEPs' outcome preferences into policy preferences, which explains why Gabel and Hix (2007) show a significant party effect even when controlling for the individual preferences of legislators.

However, while these authors conclude from their findings that parties must be able to induce their members to vote together despite disagreements over policy, I maintain that the true party effect in EP politics lies in the predominant importance of the "party label" in the PPC dynamic; Gabel and Hix simply reveal the errors in nonexperts' perceptions of preference coherence.

My argument about how individual MEPs make decisions thus makes sense of what has been one of the most striking empirical puzzles in EP politics, namely the observation of high levels of party group cohesion in a legislature featuring structurally weak party organizations. Critically, my account of EP politics provides for the micro-foundations necessary to satisfactorily explain MEP policy choice and EP party cohesion. It does not reach conclusions about individual-level behavior on the basis of aggregate-level observations, but explains how individual behavior is aggregated via the policy-making process and provides for the political outcomes we observe.

In the end, the PPC dynamic provides important advantages to everybody involved. It allows individual members to concentrate their limited personal resources on a narrow set of issues while having confidence that their outcome preferences are properly represented when they follow their expert colleagues in plenary voting. This is more than just a system of reciprocity, as the distributional committee perspective would suggest, since MEPs do not have to trade off their most preferred outcomes in one policy area for success in another. Meanwhile, EP committees can function as repositories of expertise and as principal agenda-setters within their jurisdictions. Finally, party groups get to make up for their structural weaknesses, reap the gains of specialization, and realize their policy goals through high levels of party cohesion. Interestingly, these preferable outcomes are the product of a political decision-making process that is driven, to a significant extent, by a profound *lack* of resources, as the PPC dynamic makes up for limited informational resources and the traditional instruments of party control. Party cohesion thus results from political constraints, rather than political capabilities.

Notes

1. A third perspective, proposed by Cox and McCubbins (2005), suggests that party cohesion can be realized by party leaderships not through party discipline, but by deliberately keeping issues that may be divisive off the policy agenda. This

possibility is not considered in this book because primary legislative agenda-setting power in the EU lies with the European Commission, which means that no EP party can simply keep an issue off the agenda. To the extent that EP party groups can exercise independent agenda-setting powers, in particular by intro-ducing legislative amendments, the existing research provides no indication that agenda control affects party group cohesion (Hix, Noury, and Roland 2007: 123–31).

2. In the U.S. context, voting choice studies have shown that legislators rely heavily on information from "specialist" legislators or "trusted colleagues" who are knowledgeable on the particular issue under consideration (Zwier 1979; Kingdon 1981; Sabatier and Whiteman 1985). Matthews and Stimson (1975) describe the "normal" decision-making process in the US Congress in similar terms. Their argument emphasizes "cue-taking" but defines these cues more broadly than the PPC model, as the basis for adopting the position of an expert colleague can be friendship, trust, and reciprocity, aside from similar preferences.

3. Hix, Noury, and Roland (2007: 42–3) hint at a similar logic but do not specify the basis of and mechanism by which information is exchanged between experts and nonexperts. They also do not elaborate on the implications of this dynamic for interest aggregation and party cohesion.

4. The only fully reliable way for a nonexpert MEP to determine which expert colleague's policy position most closely matches her outcome preferences would be to determine her own policy preferences, which is not feasible given informational constraints and would defeat the very purpose of specialization and a division of labor in the legislature.

5. The PPC model is reminiscent of the work by Asbjørn Skjæveland on the Danish *Folketinget* (2001). It goes beyond his "division of labor" argument, however, in that it specifies the bases on which legislators follow their expert colleagues, namely perceived preference coherence (and/or focal points, as discussed in Chapters 4 and 5).

6. For the 2004–9 legislative term, the exceptions were Belgium, France, Ireland, Italy, Poland, and the United Kingdom. For the 1999–2004 parliamentary term, the subject of the empirical analyses in this book, MEPs from Belgium, Ireland, Italy, and the United Kingdom, plus the German Christian-Democrats, were elected in subnational constituencies.

7. See Corbett, Jacobs, and Shackleton [2007: 99–101] for details.

Chapter 3

Committees, Parties, and Voting in the European Parliament

This first empirical chapter is structured around the hypotheses laid out in Chapter 2 and confirms the expectations of the perceived preference coherence (PPC) model. Drawing on two sets of data, it demonstrates how individual members of the European Parliament (MEPs) make decisions, how these decisions are aggregated and, by extension, how party cohesion in the EP comes about. First, it relies on qualitative data from a series of 90 in-depth interviews with members of the European Parliament (EP), parliamentary officials, and a small number of representatives from other European Union (EU) institutions.[1] Second, it presents the results of quantitative analyses regarding the link between committee positions and voting outcomes on the EP floor using a large sample of plenary roll-call votes. The analyses of these data support the propositions of the PPC model and thus draw a picture of EP politics that differs substantially from the received wisdom regarding decision-making in the EP, in that it challenges the usual focus on party control as the driving force behind EP policy choice.

The analysis of the qualitative data confirms the existence of what the previous chapter has labeled an "informational deficit" in the EP. MEPs generally lack detailed information about the content and consequences of most legislative proposals. However, specialization in the EP committees serves as a way to alleviate this shortcoming. Specialized committee members constitute the primary providers of information to nonexpert legislators, and the formal positions that EP party groups assume toward particular policy proposals are the result of consideration, deliberation, contestation, and cooperation *in the responsible EP committee*. Party positions, in the form of the formal voting recommendations issued by party groups, are thus endogenous to the political process in committee, rather than imposed from above by the party group leadership or the leadership of national party delegations. There are usually no party positions independent of or parallel to what has been formulated in committee.

However, the reality that EP party group positions are endogenous to deliberation and negotiation in committee does not, in itself, undermine the notion that party groups and their leaderships are critical in ensuring high levels of party cohesion through successfully enforced party discipline. After all, the party leadership might well leave the creation of the formal party line to the experts, but then serve as the guarantor of party unity once a proposal reaches the EP floor. This, however, depends on the answer to two critical questions: Are the party groups capable of fulfilling this function, and is there actually much *need* for disciplining action? The evidence presented in this chapter suggests that party groups are not capable of controlling their rank and file either through punishments or rewards. In fact, their abilities to enforce party discipline are even more limited than the existing literature assumes. This is not a major problem for the party groups, however, since there is very little need for active party leadership control of their members.

The quantitative analysis of votes on the EP floor demonstrates that nonexpert legislators adopt the positions of "their" representatives in the responsible committee, that is, those colleagues with whom they perceive to share outcome preferences. These colleagues are usually members of the nonexperts' national party delegations, with whom they perceive to share both policy- and constituency-based outcome preferences. Not all MEPs are represented in the responsible committee by a member of their national party delegation, however, in which case they adopt the position of their party group colleagues, as the next-best approximation of their outcome preferences. The implication of both of these findings is that party groups stand united behind a particular legislative proposal by the time it arrives on the EP floor, as long as their representatives in the responsible committee are successful at coordinating and agreeing to a common position. This is not only a critical responsibility of the committee delegation—and very much perceived as such—it is also an empirical reality: Committee members of the same party group present a united front in the vast majority of cases.

The conclusions drawn from this chapter are the product of the mixed methods approach used throughout this book. In fact, a quantitative approach alone would not allow us to recognize the important features of EP politics it highlights, because the propositions of the party control argument, the shared preferences thesis, and the PPC model are observationally equivalent when it comes to voting behavior on the EP floor. In each case, we would expect to see cohesive party groups. We therefore cannot fully understand EP policy-making processes and outcomes by only examining voting behavior. The analysis of both qualitative and quantitative data, however, allows us to evaluate the respective applicability of the three theories.

This chapter begins by providing evidence that undermines the propositions of the shared preferences and party control models. In Part 1, it discusses the EP's informational deficit and casts doubt on the notion that individual MEPs are sufficiently informed about the content and likely consequences of the majority of legislation they vote on. This makes it unlikely that the policy choices of individual MEPs and, by extension, the aggregate positions of EP party groups can be attributed to shared policy preferences. Simply put, MEPs do not know enough about most legislative proposals to develop well-defined policy preferences. To alleviate this shortcoming, they rely on their colleagues in the responsible committee for information that facilitates their policy choice.

It is these expert colleagues who formulate the formal "party lines" of their respective party groups. This undermines one of the key propositions of the party control model, since party group leaderships do not have well-defined policy preferences regarding individual legislative proposals either, as Part 2 demonstrates. Just like their nonexpert rank and file, party leaderships adopt the positions of their expert specialists in committee. They do not, however, engage in active disciplining to ensure that these positions are followed on the EP floor, as their capacities to control their members are even more limited than the extant literature suggests and because the PPC dynamic, most of the time, assures cohesive voting in the plenary.

Part 3 of this chapter provides support for the propositions of the PPC model. It illustrates how the party group positions that are an endogenous product of decision-making in the responsible committee are aggregated into common party positions. It highlights, in particular, the importance of coordination among committee colleagues when formulating these positions and emphasizes the importance of this coordination effort, rather than coercive action, in ensuring party unity. Finally, statistical methods are used to demonstrate that nonexpert MEPs adopt these positions when voting on the EP floor.

Part 1: Incomplete information and uncertain policy preferences

As proposed in Chapter 2, MEPs are indeed confronted with a distinct "informational deficit" when making policy choices. Time is arguably the most important factor constraining the ability of MEPs to translate their outcome preferences into policy positions. MEPs are confronted with high volumes of legislation: During the EP's fifth term (1999–2004), a total of 2,077 committee reports were tabled in plenary, of which 1,232 were legislative in nature. Of these, 403 were decided under the time-consuming codecision procedure, which compares to only 165 in the preceding five years (Corbett, Jacobs, and Shackleton 2007: 139, 226).

Meanwhile, time is further constrained by travel between Brussels and Strasbourg, and between the locations of the EP and the members' home districts. As one MEP notes: "So many things happen in the EP, so many different subjects are being debated in different committees, that none of us follows everything with much detail . . . You don't have the time to look at everything yourself . . . We are always under time pressure here."[2] This sentiment is widespread among MEPs,[3] and in order to assume well-founded positions on every piece of legislation they are confronted with, legislators would require more hours in the day or a larger staff that competently evaluates the content and expected consequences of most legislative dossiers. This is a genuine problem for members of the EP, as the average number of assistants per MEP is only two.[4] While legislators in national parliamentary systems may have a staff size comparable to that of MEPs, the degree of autonomy enjoyed by the legislature in parliamentary systems with a fused executive and legislature is much more limited than in the case of the EP. Hence, legislators do not require the same amount of personal resources as members of the EP because they can rely on expertise grounded in national governmental ministries and in strong national party organizations. Given the role of the EP as a strong policy-influencing legislature, however, MEPs require more independent personal resources, such as a professional staff, to make informed, independent policy decisions. After all, as Cox (2000: 172) emphasizes, making legislation is more like research and development than it is like a choice among already-known alternatives. Accordingly, the resources required by MEPs are more comparable to those of legislators in separation of powers systems than to those in their national parliamentary counterparts in the EU member states. A relevant point of comparison is thus the U.S. House of Representatives, where members work with a minimum staff of 18 (Whiteman 1995: 30).

As in other legislatures, individual legislators' choices about participation in the negotiation process regarding a particular policy proposal are a function of their willingness to invest their scarce time, energy, and resources (Hall 1996). Due to the informational deficit, however, everyone in the EP focuses overwhelmingly on their own committee's affairs. Therefore, unless an assistant happens to become aware of a potential problem with a particular piece of legislation outside of the jurisdiction of the MEP's committees, the MEP might never know about it personally.[5] This necessarily means that MEPs are less informed about bills pending before other committees and more dependent for pertinent information on their expert colleagues in those committees (see Cox and McCubbins [1993: 11]).

As a result, it is quite common for members not to know very much substantive detail about the issues under consideration (see also Neuhold [2001]). A number of respondents readily acknowledges that most members generally do not know the majority of what they are voting on.[6] One explains that she knows what an issue is "basically about" from the party group meeting, but when an issue is divided into "75 votes, I really don't know each time what I vote ... If there is something that I don't care about, it must be handled by somebody who has more knowledge and interest in it."[7] Another MEP, from the Transport Committee, describes that he cannot follow what is going on in the Environment Committee with regard to animal testing "from A to Z," so he relies on his party's specialists to scrutinize those issues for him so that he knows what the basic issues and divisions are. He is provided the essential information he needs to "make up his mind" by his party colleagues, but he cannot "pay attention to Paragraph 7, Part 8, of some dossier" he is not directly involved in.[8] These findings, which support the propositions of the PPC model, illustrate that MEPs openly acknowledge lacking the capacity, in terms of expertise and resources, to form their own policy preferences autonomously from an external input. Accordingly, shared preferences alone cannot explain policy choice and party cohesion in the EP, as MEPs do not form independent policy preferences.

Specialization in committee

The informational deficit prevalent in the EP results in the delegation of decision-making authority to MEPs in the responsible legislative committee who are experts in the particular policy area under consideration. It is these few informed legislators who guide the Parliament as a whole through a given legislative process and set the parameters for action.

Following a natural division of labor between specialists on different issues, legislators tend to follow the information and advice they receive from their colleagues. As the informational perspective on the role of committees suggests (Krehbiel 1991), MEPs essentially "leave it to the experts" and follow their lead, allowing them to reap the gains from specialization.

In this context, it is striking that numerous respondents use the word "trust" unprompted during the interviews,[9] while others use similar terms such as "relying on"[10] or "following" committee experts.[11] This finding, which echoes conclusions by Whitaker (2005), matches what we know about the U.S. Congress, where analyses of vote choice have found that legislators rely on information from legislative specialists or "trusted colleagues" known to be knowledgeable about the particular issue at hand (Matthews and Stimson 1975; Zwier 1979; Kingdon 1981; Sabatier and Whiteman 1985). The PPC argument suggests that the basis of this trust is the assumption that the policy specialists with whom nonexperts perceive to share common outcome preferences—that is, experts with whom they share a common party affiliation—are unlikely to mislead them. As one senior MEP from the Environment Committee describes, when a party colleague and social policy expert who he has known for many years approaches him and suggests a position on a social policy issue, then he will, under most circumstances, follow this advice.[12] This was echoed by other respondents, who acknowledge that "if . . . you don't know anything about some other issue . . . then you are going to trust your colleagues,"[13] that "you rely on your colleagues, especially on technical issues,"[14] and that "I trust my friends in the committee, and they trust me."[15] Another MEP explains that: "You don't even read the report. You go to plenary, you have some general knowledge of what is in that report, but you just trust your colleagues from your party in that committee. You trust that they are the experts, and that they have gone through the issue in detail. It is based on mutual trust."[16]

Not everyone is a specialist on a given issue even within the responsible committee, however, especially in those with broad jurisdictions. This prompted one respondent to emphasize that "[in each party group] you only really have three specialists, or four; the rest are just following the specialists."[17] The complex and technical nature of many proposals effectively excludes most members from the detailed negotiations and deliberations even if they possess general expertise in the substantive issue areas covered by the committee.[18] For example, an expert on environmental policy might be a specialist dealing with biodiversity and remain relatively uninformed on the nitty-gritty aspects of carbon dioxide emissions; it is "double-Dutch, even for someone who is living with it every day," as one EP official maintains.[19] Moreover, time and resource constraints also affect committee members, meaning that even within single policy areas, MEPs have to pick and choose where to invest their time and resources.

For these reasons, responsibility for handling a certain dossier is delegated to a select few, even within the committee. There are usually only a small number of people who assume the leadership among their party colleagues, who try to inform the committee about the breadth of the repercussions of what is going on, and who, ultimately, delineate the policy positions of the party group as a whole.[20]

Part 2: The limits of party control

Decision-making in the EP committees is, therefore, not based on predetermined positions formulated by the party leaderships, with committee members simply representing these exogenous positions in the pre-floor negotiations.[21] It is actually quite the opposite: positions toward a legislative proposal are the product of committee deliberation and negotiation. Parties have, in the words of one MEP, "very broad lines, but there is no particular position on particular issues or particular directives. That is usually built up."[22] Hence, there is no party line dictated by the party leaderships, but rather one that is defined, represented, and propagated by the key actors in committee.[23] This confirms one of the key propositions of the PPC model and challenges a crucial aspect of the party control thesis.

The party control model is further undermined by the reality that even if parties did have well-defined, exogenous policy preferences, they would have great difficulties enforcing these positions. This is because EP party groups and their leaderships are even more constrained in their ability to engage in disciplining than is often assumed. Interviews with MEPs in leadership positions of EP party groups, national party delegation leaders, and EP officials involved in their party groups' offices responsible for legislative organization and coordination indicate that party leaderships are unable to impose a decision on their rank and file. Hence, even those who would have the greatest interest in exaggerating party control capabilities so as to attribute greater power to themselves, actually emphasize their inability to discipline their rank and file. One high-ranking party leader in the Party of European Socialists (PES), for example, emphasizes that "there is no such thing as punishment,"[24] while another party official asserts that "we would love to have something to whip people with, but we don't."[25]

What is more, EP party groups do not serve as the principal "gate-keepers" to positions of legislative power and influence, as important positions are distributed on the basis of proportional national representation, ability, expertise, and experience.[26] Hence, members are not dependent on the EU party groups for career advancement in the EP because party groups actually have few "carrots" to offer their rank and file in exchange for party loyalty.[27] For example, it is the party members in the committee who select one of their own as group coordinator, not the party group leadership. And while the formal power to make appointments to other important posts within the party and legislature lies with the party groups, in reality these positions are filled by nominees of the national party delegations, who are entitled to a number of posts proportional to their size (Kreppel 2002: 190, 202; see also Hix, Noury, and Roland [2007: 135]). Party groups have little opportunity to challenge these nominations and would do so only under exceptional circumstances when the nominee is broadly unacceptable to other national party delegations.[28] As one national party delegation leader in the European People's Party (EPP) maintains:

I can hardly imagine that my delegation or any other [puts up] Mr. Smith as a nominee for committee chair and the party group leadership comes and says no, during the most recent term he voted against the party line a certain number of times, so we cannot accept him. In this case, the will of the national party delegation prevails. They cannot make you do it.[29]

From the point of view of the party group leadership, this means that when positions are distributed at the beginning of a new legislative term, "you have to find a balance: you ask people to express their priorities and you take into account the priorities of the delegations, and then you try to find a solution taking into account experience and ability;" it is not about "giving bonbons to people."[30]

It is thus not surprising that "whipping" is both less frequent and strict than in national parliaments (Corbett, Jacobs, and Shackleton 2007: 108) and that the disciplining of members who deviate from the party line is unheard of in the EP.[31] In fact, even the three most publicized cases where MEPs were expelled from their EP party groups were not the result of deviations from the party line in terms of their voting behavior, but of specific actions deemed in violation of party group solidarity, as my respondents were eager to emphasize.[32] Roger Helmer was excluded from the EPP after signing a controversial motion of censure against the European Commission under President José Manuel Barroso, which placed him "outside the solidarity of the group" (EPP 2005). That is to say, he did not get ejected for voting against the party line, but for the more serious act of initiating of a vote of no confidence against the President of the EU executive, who was a fellow member of the EPP. Daniel Hannan was expelled, also from the EPP, not for voting against the party line, but for making "unacceptable remarks in the plenary session in Brussels of 31 January comparing the interpretation by the EP President of a Parliament Regulation to the German law of 1933 giving power to the Nazi regime" (EPP 2008). Finally, Mr. Hans-Peter Martin was excluded from the PES in 2004 after going public with claims of videotaped evidence of several thousand cases of MEPs picking up their per diem allowances during parliamentary sessions while in fact remaining absent from the proceedings (Minder 2004). This shed a questionable light on how MEPs use their daily allowances, when in fact "none of the things that Mr. Martin has accused his fellow MEPs of doing are illegal" (Clegg 2004). In each of these cases, MEPs were excluded from their party groups not for voting against the party line, but for acts perceived to violate the spirit and purpose of party membership and collegiality.

Even if one were to accept the assumption that party groups could discipline their members, however, the notion of coercive action against individual legislators presupposes that parties actually systematically monitor and record the voting behavior of their members. In the EP, this is evidently not the case. In fact, respondents in leadership positions in the two largest EP party groups, EPP and PES, maintain that the party group leaderships do not systematically monitor the votes of individual MEPs.[33] The same appears to be the case for national party delegations within the party groups: With a single exception, all national party delegation leaders questioned about their practices of keeping voting records claimed that they do not systematically monitor their colleagues' voting behavior over time.[34] To the extent that voting records are kept, it is at the party group level. These databases are "not used in a punitive way," however.[35] They are used to monitor the presence or absence of members for votes in committee and on the EP floor, and to keep track of the voting behavior of entire national party delegations, not individual members.[36] This is important not for disciplinary reasons; primarily, it helps party groups determine persistent lines of division within the party group, to identify particularly sensitive or important issues, and to identify future policy priorities.[37] However, neither the party groups, nor the national party delegations that comprise them, seem to engage in the systematic monitoring of individual-level behavior necessary to successfully engage in organized party control at the party group level.

Part 3: Perceived preference coherence and EP decision-making

EP party group leaderships neither have well-defined, exogenous policy preferences independent of those formulated by their party colleagues in the responsible committee, nor would they have the ability to enforce them. Party lines are not imposed from above, but created through the committee decision-making process. They result in cohesive party group positions on the EP floor if members of the same party group in the responsible committee are able to formulate a common party position. These findings are supportive of the propositions of the PPC model, and this section focuses on the process that produces a coherent party line through the transmission of policy information and policy positions from a small number of policy specialists in the responsible committee to the party group plenary. It then demonstrates that MEPs adopt the policy positions that come out of the committee when voting on the EP floor.

The creation of a party line

The informational structure of the party groups resembles a series of information filters, originating from the rapporteur and coordinator to the committee working groups, the coordinator meetings, the party working groups, and finally the party plenary. At each of these stages, information is made available and distributed, but within the constraints of time management and, to some extent, the strategic interests of the key players. The official party line concerning a given proposal is the end result of this information distribution process.[38] In a sense, what constitutes the party's "leadership" shifts with each legislative proposal: rather than acting as representatives of an existing party line, those handling a dossier in committee are its architects.[39]

Of particular importance to developing a party line is a small group of key actors, generally comprised of rapporteurs or shadow rapporteurs, party group coordinators, and a handful of other MEPs who choose to be particularly involved in the deliberation and negotiation of a proposal. These individual actors have great opportunities of influence and can "transcend formally weak positions to shape legislation" (Collins, Burns, and Warleigh 1998: 10). Since there is only one rapporteur for each legislative proposal, this position is allocated between the party groups. The party groups who do not end up holding a rapporteurship then appoint a shadow rapporteur whose responsibility it is to monitor the dossier on behalf of his party group. These shadow rapporteurs are very influential in that they are the primary negotiation partners of the rapporteur within the committee, as well as the primary sources of information for their party colleagues.

Each party group also has a group coordinator in every committee who is, in essence, her party group's leader within the domains of the committee. The responsibilities of the coordinators are much more broadly defined than those of the rapporteurs or shadows, however, in that they do not focus on a single issue or proposal, but seek to establish a coherent approach to the entire universe of proposals under consideration in the committee. Accordingly, their outlook is more universal than that of the rapporteurs or shadow rapporteurs, as they manage the broad policy agenda of the committee members from their party group, rather than lead the deliberation and decision-making regarding specific policies. And while coordinators are formally superior to rapporteurs or shadow rapporteurs, in reality the two tend to work in tandem and jointly lead their party groups through the decision-making process.[40]

Finally, there is also an element of self-selected· participation among committee members. If an MEP, other than those in formal leadership positions in the committee, gets actively involved in a given issue based on personal interest or motivation, "you have to count him in," as one MEP puts it.[41] Most often, this participation is determined by the particular area of expertise of committee members, since even within a committee's jurisdiction particular members possess specific areas of specialization.

All together, then, it is usually only a handful of experts from each party on a committee who really treat a legislative proposal in detail and bargain among themselves with regard to matters of public policy,[42] and the set of active participants shifts across bills (see also Hall [1996: 8]).[43] Only when an issue is especially controversial does the number of actively involved actors increase. In the words of one official, most of the committee members, just as the remaining MEPs outside the committee, "are following what their leaders [in the committee] are telling them."[44] Once these key players in the committee have established their positions—often already targeted at a compromise with the other shadow rapporteurs and even taking into account the position of the Council of Ministers—they establish a common position with their party colleagues in committee during the meetings of the *committee working group*. These working groups consist of all members of a party group sitting on the committee. Of course, committee working group meetings are often preceded by informal or formal meetings between members of the same national party delegations, who then promote their national party positions in the committee working group meeting. Finding agreement in the committee working group is a critical step, however, as it is usually at this stage that a unified line for the party group is generated.

Once a common position has been established among committee members from the same party, this position is presented either directly to the party plenary or to another set of intermediaries, namely the *coordinator meetings* (where the coordinators from different committees exchange information) and the *party working groups*, which in the larger party groups (EPP, PES, and Liberals) coordinate the parliamentary work of the party group members across different committees with overlapping policy competences.[45] These steps are very important, as potential controversies are detected and discussed with members of the other committees who may have a stake in and some degree of expertise on the issue. The party working groups in particular are designed to reduce and relieve the workload of the party groups. In the words of one Socialist MEP, they "filter out"[46] the most important aspects of a proposal and solidify a common party group position.[47]

If a common position comes out of the party working group, it is unlikely to be questioned by the party plenary and stands as the official party line. This party line is then formally communicated, in the form of voting instructions or "voting lists," by the party leaderships.[48] In the words of one long-serving EP official, "sometimes the plenary of the group can depart from what is proposed by the working party people, the coordinator on the issue, or the shadow, but that is uncommon. Very, very uncommon."[49]

Only if it is a very important issue for a national constituency or a matter of conscience will national party delegations or individual actors deviate from the party line, following the so-called "conscience clause." Party groups are actually quite accepting of dissenting views and policy positions, *as long as* these positions do not come as a surprise. Hence, if a particular group of party members or a national party delegation intends to deviate from the party line, the expectation is that this deviation will be announced to the party before the time of the vote, in part because this will provide another chance to make a renewed effort at finding a compromise position.[50] While a deviation may not be desirable from the point of view of the party group leadership, it is much preferred to a sudden and unexpected change in the political arithmetic. In the rare situation when a national party intends to dissent from the party group line, a separate voting list is supplied by the national party delegation, allowing the individual nonexpert MEPs to learn about the details of a proposal to compare and contrast positions. The decision-making process regarding a recent legislative proposal on "liability with regard to the prevention and remedying of environmental damage" (COD/2002/0021) provides an example for such a situation and is discussed in more detail in Chapter 5. In this case, there were two voting lists in the European Liberal Democrat and Reform Party (ELDR) for the first reading floor vote. This document actually had two columns providing contradictory voting instruction. One was the vote suggestion of the rapporteur in the lead committee, Toine Manders, while the other one was the proposed positions of a senior Liberal member of the Environment Committee, Chris Davies. Liberal MEPs could then decide which one of their colleagues they wanted to follow when making their own vote choice.

This kind of division among party colleagues in the responsible committee is quite unlikely, however, as committee experts recognize the importance of providing a coherent line to their colleagues in the party plenary. Since nonexpert members rely on their national party representative in the responsible committee when taking a position on the floor, a common position among the committee members from the same party group almost certainly entails a cohesive party line on the EP floor. Well aware of this reality, the current *de facto* party group leadership, most importantly the rapporteur or shadow rapporteur and the committee coordinator—often in cooperation with party group advisors—work in tandem to secure a party group position that is as broadly acceptable as possible to the maximum number of national party delegations. In fact, what is considered to be successful committee work is that the party line that comes out of committee is as broadly acceptable as possible to the greatest number of national party delegations, and thus the party group as a whole. This is "the yardstick applied to coordinators,"[51] because successful coordination in committee allows the party group to maximize its power in voting as cohesively as possible. The role of key actors in committee is thus a coordinating rather than a coercive one. That is, given their inability to actually force a given committee member to accept the party line and promote it within his or her national party delegation, the (shadow) rapporteur and coordinator seek to coordinate by way of deliberation, discussion, persuasion, and even through further negotiation to bring as many members of the committee working group on board as possible.[52] Rather than "whipping" their fellow colleagues into accepting their line, key committee actors have to "sell" it convincingly, which can be "a long process of building up a common position taking into account different sensibilities and interests."[53] As one respondent put it, "it is much more about consensus building and about persuasion and about dialogue than about some forceful instruments or means to achieve unity or discipline."[54] Another maintains that "definitely the aim of the group is to try to find a compromise and a common line. We reach this compromise 90 percent of the time."[55]

This is in part a result of a distinct norm of consensus that operates both within party groups and across partisan lines in the EP (Schneider, Steunenberg, and Widgrén 2006; Benedetto 2007). "The way we work here is to seek a compromise," according to one senior party group official.[56] However, there are also good strategic reasons for these efforts, as a coherent party position among policy specialists benefits legislative experts, nonexperts, national party delegations, and EP party groups and their leadership. First, it maximizes the policy influence of experts, because a common position among a party group's policy specialists is likely to be adopted as the formal party line. Moreover, since the position of the committee working group is usually the product of extensive negotiations among members of the same party in committee, rapporteurs and committee coordinators have a distinct interest in preventing the committee working group position from unraveling during the party group meeting.[57] As one shadow rapporteur put it: "In the end, when I have done the negotiations, they better follow me!"[58] Second, a common position among party group colleagues in committee maximizes the confidence of nonexperts in their preference coherence with committee colleagues, because there is no disagreement among those experts with whom they are most likely to perceive to share outcome preferences. In that sense, it "maximizes" perceived preference coherence. Finally, a common policy position in committee is of value to national party delegations and the party group as a whole, because it maximizes the probability that the party will vote cohesively on the EP floor. National party delegations know that they do not have "the numbers in the delegation to change the direction of a vote. We can contribute to the coherence of the decision, but if we are keen to achieve things in the Parliament then we have to work primarily through the [party] group."[59] Meanwhile, EP group leaderships are well aware that they are unable to enforce party discipline and that a common position in committee is their best bet in achieving a cohesive vote on the EP floor. A common position in committee has an additional benefit, however, in that it ensures that valuable time and resources are not spent unnecessarily on discussion of issues that are relatively uncontroversial. There simply is no time for every proposal to be discussed in detail in the party group meetings prior to voting sessions in Strasbourg, which means that coordination among the relatively small number of specialists in the responsible committee greatly facilitates intra-party decision-making. It is also a strong indication that there is no real controversy to be settled, which allows the party plenary to focus on those issues with the potential for genuine disagreement. A common position among party colleagues does this while providing a strong indication to the party as a whole, and its leadership, that the proposed position is unlikely to deviate too far from the party median.

In fact, one of the key purposes of the decision-making process being led by specialists is to avoid lengthy discussion of technical details in party group or EP plenary.[60] Controversies are supposed to be settled among the specialists unless broader issues of controversy are raised. The technical aspects of a dossier might make it into the broader setting if they cannot be settled in committee, but this is not very common, especially with highly technical dossiers.[61] In other words, EP committees are not just informational to the chamber as a whole, but party delegations within the committees are informational to their party groups.[62] The party plenary as a whole enters the picture only toward the end of the negotiation process, when committee deliberation is almost complete. It determines if there is a need for adjustment of the committee position, but in the words of one MEP, "it is rare for enough people in the full EP to study the question who are not on the committee, who actually want to change the whole thing."[63]

As agents of the chamber, the committee members possess a significant amount of policy influence and leadership opportunities. As in any principal-agent relationship, the possibility of agency loss is therefore ever present. Since party positions come out of committee, party groups have to be concerned about the possibility that the positions arrived at in committee do not represent the positions of the party as a whole, or that they are perceived as deviating from the collective interests of the party group. This would threaten the PPC dynamic and thus the voting cohesion of the party group because it would undermine the party members' perception that these positions most closely match their own outcome preferences. There are a number of checks and balances built into the process of building a party line with regard to a particular legislative

63

proposal, however. As a number of respondents maintain, it would be very difficult to "sneak" something of substantial controversy through the different screening stages without somebody noticing along the way.[64] In other words, the party line proposed by the committee members has to be acceptable to the group and the process of information transmission is not simply an unchecked "one-way street."[65] Yet, all intermediary forums for deliberation falling in between the committee and plenary stage operate under significant time constraints,[66] meaning that real controversy will only erupt if the issue contains provisions that some find simply unacceptable. Party groups are relying on a "fire-alarm" monitoring system, where potential problems or controversies can be brought to the group's attention in different settings by attentive members, or groups of members, who are not in the responsible committee. In most cases, however, a majority position from the committee working group is likely to prevail in the party working group, which will then also succeed as the official party line in the party plenary. This is, in part, because it is a rare circumstance that members outside of the committee will have followed the details of a proposal carefully enough to challenge the position proposed by the committee working group. As a result, the transmission mechanism from key players in committee to the committee as a whole, and then further into the party groups and the EP plenary, functions quite smoothly. In fact, this transmission from specialist to regular legislator appears to be the default process. This is partially for practical reasons because, as one respondent explains: "If we [in the committee] were to go to the full group with very sensitive issues that we could not agree on among ourselves, all hell would break lose. Because then you know what happens? Members actually read the amendments! And this is not good."[67]

Committee decisions and voting on the floor

One of the principal findings of the previous sections in this chapter is that it is members of the standing EP committees who are the architects of a party group's positions toward specific policy proposals. Unlike traditional parliamentary systems, where party positions are largely determined by strong party leaderships and based on a distinct government-opposition cleavage, a party line in the EP is not established prior to the deliberation in the first reading phase of the legislative decision-making process. Rather, it is the result of this deliberation process, with committee members establishing and proposing the positions their parties are to assume toward a policy proposal. While it is not a foregone conclusion that a majority in committee will automatically translate into a majority on the floor,[68] it is commonly suggested that "the work that is done at the committee level is accepted by the plenary."[69] This is because "once you have something approved by a committee, usually that [committee's members] manage to get it approved by their political groups."[70] One respondent spells this out as follows: "The consensus that arises from the committee is hoisted on the plenary as a whole ... The majorities in the committee are the same as the majorities in plenary. Parliament rarely goes against what the committee says ... Once an issue goes through the committee, it is going to invariably also make it through Parliament."[71]

However, this accepted wisdom among MEPs has not yet been systematically tested, a shortcoming that the following analyses seek to rectify. They determine that, as hypothesized, the positions of committee members constitute significant predictors of voting patterns in the EP plenary. More specifically, the findings support the expectations outlined in the previous chapter: MEPs primarily follow their national party delegation colleagues in the committee responsible for a piece of legislation when voting in the EP plenary, but only when they actually have a colleague from their national party delegation in the committee. This is not the case almost fifty percent of the time, however. When not represented in committee by a national party colleague, MEPs follow their party group representatives, while national affiliation hardly explains any of the variance in voting patterns.

This analysis is based on the entire population of plenary roll-call votes on legislative resolutions taken during the 1999–2004 parliamentary term under the codecision procedure when the final votes in either the first or third reading stages were recorded by name.[72] This yields a total of 122 roll-call votes and 52,363 individual-level observations. By focusing on final legislative reports under the codecision procedure, I am subjecting my theoretical propositions to the most rigorous empirical test because these are the highest profile EP votes and, therefore, nonexpert legislators would be most likely to be better informed about the content and likely consequences of these pieces of legislation. This is for two reasons. First, if MEPs ever have an incentive to expend time and resources on determining their positions toward policy proposals outside of their realms of expertise, it would be on these high-profile votes. Second, the EP has the highest public profile as an equal partner of the Council of Ministers under codecision, where the EP has the powers of veto and amendment. It is in the case of these high-profile votes that MEPs are most likely to be held accountable if they make the "wrong" decisions; therefore, they should be least likely to simply accept the voting advice of their colleagues in committee in lieu of determining their own positions independently. In sum, MEPs have the greatest incentive to *deviate* from the positions of their committee experts when making decisions under the codecision procedure and when voting on final legislative acts.[73]

It is important to recognize, however, that this analysis does not test the PPC model against a theoretical alternative. Its more modest ambition is to test for the existence of a PPC effect against a baseline of "no PPC effect." This is because the most important alternatives to the committee-based PPC effect shown in the analysis would be a party effect that exists independently of this committee input, or a shared preferences effect where MEPs vote with their committee colleagues not because the EP's informational deficit forces them to do so, but because their policy preferences coincide. The quantitative data alone does not allow us to differentiate between the three explanations, however. We cannot account for joint policy preferences because, as Part 1 of this chapter shows, most MEPs do not have well-defined policy preferences concerning most legislative proposals. Similarly, it is not possible to measure an exogenous party effect because there are no party positions independent of what happens in committee with regard to the great majority of votes. As Part 2 of this chapter demonstrates, party leadership in the EP is a fluid concept, with party representatives in the responsible committee acting as the *de facto* leaders of their parties with regard to a particular policy proposal. The causal sequence thus runs from committee to individual MEP, rather than from party leadership to individual MEP. It is this effect that the quantitative analysis seeks to account for.

Table 3.1: Frequencies, categorical variables in roll-call vote analyses

	Frequencies				
	Yes votes	No votes	Abstentions	Missing	Total
Vote	44,049	5,838	2,476	0	52,363
Common position, EP party group	44,245	4,419	927	2,772	49,591
Common position, National group	39,307	2,946	453	9,657	42,706
Common position, National party delegation	24,475	2,923	946	24,019	28,344

Because the dependent variable is categorical, I analyze the data using a multinomial logit regression model. The model simultaneously estimates the probability of any given legislator voting Yes, voting No, or abstaining. Abstentions represent the baseline category; Yes and No are the predicted categories. I use the positions of EP Party Group, National Group, and National Party delegations in the responsible EP committees as predictors for individual-level votes on the EP floor.[74] Table 3.1 provides frequencies of the different categories for these variables.

Table 3.2 displays the multinomial logit regression estimates, with "Abstention" as the omitted baseline choice.[75]

These results show the coefficients representing common positions of the EP party group and the national party delegation to be highly statistically significant, indicating that both common positions are potent predictors of Yes and No votes in the EP plenary. The coefficient for the national party position, however, is quite a bit larger than that of the EP party group, meaning that MEPs are most likely to follow their national party delegation members. A common position of the national group, in contrast, fails to achieve statistical significance.[76]

Since these coefficients are substantively difficult to interpret, the results are converted and presented in the following text as conditional predicted probabilities, which indicate the mean probabilities of a given outcome occurring at different combinations of common positions in committee.[77]

Table 3.2: Multinomial logit regression estimates, including National Party Delegation predictor

	No vote	Yes vote
EP party group	−5.44***	−1.85***
	(.40)	(.28)
National group	−.27	−.01
	(.31)	(.23)
National party delegation	−8.91***	−4.02***
	(.38)	(.21)
Constant	14.54***	10.22***
	(.54)	(.40)
Number of cases	25,093	
Log pseudo-likelihood	−3771.97	
Pseudo R^2	0.57	

Note: Table entries are multinomial logit estimates. The omitted (baseline) choice for each column is "Abstention." Cluster adjusted standard errors (cluster: MEP) appear in parentheses. Statistical significance is indicated as follows: $p < .05^*$, $p < .01^{**}$, $p < .001^{***}$

Table 3.3: Number of observations, various combinations of values of predictor variables

	Common position		# of observations
EP group	National group	National delegation	
Yes	Yes	Yes	22,279
Yes	Yes	No	155
Yes	Yes	Abstention	156
Yes	No	Yes	422
Yes	No	No	410
Yes	Abstention	Yes	34
Yes	Abstention	Abstention	88
No	Yes	Yes	207
No	Yes	No	402
No	No	Yes	6
No	No	No	684
No	No	Abstention	0
No	Abstention	No	0
No	Abstention	Abstention	23
Abstention	Yes	Yes	35
Abstention	Yes	Abstention	71
Abstention	No	No	8
Abstention	No	Abstention	18
Abstention	Abstention	Yes	2
Abstention	Abstention	No	0
Abstention	Abstention	Abstention	58
Yes	Yes	(not applicable)	12,438
Yes	No	(not applicable)	831
Yes	Abstention	(not applicable)	155
No	Yes	(not applicable)	1,269
No	No	(not applicable)	306
No	Abstention	(not applicable)	48
Abstention	Yes	(not applicable)	325
Abstention	No	(not applicable)	53
Abstention	Abstention	(not applicable)	14

The raw numbers of observations for these different combinations of values of the dependent variables are listed in Table 3.3.

The first set of predicted probabilities are presented in Table 3.4. The first column displays the predicted probabilities of MEPs voting in favor of a legislative proposal on the EP floor as a function of different configurations of positions among committee actors, that is, the predicted probabilities of a Yes vote in the plenary vote at different values of the other independent variables.

It demonstrates that the average predicted probability of an MEP voting in favor of a proposal in plenary when her party group, national group, and national party delegation representatives in the responsible committee assume common positions against it is negligibly small, at only 1.4

Table 3.4: Predicted probabilities of Yes and No votes, including National Party Delegation predictor

Common positions	Probability of YES vote	Probability of NO vote
EP group: No National group: No National delegation: No	.014 (.008, .002)	.986 (.978, .992)
EP group: No National group: Yes National delegation: No	.018 (.011, .028)	.982 (.972, .989)
EP group: No National group: No National delegation: Yes	.637 (.478, .772)	.361 (.226, .552)
EP group: Yes National group: No National delegation: No	.328 (.266, .392)	.672 (.608, .734)
EP group: No National group: Yes National delegation: Yes	.700 (.603, .784)	.298 (.214, .396)
EP group: Yes National group: Yes National delegation: No	.393 (.300, .495)	.607 (.505, .700)
EP group: Yes National group: No National delegation: Yes	.972 (.962, .980)	.015 (.010, .022)
EP group: Yes National group: Yes National delegation: Yes	.976 (.974, .979)	.011 (.010, .013)

Note: Table entries are mean predicted probabilities. Upper and lower 95 percent confidence intervals reported in parentheses.

percent.[78] A common position in favor by the national party delegation only marginally increases this probability to 1.8 percent if the EP party group and national party delegation remain opposed. In contrast, if the committee members from the MEP's party group vote in favor, the mean predicted probability of a Yes vote increases to a total of 32.8 percent, even if the national group and the national party delegation vote against. The most powerful predictor, however, is the common position of the national party delegation: Even if the party group and national group members in the responsible committee oppose a proposal, the average predicted probability of the MEP following the common position of her national party colleagues is 63.7 percent.

The average predicted probability of a Yes vote on the EP floor changes when different configurations of the committee groupings support a proposal. The average predicted probability of a Yes vote when national group and national party delegation assume a common position in favor of a proposal while the party group opposes is 70 percent, while party group and national group sharing a common position in favor with the national party delegation opposing entails an average predicted probability of a Yes vote of only 39.3 percent. A vote in favor is all but assured, however, when party group and national party delegation support a proposal even if the position of the national group opposes; in this case, the average predicted probability of a Yes vote is 97.2 percent. This is almost the same as the average predicted probability of a Yes vote percent when all three groupings support the proposal, which is 97.6 percent. This once again demonstrates the marginal impact of the national group position on voting patterns in the EP plenary.

These results show that MEPs seem to "triangulate" the information they receive from their party group and national party delegation representatives. Specifically, MEPs do not rely solely on the national party delegation or EP party group committee position, but they seem to compare the positions of their subsets of party colleagues in the committee when making a vote choice. As a result, an individual-level plenary vote is quite uncertain when the positions of committee representatives of the national party delegation and the EP party group representatives diverge, while MEPs are almost certain to follow the committee lead when there is a common position among national party and party group representatives.

The second column in Table 3.4 shows the predicted probabilities of a No vote in plenary and confirms the pattern from above.[79] Starting from a baseline average predicted probability of voting against a proposal of 1.1 percent when party group, national group, and national party delegation support a directive, the pattern of increases in the average predicted expected probabilities is almost identical to the probabilities of Yes votes on the EP floor. The probability of a No vote is 1.5 percent when both party group and national party delegation representatives vote in favor, with the national group voting against. Party group members opposing the proposal raise the probability to 29.8 percent, while a common national party delegation position against the proposal yields a 60.7 percent probability of MEPs opposing a proposal on the floor. Once again, a joint common position of party group and national party delegation members in opposition to a proposal entails a very high, 98.2 percent average predicted probability of MEPs voting No in plenary. In contrast, the probabilities resulting from joint positions of national group and national party delegation (67.2 percent) and between party group and national group (36.1 percent), while the third group opposes, are considerably lower.

Table 3.5 presents the mean predicted probabilities of an MEP abstaining on the EP floor, as a function of the common positions of her party group, national group, and national party delegation representatives in the responsible committee.[80] The results, although less instructive due to the smaller number of observations in the Abstention category, confirm our findings concerning Yes and No votes.[81] First, the common position of national party delegation members in committee is the most powerful predictor of abstentions on the floor. Second, the common position of EP party group representatives is the second most potent predictor (although its expected impact is less pronounced than in the case of Yes and No votes). And third, MEPs are most likely to abstain in the plenary when their national party delegation colleagues and EP party group colleagues in the responsible committee abstain collectively.

In these analyses, any cases with missing data on one or more of the variables are dropped, which means that only those cases are included when MEPs are represented by colleagues from their party groups, national groups, and national party delegations in the responsible committee. This, however, is often not the case, as MEPs are frequently not represented by members of their national party delegation: Of the total N of 52,363 valid individual votes, 24,019 (or 46 percent) are missing because MEPs do not have a member of their national party delegation taking part in the committee vote. So the question is: Who do MEPs follow when they do not have a national party delegation representative in the committee? The aforementioned analysis suggests strongly that they would follow their party group representatives. To ascertain this pattern, I run an additional analysis excluding those cases where MEPs are represented by national party delegation colleagues in the committee.

Table 3.6 displays the multinomial logit regression estimates for those votes where legislators do not have a national party representative in the responsible committee. Again, "Abstention" is the omitted baseline choice.

The table shows that only the coefficient representing the common positions of the EP party group is statistically significant for both Yes and No votes. This result indicates that a common party group position in committee is a more potent predictor in the EP plenary than a common position of the national group. Hence, MEPs are most likely to follow their party group colleagues on the responsible committee when they lack representation by members of their own national party delegation.

Table 3.5: Predicted probabilities of abstention, including National Party Delegation predictor

Common positions	Probability of Abstention
EP group: No National group: No National delegation: No	0
EP group: Yes National group: Yes National delegation: Yes	.012 (.011, .014)
EP group: No National group: Abstain National delegation: No	0
EP group: Yes National group: Abstain National delegation: Yes	.013 (.008, .017)
EP group: No National group: No National delegation: Abstain	.109 (.043, .219)
EP group: Yes National group: Yes National delegation: Abstain	.414 (.335, .499)
EP group: Abstain National group: No National delegation: No	.002 (.001, .003)
EP group: Abstain National group: Yes National delegation: Yes	.076 (.045, .125)
EP group: No National group: Abstain National delegation: Abstain	.105 (.046, .204)
EP group: Yes National group: Abstain National delegation: Abstain	.412 (.310, .522)
EP group: Abstain National group: Abstain National delegation: No	.002 (.001, .004)
EP group: Abstain National group: Abstain National delegation: Yes	.077 (.038, .133)
EP group: Abstain National group: No National delegation: Abstain	.811 (.691, .905)
EP group: Abstain National group: Yes National delegation: Abstain	.813 (.730, .882)
EP group: Abstain National group: Abstain National delegation: Abstain	.810 (.712, .891)

Note: Table entries are mean predicted probabilities. Upper and lower 95 percent confidence intervals reported in parentheses.

Table 3.6: Multinomial logit regression estimates, excluding National Party Delegation predictor

	No vote	Yes vote
EP party group	−6.48***	−2.35***
	(.36)	(.28)
National group	−1.04***	.16
	(.18)	(.14)
Constant	7.25***	5.06***
	(.44)	(.38)
Number of cases	14,439	
Log pseudo-likelihood	−6243.22	
Pseudo R^2	0.29	

Note: Table entries are multinomial logit estimates. The omitted (baseline) choice for each column is "Abstention." Cluster adjusted standard errors (cluster: MEP) appear in parentheses. Statistical significance is indicated as follows: $p < .05$*, $p < .01$**, $p < .001$***

Table 3.7 makes the substantive impact of these coefficients more accessible by presenting mean predicted probabilities of a Yes vote on the EP floor. It shows that a common position in favor of a proposal on the part of the national group representatives, with the party group against, yields only a 27.1 percent average predicted probability of an MEP voting in favor on the floor, while this probability is 82.5 percent when party group members vote in favor and the national group is against. This pattern applies in the case of No votes as well: A common EP party group position in opposition to a proposal in committee entails a 72.8 percent average predicted probability of members voting against the proposal in the subsequent plenary vote, while there is only a 12 percent probability with a common national group position. When national group and party group share a common position, the probabilities of MEPs following on the EP floor are 90.8 percent for Yes votes and 89.8 percent for No votes.

Finally, the EP party group position also constitutes the most potent predictor of abstentions in plenary, which are presented in Table 3.8. It demonstrates the average predicted probability of abstaining when the EP party group members in the responsible committee abstain collectively, which is 41.1 percent when the national group members vote against the proposal and 37.5 percent when they support it. In contrast, national group members abstaining together in committee barely affects the probability of MEPs abstaining in plenary.

Comparing the results of the analyses including MEPs who are represented by at least one national party colleague in committee and those who are not supports the thesis that MEPs seem to triangulate the

Table 3.7: Predicted probabilities of Yes and No votes, excluding National Party Delegation predictor

Common positions	Probability of YES vote	Probability of NO vote
EP group: No	.102	.898
National group: No	(.080, .126)	(.873, .920)
EP group: No	.271	.728
National group: Yes	(.242, .302)	(.695, .757)
EP group: Yes	.825	.120
National group: No	(.795, .851)	(.097, .145)
EP group: Yes	.908	.040
National group: Yes	(.896, .921)	(.034, .046)

Note: Table entries are mean predicted probabilities. Upper and lower 95 percent confidence intervals reported in parentheses.

information they receive from their party group and national party experts. They show that MEPs who are in a position to triangulate, because there is a member of their national party in the responsible committee, are more likely to adopt the EP party line that comes out of committee, as long as this party line reflects a common position shared by their EP party group and national party delegation representatives. For these MEPs, the mean predicted probability of following the common position that comes out of committee is 97.2 percent for a Yes vote, 98.2 percent for a No vote, and about 80 percent for an abstention. In contrast, MEPs who do not have a national party colleague in the responsible committee and cannot triangulate the information they receive from their EP party group

Table 3.8: Predicted probabilities of abstention, excluding National Party Delegation predictor

Common positions	Probability of Abstention
EP group: No	.001
National group: No	(0, .002)
EP group: Yes	.052
National group: Yes	(.043, .062)
EP group: No	.003
National group: Abstain	(.001, .005)
EP group: Yes	.047
National group: Abstain	(.032, .065)
EP group: Abstain	.411
National group: No	(.302, .525)
EP group: Abstain	.375
National group: Yes	(.282, .473)
EP group: Abstain	.341
National group: Abstain	(.227, .466)

Note: Table entries are mean predicted probabilities. Upper and lower 95 percent confidence intervals reported in parentheses.

colleagues in committee are less likely to adopt their party group's common position, with predicted probabilities of 82.5 percent for a Yes vote, 72.8 percent for a No vote, and about 40 percent for abstentions. These differences in predicted probabilities indicate why previous research has found a positive correlation between party size and party cohesion (Hix, Noury, and Roland 2005): MEPs from large party groups are more likely to be represented by a member of their national party delegation in the responsible committee, which allows them to triangulate the information they receive from their party group and national party delegation colleagues in committee. If these two groups share a common position, which is the case most of the time, it is almost certain that nonexpert MEPs will follow on the EP floor. In contrast, MEPs from small party groups are less likely to have a national party colleague in the responsible committee, and they are (somewhat) less likely to adopt their party group line.[82]

Conclusion

This chapter demonstrates that party positions in the EP are the product of the committee decision-making process, rather than an exogenous input imposed from above by the party group leaderships. In fact, there is little to suggest that EP parties have positions that are independent of what emerges from committee, which undermines the proposition of hierarchical party control in EP politics. Moreover, the qualitative evidence presented in this chapter casts doubt on the argument that EP party groups are truly capable of disciplining their rank and file. In fact, their capacity in this regard is weaker than is commonly assumed, which explains why actual cases of punitive measures against individual MEPs for deviating from the party line are virtually unheard of. Importantly, party groups are quite constrained when it comes to distributing posts and positions within the EP, which challenges the suggestion that the EP party groups' real power lies in their role as gatekeepers to influential positions within the legislative or party organizations. In reality, party group leaderships are bound by norms of intra-party proportionality, which inhibit the extent to which they can actually choose to reward party loyalists or withhold promotions from dissenters. They also do not systematically monitor the voting patterns of individual MEPs, which would be a prerequisite for the methodical execution of party control. For these reasons, it is highly questionable that party control—whether in the form of carrots or sticks—is a sufficient explanation for the high levels of party cohesion on the EP floor.

This is not to suggest that party discipline can play no role in shaping the behavior of individual MEPs, but rather to question the notion that party control is the principal factor explaining cohesive party group positions in the EP and to challenge the assumption that party cohesion would be substantially lower were it not for the ability of EP parties to control their members. The results in this chapter suggest that party control is neither a necessary nor a sufficient condition for EP party group cohesion. Yet, we also cannot simply attribute party cohesion to shared preferences among MEPs from the same party group because this would imply that MEPs have well-defined, exogenous policy preferences concerning most legislative proposals. In reality, MEPs do not know what their positions with regard to most legislative proposals ought to be because they lack the time and staff to collect and evaluate relevant information on every single legislative proposal before them.

The implication of these conclusions is that "politics" in the EP is about more than just shared preferences or party control. Instead, a dynamic process, involving deliberation, contestation, and coordination among policy experts, defines the policy positions that come out of committee, which become the formal party lines of the different EP party groups. Nonexpert legislators, who are too constrained by the EP's informational deficit to independently determine their policy preferences and positions concerning most policy proposal, adopt their expert colleagues' policy positions when making decisions on the EP floor. They do this on the basis of perceived preference coherence.

As the quantitative analysis demonstrates, MEPs rely primarily on their national party delegation colleagues in the responsible EP committee when voting on the EP floor. This is because levels of perceived outcome preference coherence are highest when legislators believe that they share both ideological and constituency interests with their expert colleagues. When MEPs are not represented by "one of their own," however, which is 46 percent of the time, they are most likely to follow their EP party group representatives, with a mean predicted probability of 82.5 percent for a Yes vote, 72.8 percent for a No vote, and about 40 percent for abstentions. Crucially, MEPs seem to triangulate the information they receive by comparing the positions of their different representatives in the committee, especially those of their party group and national party delegation colleagues. When these positions diverge, the resulting votes in plenary are quite uncertain. In the 92 percent of cases when both share a common position, however, the probability of nonexpert MEPs voting accordingly in plenary is very high: As Tables 3.4 and 3.5 show, the mean predicted probabilities are 97.2 percent for Yes votes, 98.2 percent for No votes, and just over 81 percent in the case of abstentions. The implication of these findings is that we should expect EP party group cohesion to be high simply on the basis of perceived preference coherence. For votes in favor of a given policy proposal, for example, 54 percent of MEPs have a 97.2 percent predicted probability of adopting a common position formulated by their national party and party group representatives in committee for the 92 percent of cases where the two groups agree with each other; the remaining 46 percent of MEPs have a 82.5 percent predicted probability of adopting the common position of their party group colleagues in committee. This adds up to cohesive party groups.

This evidence supports the propositions of the PPC model, but only in combination with the qualitative data can we truly evaluate its ability to explain EP decision-making. This is because both the shared preferences thesis and the party control argument would predict equivalent voting patterns on the EP floor. The interview data, however, shows that policy preferences and positions in the EP are neither imposed from above by the party group leaderships and then pursued in committee, nor derived autonomously by individual MEPs. Instead, they originate in committee and are aggregated to the EP floor through the PPC dynamic. Mixing qualitative and quantitative approaches thus enables us to not only recognize important nuances in EP decision-making, but more importantly to assess the applicability of three competing explanations.

While neither shared preferences nor party control predetermines EP decision-making, preferences and parties do play important roles. Shared preferences come into play in the form of perceived shared outcome preferences between experts and nonexperts, which provide the basis for the PPC dynamic. Meanwhile, a common party label serves as a proxy for these shared outcome preferences between expert and nonexpert legislators. Common outcome preferences and shared party affiliation thus have a mutually conditional effect on MEP policy choice.

There is a second important party effect, however, because the votes of individual MEPs are quite uncertain if their party group and national party representatives in the responsible committee assume different positions concerning a particular policy proposal. For this reason, coordination in committee between party group colleagues from different national party delegations is of critical importance if party groups seek to present a united front in the EP plenary. This coordination effort is structured along party group lines, as small groups of active participants in the deliberation of particular legislative proposals seek to build party group positions that are broadly acceptable across national party delegations. Notably, this coordination is based on deliberation and negotiation, rather than coercion; its aim is to find broad consensus, not to outvote a dissenting minority and force it to accept the majority position. Moreover, coordination is mostly successful and common positions are established well before a proposal reaches the party working group or the EP floor. Intra-party group divisions do not usually arise as a result, as one MEP emphasizes: "It rarely happens that the head of the [EP party] group insists that the party group follow one line under all circumstances. There is also no need for that because most of the time we vote together anyway."[83]

These findings about coordination in committee and the creation of a party line explain why it is a rare occurrence that national party delegations deviate from their EP party group line. That is, they help us understand how EP party groups and their national party delegations manage to take common positions on most issues on the EP floor. It is not so much that the national party will voluntarily decide not to vote against the party line (Hix, Noury, and Roland 2007: 133), but rather that under most circumstances the position of the EP party group reflects a compromise agreement between national party delegations, where the particular concerns of individual national party delegations have been taken into account. This result is achieved through the delegation of policy-making authority on particular issues to a small subset of expert legislators in the responsible committee whose stated responsibility it is to define a party line that is as broadly acceptable as possible to the greatest number of national party delegations. This system of delegation works for three reasons. First, committee membership is distributed proportionally across national party delegations to maximize the representativeness of the committee delegation. Second, deliberation and negotiation is left to policy experts who can credibly claim to make "good" policy. Third, negotiations take place among a small number of actors, which facilitates the process and increases the likelihood that compromises can be agreed upon.

Previous research fails to recognize this pattern because it treats national party delegations as unitary actors, when in fact it is not only instructive, but quite important, to specify whom we are referring to when we assign significance to the actions of "national party delegations" in the EP party groups. In particular, we have to be clear that when national party delegations in the EP take policy positions toward particular pieces of legislation, these positions are proposed by their own in-house expert legislators and are usually reflective of a broader compromise reached among committee representatives from different national party delegations. Except in a small number of cases that are deemed to be of fundamental importance, in which case some national parties may provide exogenous policy positions (Raunio 2000: 218), the positions of national party delegations are endogenous to the decision-making process in committee. This is critical because the policy positions of both the party groups and the national party delegations that comprise them are the result of the same pre-floor deliberation and negotiation process. In other words, EP party groups and national party delegations arrive at their policy positions in a single process that maximizes the probability of consensus. It is thus not surprising that, most of the time, party groups and national party delegations vote together.

Just like the party lines of the EP party groups, the positions of national party delegations come out of committee and are then adopted in plenary on the basis of perceived preference coherence. The implication is that cohesive voting is the default option in national party delegations, which is reflected in the comments of one national party delegation leader who maintains that he is not "obliged" to discipline his national party delegation colleagues "because there hasn't been an instance of serious divergence."[84] These findings again suggest that party cohesion would be quite high even in the absence of party discipline. However, while the link between party discipline and cohesive voting patterns has not been convincingly demonstrated in the case of EP party groups, there actually is meaningful evidence that at least some national party delegations seem capable of controlling the behavior of their MEPs (Faas 2003; Hix 2004). Even in the case of national party delegations we have to be cautious not to overstate the effect of this party control element, however, as the PPC logic suggests an alternative explanation for why MEPs are more likely to vote with their national party delegations, rather than their party groups, if the two are in disagreement over a particular policy: They are because levels of perceived outcome preference coherence are greater between legislators that share both ideological and constituency interests than between legislators that only share ideological outcome preferences. Hence, when the positions of their national party representatives and their EP group representatives in committee diverge, they are more likely to follow their national colleagues. If the groups share a common position, however, party cohesion ensues. Because of this reality, "the national party delegation leader is not as important in forming a united position of the group as the rapporteur or shadow rapporteur, or the coordinator," as one MEP explains.[85]

It is thus important to consider the role of parties and committees jointly, just like we have to think about the joint effects of parties and preferences. A micro-perspective that focuses on individual legislators allows us to consider these mutually constitutive effects. In the case at hand, the answer to the question of how common policy positions between EP party groups and their national party delegations come about lies in the pre-floor deliberation and negotiation process in committee. We know this because asking how individual legislators make decisions concerning particular policy proposal forces us to simultaneously consider the effect of both parties and committees. It also compels us to focus not just on the capabilities of political actors, but to be equally sensitive to the constraints they face in the policy-making process. In the case of EP party groups, this means their inability to enforce party discipline; for individual legislators, it means the uncertainty imposed by the EP's informational deficit. The PPC dynamic provides a solution to these problems while facilitating the realization of several key goals in legislative politics: It allows small groups of expert legislators to efficiently make policies of high substantive quality; it enables members of Parliament who are uninvolved in the deliberation and negotiation process to make informed choices on policy proposals outside their realms of expertise; and it facilitates the creation of cohesive party positions despite the EP party groups' structural weaknesses.

Appendices

Appendix 1: Interview data

To maximize the validity and the reliability of my interview data, I relied on three strategies. First, I conducted a large number of interviews, allowing for consistent themes to emerge across respondents. For each case study, detailed in Chapter 5, I conducted between 9 and 13 interviews, reaching a point of saturation both with regard to the specific policy proposal and the general questions relating to processes of policy choice in the EP. Second, I conducted interviews not just with politicians: While 51 of the 86 respondents are MEPs (two of whom were interviewed twice between 2003 and 2005), 28 are EP officials (2 were interviewed twice between 2005 and 2008), three are Commission officials, and four are Council officials. Once again, consistency of responses across this diverse range of respondents enhanced their credibility. Finally, I sought to interview a sample of respondents representative of the EP population, which was particularly successful with regard to political affiliation. The interviews involved representatives from all seven major party groups in the EP and are roughly distributed across these party groups proportionately by party strength (measured as total number of MEPs). In this regard, the sample of respondents does represent a "microcosm" of the Parliament. Concerning the countries of origin of my respondents, however, the interviews are not distributed as proportionally, partially due to linguistic constraints, but also to availability and willingness to be interviewed. Specifically, Austria, Finland, Ireland, the Netherlands, and Sweden are overrepresented, while France, Italy, and Spain are underrepresented. Respondents from Belgium, Denmark, Germany, Greece, Luxembourg, Portugal, and the United Kingdom (UK) are represented more or less proportionally. It is important to note, however, that my sample includes respondents from all the 15 countries that were EU members during the 1999–2004 legislative term.

Appendix 2: Operationalization

For each roll-call vote used in the statistical analyses, I identify the positions of the members of the EP committee responsible for the particular legislative dossier who participated in the final committee vote on the legislative report before it was transferred to the EP floor. I determine this position on the basis of their subsequent vote in plenary, since committee votes are not recorded by name. I then treat these individual-level votes as predictors of plenary voting behavior. In light of the finding that MEPs determine how to vote based on the positions of committee experts, there are three possible groups of experts who could serve in this position-setting role: First, the general population of MEPs may follow the vote recommendations of their party group colleagues in the committee. Second, they may follow the representatives of their national colleagues, rather than party group colleagues, when voting in plenary. Finally, they may focus specifically on the members of their national party delegations when considering how to vote. To operationalize these variables, I determine three types of "majority positions." First, the majority position among committee members from the same EP party group. Second, the majority position of each national group. And finally, the majority position of each national party delegation.

I define majority position as a qualified majority of 60 percent. I choose this threshold based on the following reasoning: Using the common majoritarian threshold of 50 percent would entail that we identify a "common position" even when a grouping is, in fact, dramatically divided. For example, we would code a ten to nine majority in one of the large party groups as a common party position on an issue. At the same time, a threshold of two-thirds would be quite restrictive. We would, for instance, fail to recognize a common position when five of eight members of a small party group vote together. The threshold of 60 percent is chosen to capture the middle ground. It is important to note, however, that most majority positions are quite robust and thus not sensitive to this cutoff point. The general patterns of the analyses would likely be observed with different threshold specifications as well, while some of the actual values might vary somewhat.

I then create variables for these common committee level positions of the EP Party Group, National Group, and National Party Delegation as predictors for the votes of all party group, nationality, and national party delegation members in plenary, respectively. Just like the dependent variable, which is simply the votes cast by the individual MEPs in the plenary, the three predictors can take three values: zero for a No vote, one for a Yes vote, and two for an abstention. If there was no majority position, or if an individual MEP did not have a representative of his party group, national group, or national party delegation in the committee, it is coded as a missing value. Since it is not possible to establish the EP Party Group predictor for nonattached MEPs, they are excluded from the analysis. These operationalization details also apply to the second analysis that focuses on MEPs who are not represented by members of their own national party delegation in the responsible committee, except that the variable for the common position of the national party delegation is not included in the model.

It is important to emphasize that this operationalization reflects the key proposition of the PPC model that nonexpert members rely on *perceived* preference coherence with their expert colleagues in the responsible committee when taking positions on the EP floor, rather than *actual* preference coherence. Legislators have no way of knowing whose policy preferences actually reflect their own outcome preferences. In fact, the only way for a nonexpert MEP to determine which expert colleague's policy position most closely matches her outcome preferences would be to figure out her own policy preferences, which defeats the very purpose of specialization and a division of labor in the legislature. This is why MEPs have to rely on a proxy for shared outcome preferences, which provides the key piece of information nonexperts rely on when making policy-specific decisions.

Notes

1. See Appendix 1 for further details on the interview data.
2. Respondent #48.
3. Respondents #6, 9, 18–19, 38, 51, 68, 72; see also Corbett, Jacobs, and Shackleton (2007: 57–8).
4. According to the EP Web site (http://europarl.europa.eu), accessed on April 2, 2007, there were 1,416 full-time assistants for 785 MEPs. Members are provided with a secretarial allowance to employ personal assistants and have considerable freedom in using these funds. They may choose to employ two well-paid assistants or several less-well paid or part-time employees (Corbett, Jacobs, and Shackleton 2007: 67).
5. Respondent #9.
6. Respondents #2, 7, 9, 19, 35, 68. See also Rasmussen and Shackleton (2005: 3, 16), who maintain that the "vast majority" of MEPs are only able to "follow with difficulty the progress of negotiations before they are invited to vote at first or second reading" and that "the time available to verify an agreement is normally shortest at second reading, with the vote often taking place only a matter of days after the conclusion of negotiations. Necessarily this reduces the scope for challenges to an agreement, with other members obliged to accept or trust that they should vote in favor."
7. Respondent #7.
8. Respondent #19.
9. Respondents #4, 6, 7, 11, 19, 22, 35, 38, 42, 44, 47–48, 64, 68, 72.
10. Respondents #14, 34.
11. Respondents #1, 8, 18, 51, 55, 69.
12. Respondent #22.
13. Respondent #72.
14. Respondent #14.
15. Respondent #11.
16. Respondent #35.
17. Respondent #18.
18. Respondents #17, 19, 38, 45, 49, 51, 72, 77.
19. Respondent #51.
20. Respondents #6, 18–19, 32–33, 38, 45, 47–49, 68.

21. Respondent #37.
22. Respondent #45.
23. Rasmussen and Shackleton (2005: 12) also argue that the grounds for deliberation and negotiation of particular legislative proposals is determined by the rapporteur and other key negotiators in first reading, when the formal positions of EP and Council are yet to be determined.
24. Respondent #79.
25. Respondent #9; also Respondents #80, 82, 85, 86.
26. Respondents #64, 79, 81, 84, 85.
27. The only "carrot" exclusively in the hands of the party groups is speaking time (Respondents #64, 85). Kreppel (2002: 204) maintains, however, that national representation is also taken into account when it comes to speaking time.
28. Respondents #9, 82, 85, 86.
29. Respondent #86.
30. Respondent #79. It is thus not surprising that Kreppel finds that PES and EPP members who received numerous terms as committee chair or an unusually high number of rapporteurships were no more supportive of the party line than the average for their party (Kreppel 2002: 201).
31. Respondents #79, 84, 86.
32. Respondents #64, 80, 86.
33. Respondents #64, 85.
34. Inquiries were made in person or in writing to the heads of the 20 largest national party delegations in the EP, which together make up 50 percent of the EP's total membership; 14 responses were received, for a response rate of 70 percent. Of these 14 delegations, which together account for 36 percent of the EP's total membership, only a single delegation leader maintained that he carefully monitors his member's voting records.
35. Respondent #64.
36. Respondents #9, 64, 79, 82, 85.
37. Respondents #64, 80.
38. Respondents #2, 17, 34, 45, 47, 72, 80, 83, 85.
39. Respondents #1–2, 9, 16, 18–19, 22, 33, 44–45, 48, 56, 69, 72, 79, 85.
40. EP party groups also have political advisors in charge of following the proceedings of different committees. These advisors often work closely with the co-ordinators and rapporteurs of their party groups in the committees for which they are responsible. The party advisors can play important roles, especially in terms of coordinating various positions among party members; yet, the actual political responsibilities lie with the actors in the lead committee.
41. Respondent #45; also Respondent #18.
42. Respondents #6, 18–19, 32–33, 38, 45, 48–49, 68.
43. Rasmussen and Shackleton (2005: 4) argue that MEPs have little informal control over the work of key negotiators, while Farrell and Heritier (2003a: 8)

argue that "it is often extremely difficult for others within the Parliament...to have any idea of what exactly is going on."

44. Respondent #18.
45. The EPP, for example, has five working groups: Working Group "A" (responsible for: Committee on Foreign Affairs, Human Rights, Common Security and Defence Policy, and Committee on Development and Cooperation); Working Group "B" (Committee on Industry, External Trade, Research and Energy; Committee on Employment and Social Affairs, Committee on Culture, Youth, Education, the Media and Sport, and Committee on Women's Rights and Equal Opportunities); Working Group "C" (Committee on Budgets; Committee on Budgetary Control; Committee on Agriculture and Rural Development, and Committee on Fisheries); Working Group "D" (Committee on Legal Affairs and the Internal Market; Committee on Citizens' Freedoms and Rights, Justice and Home Affairs; Committee on Constitutional Affairs, and Committee on Petitions); Working Group "E" (Committee on the Environment, Public Health, and Consumer Policy; Committee on Regional Policy, Transport and Tourism, and Committee on Economic and Monetary Affairs).
46. Respondent #56.
47. Respondents #2, 72.
48. Respondents #2, 33–34, 43, 45, 58, 72.
49. Respondent #72.
50. Respondents #64, 79, 83.
51. Respondent #64.
52. Respondents #22, 45, 56, 83.
53. Respondent #80.
54. Respondent #86.
55. Respondent #64.
56. Respondent #64.
57. Respondents #7, 33, 48, 58.
58. Respondent #7.
59. Respondent #81.
60. Respondents #33, 38.
61. Respondents #33, 45.
62. Whitaker (2005) suggests that committee delegations are informational even from the perspective of the national party delegations.
63. Respondent #48.
64. Respondents #14, 48.
65. Respondent #47.
66. Respondent #48.
67. Respondent #9.
68. Respondents #2, 38, 44.
69. Respondent #72.

70. Respondent #45; Respondents #14, 37, 48, and 55 provided similarly quotable statements.
71. Respondent #16.
72. Excluded are those cases for which there was no preceding vote in committee, or when the committee vote did not take place in the same legislative term.
73. This logic also addresses potential concerns about the use of roll-call vote data to test the PPC logic. The use of roll-call vote data in analyzing EP voting patterns has been critically evaluated in the recent past. Carrubba et al. (2006) show that the recorded votes in the EP differ along several dimensions from the remaining votes in the EP (e.g., by requesting party group and substantive issue area), indicating that the roll-call vote sample may be biased. Moreover, legislatively consequential votes under the codecision procedure seem to be systematically under-sampled. My focus on high-profile votes, however, means that the statistical analyses in this chapter quite likely systematically underestimate the degree to which nonexpert MEPs follow their expert colleagues on the basis of perceived preference coherence. This is because MEPs are more likely to make up their own minds when a roll-call vote is called on a politically consequential legislative proposal. In that case, they should be more willing to expend the resources necessary to form their own policy preferences, thus less likely to rely on perceived preference coherence with their expert colleagues, and therefore more likely to deviate from the party line.
74. See Appendix 2 for operationalization details.
75. The standard errors presented throughout are adjusted for clustering at the individual legislator level. Models that use clustered standard errors for each vote included in the analysis produce only marginally different predicted probabilities with slightly wider confidence intervals. Note that due to listwise deletion of missing values, the individual analyses conducted in what follows do not add up to the original N of 52,363.
76. Given high correlations between some of the independent variables, additional analyses were performed including different combinations of predictors. The results of the analyses confirm the ones presented here for the complete model.
77. Throughout, predicted probabilities are calculated using CLARIFY, a computer program that uses Monte Carlo simulation to convert the raw output of statistical procedures into results that are intuitive and of direct interest to the researcher, without changing statistical assumptions or requiring new statistical models (King, Tomz, and Wittenberg 2000). There are two levels of simulation. First, a random draw is made from a distribution of possible values for the coefficients (addressing our uncertainty about true value of these parameters). Then, a random draw is made, using the given values of the coefficients and fixing the independent variables at our selected values, but allowing for inherent randomness in a particular outcome (the stochastic component or error in the model). For each entry in the table, this process is repeated 1,000 times and

the "confidence intervals" are taken from the quantiles of the resulting observations, with point estimates taken to be the average of these results.

78. The results tables provide 95 percent confidence intervals around the predicted probabilities. We can be 95 percent confident that the values of the predicted probabilities fall between these upper and lower bounds.

79. Note that since there are three outcome categories (Yes, No, and Abstention), the probability of a No vote is not simply the opposite of the probability of a Yes vote.

80. Note that it is possible to calculate predicted probabilities despite the fact that abstentions were treated as the baseline category in the multinomial logit analysis.

81. Abstentions are often the result of individual MEPs or entire national party delegations deviating from the party line on the basis of the "conscience clause," when a particular vote is perceived to have a special impact on their constituencies. To provide one example, a member of the EPP from one of the Benelux countries interviewed in the context of the Port Services directive gave the following reasoning for abstaining in the final vote on the EP floor: "I did not want to change my mind or my vote, but also did not want to punish my [national colleagues] with a No vote. Abstaining hurt neither my [national colleagues] nor Mr. Jarzembowski [the rapporteur and party colleague]."

82. Additional analyses were performed to consider an alternative explanation for the positive correlation between party size and party cohesion, namely that MEPs from large party groups are simply more inclined to follow their expert colleagues in committee, *ceteris paribus*. To examine this possibility, I replicated the previous analyses including a party size variable. The results of these analyses are not presented here because the 95 percent confidence intervals of almost all predicted probabilities of MEPs from parties of different sizes adopting the positions of their expert colleagues in the responsible committee overlap, indicating that we cannot distinguish between them at standard levels of statistical significance. This is the case for all but a very small number of the combinations of values of the independent variables shown in Table 3.4. These differences, however, were substantively negligible. For example, the greatest difference in predicted probabilities without overlapping confidence intervals is found for MEPs from parties of different sizes voting Yes on the EP floor when their party group, national group, and national party delegation representatives share a common position in favor of a proposal. Here, the mean predicted probability of an MEP from a small party group voting in favor of the proposal on the floor is 96 percent, while the probability for an MEP from a large party group is 97.8 percent.

I also considered the possibility that MEPs from national and subnational constituencies are more or less likely to follow their expert colleagues in committee (see Farrell and Scully [2007]). As in the case of party size, these analyses do not produce predicted probabilities without overlapping confidence intervals for MEPs from different types of constituencies, except in one instance, namely for the predicted probability of MEPs from different types of constituencies voting No on the EP floor when their party group, national group, and national party delegation representatives share a common position in favor of a proposal. In this case, the mean predicted probability of an MEP with a national constituency voting against the proposal on the floor is nine percent, while the mean predicted probability for an MEP from a subnational constituency is 14 percent.

83. Respondent #84.
84. Respondent #81.
85. Respondent #86.

Chapter 4

Focal Points as Mechanisms for Policy Choice

In Chapter 2, we differentiated between actors who are policy specialists and those who are not. On the basis of this distinction, I laid out my argument about the perceived preference coherence (PPC) dynamic that drives decision-making in the European Parliament (EP). I argued that it explains how individual legislators make decisions regarding particular legislative proposals and, in the process, sheds light on the role of both parties and committees in EP politics. A critical aspect of the argument revolves around the translation of outcome preferences into policy preferences. That is, it considers how nonexpert legislators connect their preferences concerning the expected consequences of a particular legislative proposal with the positions they take toward it, based on their beliefs about how this policy action relates to their most preferred outcome.

However, while Chapter 3 described a dynamic political process *in committee*, there was little politics—in the form of deliberation, contestation, and negotiation—evident in the interaction between policy expert and nonexperts. It is particularly notable that my theoretical propositions so far have been built on the implicit assumption that nonexpert legislators do not demand any kind of justification or explanation from their expert colleagues as to why they should adopt their stated policy positions. In other words, they blindly accept the positions of the policy experts with whom they perceive to share a common set of preferences (i.e., their party colleagues).

If we were to accept the assumption that nonexpert legislators adopt the policy positions of their expert colleagues without explanation or justification, there would be no need for further discussion of the EP decision-making process. It seems problematic, however, to assume that this is indeed the case, as it would imply that nonexpert legislators do not care about *why* they vote the way they do. But it is obviously a questionable assumption that legislators are indifferent to all pieces of legislation, or that they care—or do not care—equally about all policy proposals. This supposition is problematic for a number of reasons. First, while legislators may not have well-defined policy preferences, they are predisposed to care more about some issues than others. This will influence the extent to which they perceive the need to pay attention to a given piece of legislation. That is, they may have reasons to attach different degrees of significance to some policies. Second, the extent to which they care about an issue or proposal may be affected by external factors, such as particular constituency concerns. Therefore, even if legislators do not particularly care about a specific issue, they may feel compelled to consider it to be of importance.

As a result, we not only have to consider the level of expertise individual legislators possess when they establish the link between their outcome preferences and policy preferences, but also how much importance they attach to an issue. We should assume that legislators who care more about an issue will expend at least some resources on trying to ensure a strong link between their policy positions and their outcome preferences, while those who are indifferent may not.

It is important to note that even legislators with a substantial level of expertise in a particular policy area have to invest some degree of effort and resources into actually determining the link between their own outcome and policy preferences. This may simply mean actually reading the policy proposal in detail, or having an assistant prepare a content report. Depending on the complexity of the dossier, however, it may require expending significant amounts of time and effort on the collection of all necessary information about the content and consequences of the legislation. Hence, participation is not without cost even for expert legislators (Hall 1996). Like nonexperts, they have to make a decision to expend some resources to establish the link between outcome and policy preferences, and to choose the policy positions that most likely entail their most preferred outcomes. In other words, *every* legislator has to make an initial strategic choice about the extent to which they pay attention to particular policy proposals: some will receive a great deal of attention, while others will necessarily fall to the side. The decision to pay attention to a proposal or not, and how much attention the proposal deserves, depends on how important the legislator considers the proposal to be. If she considers the proposal to be less relevant to her interests, she is unlikely to pay much attention to it. Only if she views the proposal as important enough to warrant her attention will she seek at least a minimum amount of information about the congruence between the likely consequences of the proposal upon implementation and her outcome preferences.

Invested and indifferent experts and nonexperts: a typology of legislators

While both expertise and the relative significance a legislator attaches to a given issue should be conceptualized as continuous variables, I discuss them in dichotomous terms here for simplicity's sake. That is, actors can be either experts or nonexperts who consider an issue to be either important or not important. This provides for the matrix in Figure 4.1.

Actors in the lower right-hand quadrant (*invested experts*) are legislators who consider a policy proposal to be of significance and who possess the necessary policy expertise to meaningfully connect their policy preferences with their outcome preferences. The decision-making process for these expert legislators resembles the committee voting model discussed in Chapter 2, where a small number of actors has full information and well-defined preferences, and can properly evaluate the content and likely consequences of a policy proposal. Moreover, since they are invested, these experts are also willing to expend the resources necessary to make informed decisions. Invested experts should thus play an active role in the deliberation and negotiation process and help shape policy outcomes. After all, these are the actors who not only use their expertise and resources to make up their own minds, but also to provide the input into the PPC dynamic and thus influence the positions of their nonexpert colleagues.

Legislators in the lower left-hand quadrant (*indifferent experts*) are those who would be capable of deriving their own policy positions from their outcome preferences, but who do not bother spending the necessary resources to do so because they do not attach enough significance to the issue at hand. These may be committee members who choose not to participate in the active negotiation of a particular proposal. We would expect these

	Issue not Important	Issue Important
Low Expertise	Indifferent Nonexperts	Invested Nonexperts
High Expertise	Indifferent Experts	Invested Experts

Figure 4.1 Typology of legislators

91

legislators to act much like nonexperts in that they will follow those expert colleagues who do care about the proposal, if they bother to vote at all. Despite their high levels of expertise, however, they will not play an active part in trying to influence the behavior of their nonexpert colleagues, again because they do not consider the issue to be of enough importance.[1]

Parliamentarians who do not possess sufficient levels of expertise occupy the upper two quadrants of the matrix. These are actors who do not autonomously form their own policy preferences and rely on expert colleagues when making a policy choice. As such, they are at the receiving end of the PPC dynamic. Here again, we can differentiate between those who consider the issue at hand to be important and those who do not.

Indifferent nonexperts, located in the upper left-hand quadrant, are legislators who attach little significance to the policy proposal and who act like the stylized-version of legislative nonexperts discussed in Chapter 2. They will simply adopt the positions of their expert colleagues, based on the preference coherence they perceive, and will not demand a justification for this choice. In other words, like expert legislators who do not care about an issue, these legislators resemble voters in the mass elections model: they will either choose not to vote at all or they will cast votes based on the party label alone, be it the national party label or the EP party group label.

More interesting are those actors in the upper right-hand quadrant, the *invested nonexperts*. While they do not possess a sufficient degree of expertise to derive their own policy preferences, they do care about the issue at hand and are unlikely to blindly adopt the policy positions even of those colleagues they trust and with whom they perceive to share a common set of outcome preferences. These legislators resemble voters in mass elections who are interested and willing to expend some resources to determine what candidate they should vote for, but for whom the party label still plays an important role in making an informed choice. The impulse of these legislators is to vote the party line, but they want to be reassured that this party line approximates their ideal outcome preferences; they want a justification for their policy action.

It is, of course, important to note that individual legislators fall into different categories depending on the particular policy proposal on the table. An invested expert on environmental policy questions may be an indifferent nonexpert when it comes to gender equality issues, for example, and an invested nonexpert in the case of legislation that relates to the civil liberties of EU citizens. Independent of the policy area, however, there are different *mechanisms* by which these four ideal types of legislators connect outcome preferences with policy preferences. Legislators who do not attach any significance to a policy proposal, *indifferent experts* and *indifferent nonexperts*, will simply rely on perceived preference coherence when making a policy choice, whether or not they possess the policy expertise that would enable them to make more meaningful choices themselves. One might even say that these legislators effectively skip the determination of their policy preferences and go directly to policy choice; they do not even form a distinct preference concerning the policy before adopting their expert colleagues' positions. Hence, for indifferent legislators the theoretical discussion in Chapter 2 provides a sufficient conceptualization of the mechanism of policy choice and, when casting a vote on the EP floor, their default choice is to follow the party line formulated in the responsible committee. In fact, since indifferent legislators do not consider the proposal to be of sufficient importance, they have no incentive to vote against this party line in the first place.

Policy specialists who view a proposal as important will use their expertise to determine what their policy preferences, and thus policy positions, should be. For these *invested experts*, the mechanism linking outcome preferences to policy preferences and policy choice consists of a personal evaluation of the content and likely consequences of the legislation upon its implementation. However, as policy experts and agenda-setters for the chamber as a whole, these legislators do not act purely on the basis of their genuinely most preferred outcome, but also as strategic actors engaged in formulating a policy that has a chance of being approved on the EP floor. In other words, the positions proposed by invested experts in the responsible EP committees to the Parliament's nonexperts are the outcome of a political deliberation and negotiation process that involves experts from other national and party delegations.

This leaves *invested nonexperts*, who consider a policy proposal to be important, but who do not possess sufficient expertise or access to necessary resources to conduct their own evaluation. Since the informational uncertainty of EP politics constrains their ability to determine the link between outcome preferences and policy preferences, they cannot make an independent, truly informed choice.[2] Invested nonexperts still have to rely on the assistance of their expert colleagues when translating outcome preferences into policy preferences, but they demand some reason to justify their policy choices. In other words, these legislators want to know *how* their outcome preferences connect to their policy preferences and policy choices. For invested nonexperts, therefore, it does not suffice to point to the PPC dynamic as the instrument for policy choice. We have to be more explicit in specifying this mechanism.

Focal points as mechanisms for policy choice

This section identifies the mechanism by which invested nonexperts link their policy preferences to their outcome preferences. This requires us to go back to the specification of member of the European Parliament (MEP) outcome preferences discussed in Chapter 2, where I maintain that outcome preferences in legislative politics can usefully be categorized as preferences deriving from legislators' ideological and constituency interests. Here, I conceptualize ideological (or policy-based) outcome preferences as the ideal points of MEPs on the two substantively important dimensions of political contestation in the EP: the traditional left-right ideological divide and a pro-/anti-EU dimension (or sovereignty-integration dimension) ranging from less to more support for the European integration process. I thus conceptualize the space structuring EP politics as a two-dimensional *ideological space* (Hinich and Munger 1994, 1997) and view legislators' policy-orientation as principally ordered by these two dimensions.[3] In this ideological space, actors are assumed to choose policy alternatives that are closest to their ideological ideal points (see, among many others: Hotelling [1929], Downs [1957], Black [1958], Arrow [1963]). These ideal points are stable normative positions representing long-standing and durable norms and values. Unlike policy preferences, which are a product of the decision-making process, these ideological ideal points are assumed to be exogenous (Marks and Wilson 2000; Scott 2001).

However, legislators are not simply motivated by their own ideological predispositions, but also by what is important to the constituents they represent. If this constituency element is adequately pronounced, legislators may even choose to disregard their own ideological outcome preferences, either because they are concerned about their electoral fortunes in future elections or because they see themselves as genuine representatives of those who elected them. MEPs do not face constituency pressures comparable to some of their national counterparts, however, for the reasons discussed in Chapter 2. First, most MEPs are not elected in single- or multiple-member electoral districts where they are directly accountable to a territorially defined subgroup of voters. Second, the link between legislators and their electoral districts is less developed than in other district-based electoral arenas. And third, public awareness of the EP and the salience EU citizens attach to it is low compared to national European arenas. As a result, most MEPs can—at least most of the time—safely assume that they will unlikely be punished for one particular policy choice. Nonetheless, potential constituency concerns cannot be completely discounted, particularly if a policy proposal is of particular public prominence. Hence, they ought to be considered part of the outcome preferences underlying the policy choices of European parliamentarians. Following the logic laid out in Chapter 2, these constituency interests are best conceptualized as the national interests of MEPs from particular member states.

Deriving policy preferences from this set of outcome preferences involves the process of balancing potentially conflicting outcome preferences, since most political issues are multidimensional in nature (Baumgartner, Jones, and MacLeod 2000: 325). Legislators may thus be confronted with circumstances in which they face trade-offs between competing ideological preferences (Hinich and Munger 1997: 200) or between ideological preferences and constituency interests (Aldrich and Rohde 1997–8, 1998, 2000, 2001). Hence, the translation of outcome into policy preferences is a matter of causal and normative beliefs. Policymakers must relate the content and consequences of a given policy proposal to their outcome preferences. This, however, is hindered by the absence of "cause-and-effect knowledge" regarding the effects of implemented legislation and by the constraints imposed on MEPs by the informational uncertainty of EP politics. Under conditions of uncertainty about what outcome preference—or what dimension of political conflict—is relevant to a particular policy decision, the political space comprised of MEP outcome preferences provides for an infinite number of policy solutions, or equilibrium outcomes. To overcome this problem, individual legislators effectively have to select one outcome preference as more pertinent to the decision at hand, which in turn facilitates the determination of a policy solution. Given the EP's informational deficit, however, MEPs have to rely on some external input that will allow them to make an informed choice.[4]

Garrett and Weingast (1993) suggest that "ideas, social norms, institutions, or shared expectations" can facilitate the selection of one policy solution over others.[5] In the context of EP politics, they can serve as mechanisms enabling nonexpert MEPs to translate their outcome preferences into policy preferences regarding a particular policy decision. I conceptualize these mechanisms as *focal points* linking legislators' outcome preferences with particular policies (Ringe 2005).[6] These focal points connect the outcome preference ideal points of MEPs to specific policy issues by supplying simplifying ideas or images about the expected consequences of a policy proposal once it is implemented. Focal points serve as short-hand devices for communicating information that emphasizes the respective salience of the different outcome preferences held by MEPs. They do this by providing a condensed evaluation of the likely impact of a policy action, thus shifting attention toward specific aspects of the proposal at hand. This enables invested nonexpert legislators to select which one of their potentially contradictory outcome preferences they consider to be relevant in the case at hand. Simply put, focal points affect perceptions of which outcome preferences matter with regard to a specific policy proposal, and how intensely they matter.[7] Spatial representations of this argument are laid out in the appendix.

The provision of focal points constitutes an example of what William Riker has termed "heresthetic," which describes the attempt to structure the political context in such a way as to move the process of contestation from one dimension of political conflict to another (Riker 1986, 1990). According to Riker, actors can introduce new issue dimensions, or dismiss or reinterpret existing ones, by "displaying the relevance of a dimension, recalling it from latent storage to the center of psychic attention" (Riker 1990: 54). However, while the concept of heresthetic is quite broad and includes various forms of strategic voting and agenda manipulation (Riker 1990: 50–4), the provision of focal points should be conceived of as a very specific example of heresthetic: by shifting attention toward particular aspects of a policy proposal, focal points influence policy-makers' perceptions of the relevance and salience of the dominant ideological dimensions. Hence, their introduction structures the political context by affecting the dimensional location of political deliberation and contestation, while simultaneously summarizing and simplifying the object of the political process. Yet, while Riker argues that heresthetic is a process that restructures the political space from a model where equilibrium is likely to exist to one where it is not (Riker 1990: 51), focal points work the other way around: they transform a model with multiple possible policy outcomes into one where certain outcomes are more likely. Focal points achieve this result by linking a policy proposal with the dominant outcome preference dimensions, that is, by tying the decision-making process to a lower dimensional political space. This decreases the number of dimensions considered to be salient for the decision at hand and decreases the number of possible equilibria.[8]

In the context of the EP, focal points are likely to fall into three broad categories based on the outcome preferences they "target." Focal points relating to the sovereignty-integration dimension should address the trade-off between the objective of building an "ever closer Union" and the desire to retain national sovereignty. This emphasis should prompt decision-makers to act based on their positions on the sovereignty-integration dimension. Examples for such focal points would be an emphasis on the necessity for completing specific European projects on the one hand (such as the single market, Economic and Monetary Union, EU enlargements, and a common foreign and security policy), or an emphasis on the singularity and desirability of national cultures, identities, institutions, or decision-making authority on the other.

In contrast, focal points relating to the left-right divide should emphasize traditional left-right issues and induce European decision-makers to act based on their positions on the left-right dimension. These focal points would, for example, stress the conflict between economic regulation and liberalization or the tradeoff between employee protection and business promotion.

Finally, focal points may stress the need to protect distinct constituency interests. In the case of the EU, these are most likely nationally-based, such as national economic interests. By emphasizing the positive or negative impact of a proposal for national constituencies, constituency-centered focal points should prompt decision-makers to vote in ideologically diverse coalitions, for example as national blocs.

In this way, focal points relate a particular legislative proposal to legislators' outcome preferences. If the focal point fails to establish this link, it will not have the appeal necessary to help structure policy choice. In this sense, the provision of focal points reflects and is constrained by the political space comprised of MEP outcome preferences: focal points are not "free-floating." While focal points can be used in distinctly strategic ways (by emphasizing and evaluating particular aspects of a legislative proposal), the providers of focal points are constrained by the structure of the political space within which they operate.

The basic argument advanced here is that depending on which focal point (or focal points) dominates the deliberation process concerning a particular legislative proposal, legislators not directly involved in the deliberation process will perceive of the issue in different ways. For example, a legislative proposal regulating economic policy at the EU level could be presented by the people directly involved in the dossier as a matter of *harmonization* toward the completion of the EU single market. As a result, pro-EU legislators, without complete information about the content and consequences of the legislation, would be likely to support the legislation. If, however, the issue were presented as one of *liberalization*, members of Parliament on the left side of the political spectrum would likely oppose the measure. Focal points can thus be deployed strategically to capture the greatest number of votes for or against the policy proposal on the EP floor.

All of this leaves one crucial question: Where do focal points come from? I argue that they are provided by legislative experts with private information about the expected consequences of a policy proposal. These policy specialists are those colleagues to whom less-informed and less-involved members have delegated the task of providing information relevant to the policy decision. In other words, they are the members of the EP's informational committee responsible for the particular policy proposal at hand. In reference to the four types of legislators discussed earlier, the *providers* of focal points are invested experts. *Receivers* of focal points are invested nonexperts. The focal point model thus describes the information exchange between these two types of legislators.

Invested nonexperts will not be receptive to focal points provided by just anybody, however. In order to have confidence that their outcome preferences are, in fact, approximated once the policy proposal is implemented, they still rely on the PPC dynamic when considering who is providing the relevant focal points. Only if they perceive to share a common set of outcome preferences with the invested expert providing the focal point can invested nonexperts confidently rely on it as a mechanism for policy choice.[9] Perceived preference coherence is thus of critical importance not just for the exchange of information between invested experts and indifferent nonexperts, but also for the information exchange, in the form of focal points, between invested experts and invested nonexperts.

Moreover, a common position among members from the same party group again constitutes a critical factor explaining cohesive positions on the EP floor because, in the absence of controversy, members of the same party group are unlikely to provide numerous focal points that may be in competition for invested nonexperts' attention and votes. That is, without intra-party divisions in committee, a united committee working group would be expected to provide only a single focal point (or a cohesive set of focal points) to the party's invested nonexperts.

The implication of this is that cohesive party positions on the EP floor are the likely consequence of the EP policy-making process whether or not legislators are invested or indifferent. Indifferent experts and nonexperts will adopt the positions of their invested expert colleagues simply based on perceived preference coherence; since they do not attach any salience to the proposal at hand, their motivation to oppose a party line formulated in the responsible committee is low. Invested nonexperts, on the other hand, do not simply adopt the positions of their invested expert colleagues. They rely on focal points, which relate the policy proposal at hand to their outcome preferences, as a justification for their policy choices. Yet, they are most likely to be receptive to the focal points provided by those expert colleagues with whom they perceive to share a common set of outcome preferences. Hence, perceived preference coherence between party colleagues is again critical to understanding policy choice, and the PPC dynamic provides an impetus for cohesive party positions on the EP floor.

Conclusion

In sum, the focal point model not only describes how invested nonexpert legislators make decisions that they perceive as approximating their outcome preferences, it also explains how invested experts influence policy outcomes. The exchange between the two groups, in turn, provides important solutions to key problems they face. The nonexperts seek digestible information that allows them to make informed choices that match their outcome preferences while providing a justification for the decisions they make; the experts seek to influence policy outcomes and help their colleagues make informed choices. The next chapter will illustrate and test the focal point model by analyzing a series of decision-making processes concerning six specific policy proposals.

Appendix: The impact of focal points—a spatial representation

To illustrate the impact of focal points on the preference functions of legislators, consider first the ideological space in Figure 4.2, which consists of the left-right divide and the sovereignty-integration dimension. Also assume that there are three individual legislators (X_1, X_2, and X_3) who each have ideal points (x_1, x_2, and x_3) on these dimensions. Italics are used to indicate ideal points in this ideological space.

The ideological space is not actually divorced from issues because ideologies provide a set of "linkages" with the n-dimensional space of policies; these linkages are highly uncertain, however (Hinich and Munger 1997: 191). Hence, the process of relating a policy proposal to the existing ideological space by interpreting its content and consequences in reference to the dominant ideological dimensions consists of a complete or partial transposition of the ideological space into the relevant policy space in which decision-making takes place. In the case where there are no variables,

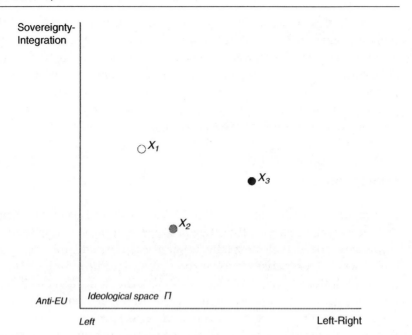

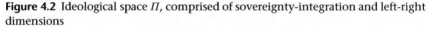

Figure 4.2 Ideological space Π, comprised of sovereignty-integration and left-right dimensions

such as focal points, intervening in the transposition of the ideological space into a given policy space, the relevant policy space looks exactly like the ideological space above. In this space, let SQ (status quo) and NP (new policy) be two competing policy options, as illustrated in Figure 4.3.

If ideological ideal points and the two policy options are thus distributed in the policy space and if the salience of the two dimensions is equal (when the legislators perceive neither dimension to be more important than the other), then SQ will be retained. As represented in Figure 4.4, equal salience of the two dimensions means that the legislators' indifference curves are of circular form. These circles have the property that all points along the indifference curves are equally far from the ideal points of the legislators X_1, X_2, and X_3. The legislators compare policy proposals on the basis of the distance from their ideal points, meaning that if the radius of the circle circumscribing their indifference curves is the distance from their ideal points to the status quo point (here: SQ), any NP that falls *inside* the indifference curve constitutes a preferred alternative to SQ. In Figure 4.4, voting for SQ is the preferred alternative for X_1 and X_2, since the new policy lies outside their indifference curves. X_3 would

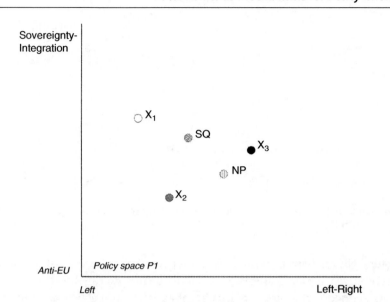

Figure 4.3 Policy space P1, comprised of sovereignty-integration and left-right dimensions

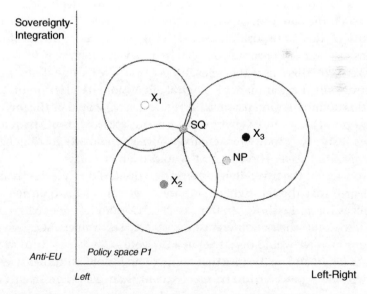

Figure 4.4 Policy space P1, salience of sovereignty-integration dimension = salience of left-right dimension for X_1, X_2, and X_3

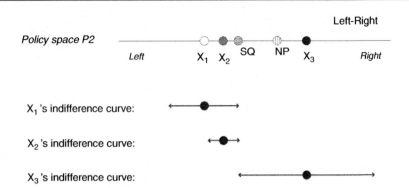

Figure 4.5 Policy space P2, salience of sovereignty-integration dimension = 0 for X_1, X_2, and X_3

prefer NP, however, which is closer to her ideal point than SQ. Accordingly, under majority rule, NP would be defeated 2–1.

As defined earlier, focal points emphasize the respective *salience* of the ideological dimensions by shifting attention toward the (perceived) consequences of a given policy proposal. In doing so, they affect the prevalent perceptions of which outcome preference matters with regard to the proposal and how intensely it matters (see also Selck [2006]). In other words, focal points affect the salience attached to the ideological dimensions when they are transposed into the policy space. The most extreme versions of this transposition would be if one of the two ideological dimensions were to become completely irrelevant, that is, if its salience were zero. In this case, the relevant policy space is one-dimensional, reflecting only the dominant ideological dimension. If the left-right divide were this dominant dimension, as in Figure 4.5, SQ would be the preferred policy option for X_1 and X_2, whose ideal points are closer to SQ than to NP. NP lies inside X_3's indifference curve, however, and would thus be her preferred alternative. Therefore, NP would again be defeated 2-1.

In contrast, if the sovereignty-integration dimension were dominant to the degree that the left-right divide was irrelevant, NP would narrowly prevail, as Figure 4.6 shows. In this case, both X_2 and X_3 prefer NP over SQ, as it lies inside their indifference curves. X_1 still prefers SQ, however, meaning that NP would defeat SQ in a 2-1 vote.

Yet, it might also be the case that neither dimension is utterly irrelevant, but that one is perceived to be more salient than the other. In this case, indifference curves are no longer circular, but have an *elliptical* shape. Specifically, if the horizontal dimension is more salient, the indifference

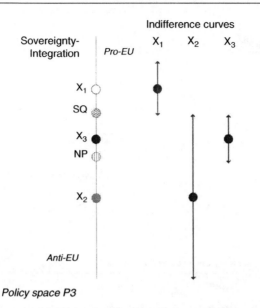

Figure 4.6 Policy space P3, salience of left-right dimension = 0 for X_1, X_2, and X_3

curves are "squeezed" from the sides because the more important a dimension is to an actor, the more small changes in the policy affect her satisfaction. In contrast, if the vertical dimension is more salient, the indifference curves are "squeezed" from above and below. Hence, if focal points affect the perceived salience of the ideological dimensions with regard to a particular policy proposal, they change the shape of the indifference curves of the decision-makers.

For example, if the provider of focal points could convince legislator X_2 that the sovereignty-integration dimension is only a bit more salient than the left-right divide when deciding between SQ and NP, X_2's indifference curve would change in such a way that voting for NP now becomes his preferred alternative (still assuming equal perceived salience of the ideological dimensions for X_1 and X_3). NP, which was previously outside X_2's indifference curve (see Figure 4.4), now lies inside his new, elliptical indifference curve, as we can see in Figure 4.7.

Next consider the case where a focal point emphasizes the salience of the left-right over the sovereignty-integration. Moreover, assume that it affects all three legislators, rather than just X_2, as was the case in Figure 4.7. In this case, illustrated in Figure 4.8, the three indifference curves are "squeezed" from the sides. As a result, SQ would again prevail as the preferred policy preference for X_1 and X_2, as NP lies outside their indifference curves.

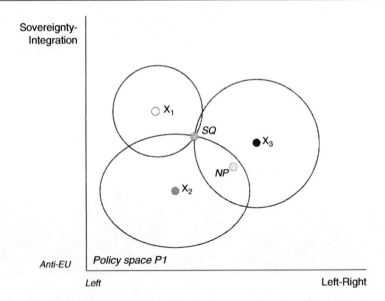

Figure 4.7 Policy space P1, salience of sovereignty-integration dimension > salience of left-right dimension for X_2

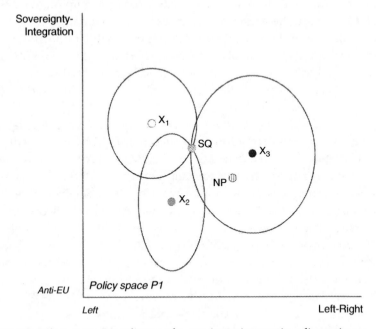

Figure 4.8 Policy space P1, salience of sovereignty-integration dimension < salience of left-right dimension for X_1, X_2, and X_3

This series of examples shows how focal points could impact policy decisions by influencing the respective salience of ideological ideal points when the two-dimensional ideological space is transposed into an n-dimensional policy space. These examples, however, assume that actors are policy-oriented. This leaves us to consider the case of office-driven politicians, who may be willing to deviate from their ideological ideal points in order to better represent or serve their constituents (and to get reelected). If this were the case, their indifference curves would change based on the degree to which the ideological dimensions' salience diminishes.

The most extreme example of this incidence would be if the ideological dimensions became completely irrelevant (i.e., their salience was zero), and were replaced by a constituency dimension where actors are aligned on the basis of the (perceived) respective gains for their constituents. Another possibility would be that the constituency element affected the salience of each ideological dimension asymmetrically. If, for example, the sovereignty-integration divide became irrelevant, while the left-right dimension retained at least some of its salience, a policy proposal would be evaluated in a two-dimensional policy space such as in Figure 4.9. In this case, NP would be X_1's and X_3's policy preference, and both would vote to defeat SQ.

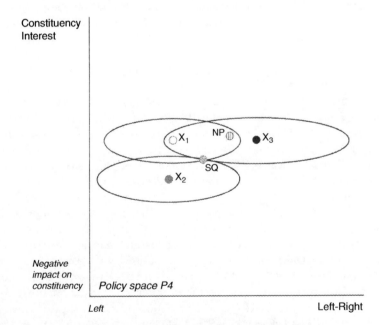

Figure 4.9 Policy space P4, salience of sovereignty-integration dimension = 0, salience of constituency interest > salience of left-right dimension for X_1, X_2, and X_3

Notes

1. The four types of legislators described here should be conceived of as ideal types specified for analytical purposes. This raises some important questions about observing these types in the real world, however, and some qualifications are worth specifying. For example, we can question the extent to which it is realistic to see legislators who do not care about a policy issue in their areas of expertise. While this may be the case in some situations, it is unlikely that an expert on environmental policy would consider an environmental policy proposal to be of negligible importance. Hence, the legislators in the lower left-hand quadrant may well be a relatively rare species in a real world legislature.

2. It is important to note that a legislator who considers a given policy proposal to be important may be willing to expend the necessary amount of resources to effectively become a policy expert, despite the constraints imposed by the informational uncertainty of EP politics. That is, she may be willing to cut resources elsewhere to enable her to allow for a personal evaluation of the proposal at hand, and thus not be dependent on her expert colleagues. However, in this case she would no longer fall into this particular category of legislators, as she would effectively become a policy expert herself.

3. While some analyses suggest that additional dimensions of conflict may also structure policy conflict in the EP, such as a libertarian-traditional dimension (Thomassen, Noury, and Voeten 2004) or a "new politics" dimension (Hooghe, Marks, and Wilson 2002), the primacy of the left-right and pro-/anti-EU dimensions has been demonstrated using a variety of methodological approaches, such as standard NOMINATE (Hix, Noury, and Roland 2007), a Bayesian application of spatial voting models (Han 2007) and expert surveys (McElroy and Benoit 2007).

4. Under circumstances when there is no one *outcome equilibrium*, the decision-making process resembles a coordination game that provides no way of distinguishing one equilibrium from another, even when the players have a shared interest in finding common ground for a policy outcome. For a two-person "pure coordination game," Schelling (1960) and Mehta, Starmer, and Sugden (1994) show that people can use different "labels" to coordinate their behavior, resulting in the selection of one single equilibrium.

5. In Garrett and Weingast's example, the member states of the European Community acknowledged the principle of "mutual recognition" to constitute an acceptable basis of an agreement, or equilibrium outcome, that led to the creation of the European single market in the 1986 Single European Act. This principle was well-established in EC politics, had been used by the European Court of Justice to settle disputes in the economic policy realm, and could serve as a universally recognized keystone for the single market. In the game theoretic literature, the link between beliefs and equilibria has been emphasized in the context of signaling games (Garrett and Weingast 1993). Kreps and Wilson

(1982), for example, elevate *beliefs* to the level of importance of *strategies* in the definition of equilibrium.

6. The original idea of focal points derives from Schelling (1960).

7. The game theoretic literature conceives of focal points as the equilibria resulting from players in pure coordination games following the coordinating "label" they consider to be most salient (Schelling 1960; Mehta, Starmer and Sugden 1994); that is, focal points are the *outcome* of the game. The term is used more broadly in the less formal literature, however. Garrett and Weingast (1993: 176), for example, maintain that focal points do not always emerge without conscious effort on the part of interested actors, but that they must often be "constructed." Hence, focal points are less the outcome of process, but *a tool facilitating this outcome.*

8. The idea of focal points reducing the number of possible equilibria is of course reminiscent of Shepsle's concept of a "structure-induced equilibrium" (Shepsle 1979; Shepsle and Weingast 1981).

9. The implication of this is that party cohesion can result even when nonexperts MEPs seek to establish policy preferences with regard to a piece of legislation. In other words, as Skjæveland (2001: 39) suggests, party cohesion is not just the result of nonexpert legislators not having opinions on policy proposals.

Chapter 5

Focal Points and Legislative Decision-Making: Six Case Studies

This chapter investigates patterns of information provision and policy choice through focal points by analyzing a series of recent legislative proposals as case studies. The cases are analyzed using interview data and statistical analyses of particular roll-call votes. The case studies concern:[1]

- Case 1: The European Union (EU) takeover directive.
- Case 2: The statute and financing of EU-level political parties.
- Case 3: Proposals on fuel quality and emission standards for motor vehicles.
- Case 4: Liability for environmental damage.
- Case 5: The liberalization of port services in the EU.
- Case 6: EU citizenship and the free movement of people.

The case studies serve as illustrations of how political processes and outcomes differ depending on the prevailing focal points presented by invested experts in the responsible committees. These focal points influence the variable interpretation of what the issue at hand is "all about," thus shifting policy preferences during the process of parliamentary deliberation beyond the committee stage, with important consequences for legislative outcomes.

As outlined in the previous chapter, focal points are demanded by and targeted at invested nonexperts, that is, those MEPs who lack expertise regarding a proposed policy but attach enough salience to it to demand information on how the proposal relates to their outcome preferences. These focal points assist invested nonexperts in translating their outcome preferences into policy preferences, which ultimately determines their policy choices. The decision-making pattern for invested nonexperts thus differs from that of indifferent nonexperts, who do not attach enough

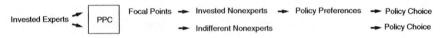

Figure 5.1 Policy choice process, invested vs. indifferent nonexperts

importance to a given policy proposal to consider how it relates to their outcome preferences. For this reason, indifferent nonexperts effectively skip the formulation of policy preferences regarding the proposal and simply adopt the position of the invested experts in the responsible committee. This difference is illustrated in Figure 5.1, which also accounts for the importance of perceived preference coherence (PPC) for both types of nonexperts: Just as the likelihood that indifferent nonexperts will adopt the policy position of invested experts is contingent on perceived preference coherence, the receptiveness of invested nonexperts to focal points provided by invested experts is conditional on whether or not they perceive to share the invested expert's outcome preferences.

We have already learned in Chapter 3 that we can predict the policy choices of members of the European Parliament (MEPs) on the basis of the policy positions of policy specialists in the responsible European Parliament (EP) committee. That analysis, however, does not allow us to differentiate between the two "paths" to MEP policy choice depicted in Figure 5.1. In other words, we cannot differentiate between the way in which decision-making patterns differ for indifferent and invested experts simply by using the positions of committee experts as predictors for voting on the floor. In particular, we cannot determine the impact of focal points as an intervening variable, because the outcome—vote choice—is the same for indifferent and invested nonexperts.

Focal points are instruments of persuasion employed by invested experts who seek to have their policy positions aggregated to the level of the party as a whole, and this persuasion plays an important role in the time period between the decision in committee and a vote in plenary.[2] At that stage, active committee members identify the key points of a legislative proposal to provide a general common understanding of why a position is taken[3] and the presentation of issues by the key players impacts to a significant extent how an issue is perceived by nonexpert party members.[4] As one MEP put it, quite bluntly, final plenary votes are not votes on the issue, but "on the issue as it is presented."[5] As there are "a number of bases on which to judge what legislation is going to do, or not going to do, and what it is about," it is often the particular focus created by those actively involved that affects vote choice.[6]

Hence, the focal point logic suggests that we should be able to predict voting outcomes on the EP floor on the basis of the prevailing focal points. In order to test this proposition, the case studies seek to determine if we can identify the dominant dimension of political contestation for a particular legislative proposal on the basis of the prevailing focal points and, in turn, if an MEP's ideal point on that identified dimension is predictive of his or her vote choice. This is based on the suggestion, laid out in the previous chapter, that focal points shape policy choice by influencing the salience of one ideological dimension over another: They affect what outcome preference invested nonexperts perceive to be relevant to a specific policy proposal and, thus, the translation of their outcome preferences into policy preferences.

The analysis of each case study shares a common structure. The first section provides a brief overview of the content of the legislative proposals and an outline of the course of events in the policy-making process. Second, qualitative analyses of the decision-making processes are based on interviews with MEPs and EU officials that were closely involved in the deliberation and/or the negotiation of the proposals. This part of the analysis serves a number of functions. It offers important details regarding the content of the proposal; it provides insights into the deliberation and negotiation process concerning each proposal and the roles of key legislators in steering the decision-making process; and it provides critical information on how the content and implications of the proposed legislation were presented to the MEPs not directly involved in the decision-making process. This is particularly important because it allows for the identification of the focal points dominating the discussion, the prevalence of which is confirmed in simple content analyses of the EP debates concerning each legislative proposal.[7]

Finally, the outcomes of the legislative decision-making processes are examined by analyzing the final votes taken on the EP floor. These analyses are performed in a binomial logit analysis framework and seek to determine if we can predict voting outcomes on the basis of the focal points prevalent in the negotiation of the proposal.[8] The dependent variables in these analyses are thus individual-level votes on the legislative report in the EP plenary; the set of independent variables is analogous across case studies.

Focal points affect what dimensions of political contestation MEPs perceive to be most salient with regard to the issue at hand. Therefore, MEPs' ideal points on the most salient dimension(s) ought to determine their vote choice. To operationalize these ideal points, MEP NOMINATE coordinates on the two primary dimensions of the European political space are used.

These coordinates represent the classic economic left-right divide and the sovereignty-integration dimension, respectively (Hix, Noury, and Roland 2007). The variables range from -1 to 1, where -1 indicates an extreme leftist position on the left-right dimension and an anti-EU position on the sovereignty-integration dimension. The expectation is that MEPs' ideal points on the sovereignty-integration dimension are statistically significant if the prevailing focal points emphasize the trade-off between further integration and a desire to retain national sovereignty; in contrast, their ideal points on the left-right dimension should be predictive of voting patterns if traditional left-right issues are highlighted.

Focal points may also emphasize particular constituency concerns, however, especially if they target specific national interests. This would prompt legislators to vote in ideologically diverse coalitions, such as national blocs. To account for this possibility, different measurements for "national interests" with regard to each legislative proposal are included. For instance, I include "type of capitalism" variables in the case of the proposals that would have economic implications for EU member states at the national level;[9] a variable indicating if member states have national legislation allowing same-sex marriages for the EU citizenship proposal; and a variable accounting for national party finance rules for the legislation on the EU party statute.

Finally, to control for the possibility that representation in the Council of Ministers (and thus national-level government-opposition dynamics) affects voting behavior in the EP, I include a dichotomous variable based on the national government or opposition status of particular national party delegations, where a value of one means that a party was part of the national government.

The case studies reconfirm some of the key findings of Chapter 3, most importantly that MEPs do not form policy preferences independently of the external input of policy experts from the responsible committee; that party positions are endogenous to the policy-making process in committee; and that shared party membership serves as a proxy for common outcome preferences in the case of invested nonexperts who make policy choices on the basis of the focal points provided by their expert party colleagues. They also support the specific propositions of the focal point model, however, and demonstrate that committee specialists create opportunities for policy choice by providing informational focal points. These focal points significantly affect how non-experts interpret the content and consequences of the proposed legislation, which shapes their policy preferences and thus policy outcomes on the EP floor.

Case 1: The EU takeover directive

The "13th directive on company law: takeover bids, protection of share-holders, workers' rights to information" (COD/1995/0341) was one of the most high-profile pieces of legislation ever to pass through the EP. Its purpose was to establish common European-wide rules regulating the rights of share-holders and the use of defensive measures in the event of corporate takeover bids. By the time it was introduced by the European Commission in 1996, the idea of establishing a European-level framework governing cross-border corporate takeovers had been on the EU agenda for many years. Early attempts to introduce Europe-wide takeover regulation date back to the early 1970s, when the Commission drafted its first directive for takeover bids.[10] The proposal was discussed for some time with representatives from the member states, but the project was ultimately abandoned due to limited interest. The directive resurfaced 10 years later, but the Commission draft was once again met with little attention on the part of the member states.

Over time, however, a considerable void in cross-border regulation in the EU became increasingly apparent. Under mounting pressure, including from the EP, the Commission presented another proposal for a takeover directive in January 1989. The proposal triggered intense debate and was criticized principally for not leaving enough latitude to national authorities. By the end of 1991 the Commission announced its intention to prepare yet another draft proposal, taking into account these arguments.

This new proposal, the 13th Directive, was presented 5 years later. It was made more consistent with existing national regulation than was the case in previous attempts of reform and proposed a "framework directive," containing general principles that member states would be obliged to follow when drafting their national takeover codes. As such, the legislation was less ambitious than previous proposals insofar as it gave member states more latitude than the previous proposals. It stipulated five general principles (Hix, Noury, and Roland 2007): (a) equal treatment for all share-holders; (b) that the target of the takeover bid receive the necessary time and information to make an educated decision on the matter; (c) that the management board of the offeree company act in the interests of the company and its shareholders; (d) that it be prohibited to create false markets in the securities of the offeree company; and (e) that offeree companies must not be hampered in the conduct of their business for any longer than necessary for a bid to purchase their shares. Another key element of the proposed legislation, following the British model of corporate governance, was a "neutrality rule" whereby companies would not be allowed to take defensive measures against a takeover bid once a bid had been launched without gaining the specific approval of shareholders for the action.

The proposed legislation was deliberated in the EP for a period of 5 years. While a compromise agreement between Council and EP seemed quite possible in the initial stage of the decision-making process, controversy concerning the proposed legislation increased dramatically over time. In first reading, which took place in June 1996, the EP approved the report of the rapporteur in the responsible Legal Affairs Committee, Nicole Fontaine, a French member of the European People's Party (EPP) group. It thus followed the recommendation of the committee, which had voted almost unanimously in favor. The EP proposed 22 amendments to the Commission proposal, including demands for definitional clarifications and measures to strengthen the rights of employees and their representatives. Subsequently, the Commission's amended proposal, as well as the Council's unanimous common position, incorporated most EP amendments without challenging the proposal's general principles.[11]

Following the EP election in June 1999, Ms. Fontaine became the president of the fifth EP and passed the rapporteurship of the takeover directive to her German EPP colleague Klaus-Heiner Lehne. The new rapporteur, however, assumed a position in the second reading that was "180 degrees opposite to the first reading," according to a Commission official involved in the dossier.[12] Under Mr. Lehne's leadership, the EP amended the Council's common position substantially with measures discouraging hostile takeover bids. Most importantly, it proposed amendments making it easier for the boards of target companies to use defensive measures; effectively replacing the British-style "neutrality rule" with the German practice (Berglöf and Burkart 2003: 187). Due to this rejection of the Council's common position, the legislation went into conciliation. Following a long and intense conciliation procedure and an 8–7 vote by the EP delegation in favor of a compromise agreement, the takeover directive was rejected on the EP floor in July 2001 with a vote of 273 in favor, 273 against, and 22 abstentions, as the Parliament's Rules of Procedure specify that a tied vote equals a rejection.

Qualitative analysis: focal points and the legislative process

The qualitative analysis of the decision-making process concerning the takeover directive supports the proposition that strategically deployed focal points shifted the policy preferences of those MEPs not directly involved in the deliberation of the legislation. This shift in policy preferences, in turn, critically shaped policy outcomes. Three focal points shaped the process of deliberation surrounding the takeover directive and took prominence at different points in time. In the early stages of the deliberation process, a focal point relating to the sovereignty-integration dimension was particularly pronounced. This focal point stressed the significance of completing the European *single market* in the realm of company law and was particularly notable during the first reading stage. It was gradually replaced, however, by two alternative focal points in the second and third reading stages, namely the issue of *workers' rights* and the notion of creating a *level playing-field* across the EU. The first of these two new focal points relates to the left-right divide by emphasizing the question of employee information and consultation in the case of a takeover or merger. The second raises concerns about the impact of the proposal on businesses in the different member states, a core constituency of all MEPs, by suggesting that the takeover directive would favor businesses in certain countries while putting others at a comparative disadvantage.

These focal points were introduced strategically at different stages of the proposal's life cycle by the primary legislative actors in the EP, who framed the political process in ways advantageous to their objectives. These actors were mainly members of the Committee on Legal Affairs and the Internal Market and, in particular, the two rapporteurs handling the dossier. Early on in the legislation decision-making process, the proposal was considered by the fourth EP (1994–9) and treated by rapporteur Fontaine. Ms. Fontaine was strongly in favor of the directive. Upon presenting her report to the plenary on June 25, 1997, she declared that she hoped "with all my heart" that the EP would vote in favor of the proposal.[13] She presented the dossier as a necessary step toward the completion of the European single market with due consideration to the principle of subsidiarity, thus tying the issue to the sovereignty-integration dimension.[14] Accordingly, and as the focal point model would predict, deliberation in the Parliament under her rapporteurship was dominated by the issues of harmonization and subsidiarity, with a particular focus on the question of what type of directive would best ensure an appropriate balance between the two.

Mr. Lehne, however, the new rapporteur who replaced Ms. Fontaine after the 1999 EP election and before the second reading, presented the proposal to the incoming Parliament in a dramatically different fashion. He portrayed the issue as being about the creation of a level playing-field across the EU, rather than about completing the single market. Thus simplifying the technical content of the proposal for his fellow parliamentarians, he shifted attention toward imbalances with regard to defensive measures that companies could take to protect themselves against hostile takeovers,[15] despite the fact that the essence of the proposal was the same as in first reading. While the takeover directive required shareholders to approve any defensive measures enacted by managerial boards, the position of the rapporteur stressed the German corporate tradition giving the board of the target company substantial autonomy and authority to frustrate a takeover attempt. Mr. Lehne maintained that the directive, as proposed by the Commission, would put certain national companies at a disadvantage both relative to companies from other European countries and from the United States, allowing some corporations to initiate cross-border takeovers while being protected against hostile takeover bids themselves.[16] In other words, he emphasized how the issue related to particular national constituency concerns.

The second issue gaining prominence throughout the political process was that of employee information and consultation in takeover and merger activities. The discussion revolved around the specific question of employee consultation and information in the event of mergers and takeovers, but also featured an ever more prominent discussion about the desirability of mergers, and the question of shareholder versus stakeholder value. Once again, the complex repercussions of the legislative proposal were simplified, this time in terms of workers' rights, which tied the content and consequences of the proposal to the left-right dimension. The issue continuously gained in visibility throughout the legislative process,[17] which was somewhat surprising from the Commission's point of view since the issue had been discussed early on in the informal trialogue meetings between Commission, Council, and Parliament. According to a senior Commission official, a member of the Socialist group in the EP had been invited to the meetings specifically to ensure that issues relating to the consultation and information of employees were adequately addressed.[18] In these meetings, the issue was thought to have been satisfied by means of cross-references to existing legislation, to which the Socialist EP representative did not object.[19]

The shift in focal points during the course of the decision-making process concerning the takeover directive is evident in the parliamentary debates in first reading (June 25, 1997), second reading (December 12, 2000), and third reading (July 3 and 4, 2001), as Table 5.1 shows.

In the debates, the single market focal point gets sidelined throughout the decision-making process.[20] While in first reading, this focal point is referred to 64 times per 10,000 input words, the number of references drops to 11 in second reading and seven in third reading. At the same

Table 5.1: EU takeover directive, frequencies-of-use, content analysis

	# of input words	# of references to *single market*	# of references to *workers' rights*	# of references to *level playing-field*
1st reading	10,000	64	34	0
	(4,067)	(26)	(14)	
	10 speakers	5 speakers	4 speakers	
2nd reading	10,000	11	39	30
	(5,593)	(6)	(22)	(17)
	15 speakers	4 speakers	8 speakers	5 speakers
3rd reading	10,000	7	46	30
	(11,940)	(8)	(55)	(36)
	26 speakers	7 speakers	18 speakers	11 speakers

Note: Entries report number of references to various focal points in EP debates for every 10,000 input words. Actual number of input words and frequencies appear in parentheses.

time, the workers' rights and level playing-field focal points gain in prominence over time. While there is not a single mention of the level playing-field in the first reading debate in 1997, it is referred to 30 times per 10,000 input words in both the second and third reading debates. The workers' rights focal point is referenced 34 times per 10,000 input words in the first reading phase, a number that increases to 39 in second and 46 in third reading.

Rather than driven by major exogenous events or changes in the policy proposal, individual-level perceptions of the takeover directive changed as a result of deliberate persuasion efforts. Rapporteur Lehne and the Socialist shadow rapporteur in the Legal Affairs Committee, Willy Rothley, played critical roles in this regard. According to Mr. Rothley, he and Mr. Lehne put a lot of energy into finding a majority against the proposal.[21] Their efforts were aimed in two directions: The workers' rights emphasis explicitly targeted the left and the level playing-field argument was emphasized for the political right, which was thought to be more concerned with national businesses.[22] While Mr. Lehne stressed the level playing-field argument, Mr. Rothley emphasized the workers' protection side of the story in the Socialist group—*despite* his conviction that the directive, in reality, did not infringe on workers' rights (Ringe 2005: 738).

The findings of this qualitative analysis also confirm that focal points were not created from thin air, but reflected existing ideological preferences and concerns. The increasing discussion about workers' rights shifted attention toward an aspect of the proposal that could prominently place the issue on the left-right divide. It also emphasized to the left that the proposal might negatively affect their core constituencies across the continent. At the same time, the level playing-field issue emphasized the repercussions of the directive for national businesses, another core constituency of most MEPs.

It is, moreover, evident that the focal points observable in the case of the takeover directive were indeed decision-making shortcuts, making a complex and technical proposal more tangible. Initially, the majority of parliamentarians were quite uninformed about the highly complex and technical takeover directive,[23] and opinions were "all over the place."[24] Therefore, MEPs had to rely on the few people who could evaluate the implications of the directive to lead them through the process, according to a Commission official.[25] In sum, focal points had a mediating impact on already existing ideological preferences. While ideological preferences and constituency concerns did not change, opposition to the directive emerged as the policy process progressed.[26] Following the suggestions of the dominant focal points, everybody started to discover that they had something to protect,[27] be it "the pearls of their national industries,"[28] or the employees of target companies.[29]

Voting patterns: the impact of the legislative process on voting outcomes

On the basis of the aforementioned qualitative analysis, it is possible to formulate a series of hypotheses concerning the expected outcome of the decision-making process in the case of the takeover directive.

In the first reading stage, the single market issue was most prominent in the debate about the takeover directive. Accordingly, we should find that pro-/anti-integration positions should be significant predictors of voting behavior, with pro-European MEPs voting in favor of the directive. As established earlier, however, the focal point revolving around the completion of the single market became increasingly marginalized throughout the political process and was replaced by concerns about the level playing-field and workers' protection. I therefore hypothesize that pro-/anti-integration positions should not be significant predictors of voting behavior in the third reading stage.

Following Hooghe and Marks (1999, 2001), we may hypothesize that the political left was initially in favor of the takeover directive, as it constituted a matter of market regulation at the EU level in the area of corporate governance. The political right, on the other hand, wishing to combine a continent-wide market with minimal regulation at the EU level, should be more hesitant in its support for the directive. I thus hypothesize that holding more leftist positions on the left-right dimension should increase the probability of support for the directive in the first reading stage. Given the rising focus on the workers' rights issue in later stages of the discussion, these tendencies should be reversed in the third reading stage: In the 2001 vote, more leftist positions should decrease the probability of support for the directive.

Finally, since the level playing-field focal point was entirely absent from the debate in the first reading stage, constituency interests related to the comparative gains of national businesses should not constitute a significant predictor of voting behavior in the first reading stage. As a result of the rise of the issue throughout the process, however, we should expect to find that in the third reading stage, national considerations had a substantial impact on voting patterns. Specifically, we should find that parliamentarians from member states with liberal market economies supported the directive, since their equity-based systems already placed the shareholder at the center of regulatory and legal protections against hostile takeover bids (Berglöf and Burkart 2003). For these MEPs, the level playing-field argument actually highlighted perceived gains from the takeover directive. MEPs from countries with national coordinated market economies should also be expected to favor the directive, for similar reasons. In Sweden, for example, regulations dating back to the early 1970s already required defensive actions to have shareholder approval. Moreover, the most widespread defensive practice in the Scandinavian countries is a system of dual class shares (Bennedsen and Nielsen 2004), which the takeover directive did not actually prohibit. For similar reasons, we should also observe that MEPs from partial coordinated market economies should be concerned about the impact of the legislation on the defensive actions available to their nations' companies. Finally, parliamentarians from sectoral market economies should largely oppose the directive, which was perceived as a threat to established neo-corporatist traditions at the national, sectoral, and firm levels.

The dependent variables in these binomial logit regression analyses are the votes in the first and third readings.[30] The models simultaneously estimate the probability of a given legislator voting Yes or No. The dependent variables are dichotomous, as the small number of abstentions is treated as *de facto* votes against the proposed legislation (since under absolute majority rule, abstaining has the same effect as voting against). The independent variables are the two ideology variables (left-right and sovereignty-integration), as proxied by MEPs' NOMINATE scores, the

Table 5.2: EU takeover directive, binomial logit regression estimates, first reading vote

	Floor vote, first reading
Left-right dimension	−1.83***
	(.41)
Sovereignty-integration dimension	2.57***
	(.53)
Government status	−.53
	(.50)
Liberal market economy	−3.20***
	(.69)
Partial coordinated market economy	3.01***
	(.60)
Sectoral coordinated market economy	1.13*
	(.48)
Constant	1.01*
	(.47)
Number of cases	359
Log pseudo-likelihood	−118.29
Pseudo R^2	.39

Note: Table entries are binomial logit estimates. Dependent variable: vote (Yes = 1, No = 0, Abstain = 0). "National Coordinated Market Economy" serves as the reference category. Statistical significance is indicated as follows: $p < .05^*$, $p < .01^{**}$, $p < .001^{***}$

government status dichotomous variable, and a set of dichotomous variables for "type of capitalism."

The results in Table 5.2 show that this regression model explains a substantial part of the variance in voting behavior with a pseudo-R^2 of 0.39. Also, as predicted on the basis of the dominant focal point in the first reading stage, positions on the sovereignty-integration dimension constitute a highly statistically significant predictor of voting behavior in the roll-call vote of the first parliamentary reading. Moreover, the sign of the coefficient indicates that a more pro-European attitude correlates positively with the probability of a Yes vote. Since these results are substantively difficult to interpret, the results are again presented throughout this chapter as conditional predicted probabilities.

Figure 5.2 presents the predicted probabilities of a Yes vote across different levels of EU support. This figure illustrates the substantial impact of more pro-European positions on the probability of a vote in favor of the directive, across different types of capitalism.[31]

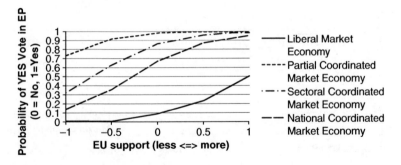

Figure 5.2 EU takeover directive, mean predicted probability of Yes vote given levels of EU support, first reading vote

The results in Table 5.2 also show that, as expected, positions on the left-right dimension are statistically significant and negatively related to the dependent variable: Leftists were more likely to vote in favor of the directive. This finding is evident in the downward-sloping lines in Figure 5.3, which represent the mean predicted probabilities of a Yes vote given positions on the left-right dimension, again differentiating between different types of capitalism.

Finally, Figure 5.4 shows the modest impact of government- or opposition-status of MEPs in their national member states, and thus their representation in the Council, which is not surprising since the coefficient in Table 5.2 does not achieve statistical significance. The slope of the graphs is surprising, however, since representation in the Council of Ministers evidently decreases the probability of MEPs voting in favor of the takeover directive in first reading.

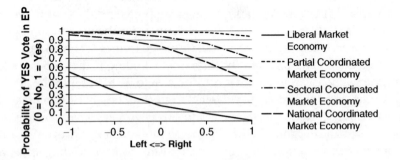

Figure 5.3 EU takeover directive, mean predicted probability of Yes vote given left-right positions, first reading vote

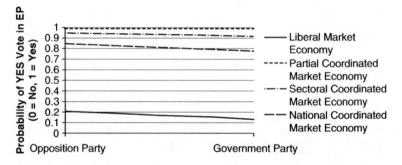

Figure 5.4 EU takeover directive, mean predicted probability of Yes vote given government status, first reading vote

Contrary to our expectations, national economic considerations are highly statistically significant predictors of voting behavior, as the "type of capitalism" variables are significant and their coefficients quite substantial. Specifically, Figures 5.2 through 5.4 demonstrate that MEPs from member states with partial coordinated market economies were most likely to support the legislation in first reading, followed by MEPs from sectoral and national coordinated market economies. Members from countries with liberal market economies were least likely to vote in favor of the takeover directive in first reading.

Comparing these results with the analysis of the third reading vote on the takeover directive demonstrates that policy preferences concerning the takeover directive were not stable across both votes. In fact, the coefficient of all predictor variables switch signs, as Table 5.3 illustrates.

These results are consistent with the expectations of the focal point model, which can account for these switches in the signs of the coefficients. The sign of the sovereignty-integration variable, for example, switches from positive to negative: While pro-Europeans strongly supported the directive in the first reading stage, the relationship between support for the EU and support for the takeover directive is now reversed (compare Figures 5.2 and 5.5).

One possible interpretation of this curious finding is that pro-European MEPs actually began to consider the directive to be harmful to the integration process as the level playing-field argument began to dominate the discussion. As a result, positions on the sovereignty-integration dimension did not become insignificant during the decision-making process. Yet, as the single market focal point was marginalized in the third reading stage, the slope of the graphs representing the changes in predicted probabilities along

Table 5.3: EU takeover directive, binomial logit regression estimates, third reading vote

	Floor vote, third reading
Left-right dimension	2.13***
	(.33)
Sovereignty-integration dimension	−.76*
	(.30)
Government status	2.42***
	(.36)
Liberal market economy	.03
	(.59)
Partial coordinated market economy	−2.38***
	(.48)
Sectoral coordinated market economy	−4.77***
	(.54)
Constant	1.59***
	(.44)
Number of cases	560
Log pseudo-likelihood	−237.50
Pseudo R^2	0.39

Note: Table entries are binomial logit estimates. Dependent variable: vote (Yes = 1, No = 0, Abstain = 0). "National Coordinated Market Economy" serves as the reference category. Statistical significance is indicated as follows: $p < .05^*$, $p < .01^{**}$, $p < .001^{***}$

the sovereignty-integration dimension is less steep than in first reading, indicating its decreasing importance over time.

The simultaneous rise of the workers' rights focal point also entails a switch in the direction of the left-right variable, as predicted earlier and illustrated in Figures 5.3 and 5.6. While left-leaning MEPs had a greater probability of voting in favor of the directive in the first reading vote, they now show a greater probability of voting against. As Figure 5.6 shows, the

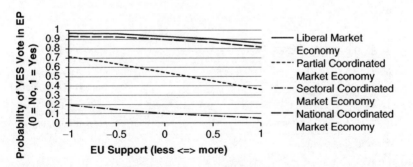

Figure 5.5 EU takeover directive, mean predicted probability of Yes vote given levels of EU support, third reading vote

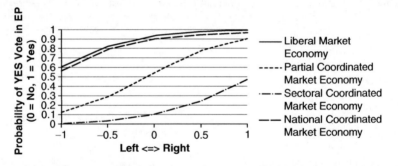

Figure 5.6 EU takeover directive, mean predicted probability of Yes vote given left-right positions, third reading vote

mean predicted probability of a vote in favor of the directive increases as values on the left-right divide shift toward the right.

Figure 5.7 shows that representation in the Council of Ministers, that is, affiliation with a national party in government at home, entails a greater probability of MEPs supporting the takeover directive in third reading. This impact is especially pronounced for MEPs from partial coordinated market economies.

Finally, considerations about the impact of the proposed legislation on national economic interests are indeed statistically significant in predicting voting behavior in the third reading stage, when the level playing-field issue was especially prominent. The findings also support our expectations. Members of Parliament from liberal market economies were indeed very likely to vote in favor of the directive, as were MEPs from countries with national coordinated market economies. In contrast, members from partial

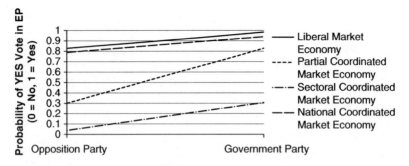

Figure 5.7 EU takeover directive, mean predicted probability of Yes vote given government status, third reading vote

coordinated market economies were less likely to support the proposed legislation, while parliamentarians from sectoral coordinated market economies were very unlikely to support it.

In sum, a critical preference shift with regard to the ideology variables was a decrease in the perceived salience of the sovereignty-integration dimension by legislative nonexperts between the first and third reading stages, paired with a simultaneous increase in the perceived salience of the left-right divide. This was not simply a shift in the perceived salience of the two ideology dimension, however, but also a critical shift in the directional impact of the two dimensions. While the more pro-EU position entailed a greater probability of voting in favor of the takeover directive in first reading, its impact in third reading was reversed. Similarly, a more leftist position in first reading was associated with a greater probability to support the proposed legislation and a decreased probability of support in third reading. A comparable shift occurred in the case of the "type of capitalism" variables representing national economic interests.

Case 1: Conclusion

The qualitative analysis of the perceptions of the takeover directive established that the interpretation of what constitutes the dominant aspect of a given legislative proposal can be traced back to one (or more) focal point(s). The analysis identified three competing focal points that took prominence at different points in time: the single market focal point, the workers' rights focal point, and the level playing-field focal point. Appealing to existing ideological predispositions, these strategically deployed focal points influenced the variable interpretation of what the issue at hand "was all about," thus shifting policy preferences during the process of parliamentary deliberation. Critical, in this regard, were a small number of specialized actors in the Legal Affairs Committee.

Subsequently, the quantitative analysis of voting behavior established that the strategically deployed focal points significantly shaped voting outcomes in the case of the EU takeover directive. It is thus evident that the policy outcome was the result of a decision-making process where strategic actors shaped policy preferences. As hypothesized, these outcomes are predictable on the basis of the prevalent focal points. That is, if we know how people perceive a proposal, we can make an educated prediction about how they will vote on it, based on their general ideological preferences.

Finally, the analysis confirms some of the central characteristics of focal points and the fashion in which they are employed in legislative decision-making. The prevailing focal points constituted very general representations of the content and consequences of the particular policy issue under consideration, while the discussion of technical details of the legislation was kept at a minimum. There was also a distinct element of persuasion involved in the deliberation of the legislation, which defies the notion of exogenous policy preferences and positions. Finally, each focal point highlighted the importance of a specific consequence of the legislation and tied it to one particular outcome preference: The single market focal point emphasized the desirability of the legislation as a step toward further integration, making it a pro-/anti-EU issue. The workers' rights focal point stressed the potential negative impact on employment and social fairness; as such, the issue was seen as a left-right question. Finally, the level playing-field focal point highlighted how unbalanced the distribution of benefits of the legislation would be across member states and thus targeted concerns about national constituents. Moreover, the case of the takeover directive demonstrates that focal points not only affect the salience of the dimensions of contestation, but also influence the direction in which the dimensions matter.

Case 2: The statute and financing of EU-level political parties

Going back to the Maastricht Treaty, the EU has recognized the importance of European political parties in developing political debate in Europe, enhancing the quality of EU democracy, and improving the functioning of EU institutions. Building on this recognition, the purpose of the legislation titled "Political parties at European level: statute and financing" (COD/2003/0039) was to define the exact nature and purpose of EU-level political parties and to create a financing framework whereby EU-level political parties would be funded in part from the EU budget.

The legislative proposal was introduced by the Commission on February 19, 2003, and proposed a total annual budget of 8.4 million Euros for party funding. It stipulated that each European party would receive a flat-rate basic grant from the EU budget, plus a second component based on its number of MEPs. Twenty-five percent of the budget of each party would still come from autonomous financing, including donations, which would have to be specified when exceeding EUR 100 and could not exceed EUR 5,000 a year per person or organization. To assure the transparency of party accounts, the Commission proposal specified that European parties that receive financing must provide annual records of their revenues, expenditures, statements of assets, and liabilities (European Commission 2003).

Eligibility for financing from the EU budget was tied to certain "minimum requirements" of democratic conduct, including provisions that EU parties must participate in EP elections, have clearly defined bodies responsible for financial management, and "respect [for] the basic purposes of the Union" with regard to freedom, democracy, human rights, and the rule of law. Eligibility was also dependent on being represented in the EP or in a reasonable number of member states. Specifically, a European political party must have elected members in the EP, or be represented in national or regional parliaments in at least one-third of the EU member states, or it must have obtained at least 5 percent of the votes in the most recent EP election in at least one-third of the member states.

Qualitative analysis: focal points and the legislative process

The proposal was treated in the EP by a German Social-Democrat, Jo Leinen, on behalf of the Committee on Constitutional Affairs. In first reading, in June 2003, the EP decided to limit the scope of the directive to the question of party financing, leaving aside the issue of establishing a genuine legal statute for EU parties. It merely stipulated that EU parties must have a legal personality in the member state in which its seat is located (Belgium, for most parties).[32] In this respect, it emphasized the urgent need for rules on party funding, given recent criticism by the EU Court of Auditors of the existing financing system.[33] The Court had suggested that the current structure where the political parties were financed through a budget line that belongs to the EP party groups was questionable, because it violated the division between party and parliamentary faction.

The EP also amended the Commission proposal to be more inclusive of smaller parties by lowering the threshold for funding eligibility from one-third of the EU member states to one-quarter and proposed that parties must have received at least 3 percent (rather than 5 percent) of the votes cast in those member states in the most recent EP election to receive funding. The EP report further specified that European parties must specify donors and donations exceeding EUR 500, as opposed to the EUR 100 proposed by the Commission. It also increased the threshold above which donations should not be accepted from EUR 5,000 to EUR 12,000 and proposed that European political parties should be allowed to charge membership fees, as long as they do not exceed 40 percent of the party's annual budget.

Finally, the EP position emphasized that funding provided by the EU budget should not be used for the direct financing of national or regional political parties, except for the financing of EP election campaigns or "party activity at any level directly associated with the politics of the EU." The Council accepted these changes in its common position and the legislation entered into force on February 15, 2005.

The criticism of the Court of Auditors put a distinct time pressure on the EP to get the finances of its parties in order and to establish European parties that were autonomous from their EP party groups before the end of the 2004 legislative term.[34] Especially at a time when the financial structures of the EP and its members had become under increasing scrutiny in the eye of the public, the need for legislation that would put European parties on a firmer, more defined, more transparent, and more accountable basis was widely acknowledged to make the system less vulnerable to criticism.[35] Yet, despite the broad recognition that a statute dealing with the financing of European parties, in particular, was urgently needed, there was considerable controversy within the EP with regard to the specifics of the proposal. Especially contested were the thresholds establishing the eligibility of parties for EU funding,[36] the extent to which donations would be permitted,[37] the purposes for which EU funding could be used,[38] and the issue of tying funding to minimum democratic requirements.[39] There was a relative consensus with regard to these issues among the committee representatives of the three largest EP party groups (EPP, PES, and Liberals), while the Greens were initially divided and the representatives of the smaller groups, who felt disadvantaged by the Commission proposal, were largely opposed.[40] With regard to the permissibility of donations, there was also a national aspect to the proposal, since certain member states already put an upper limit on direct donations.[41]

The discussion at the plenary level did not, however, reflect the complexity of the issue at hand,[42] either with regard to the question of financing or the legal status of EU parties, since MEPs "only have a general idea of how financing works."[43] Instead, the issue was treated by a relatively small number of experts in the responsible Constitutional Affairs Committee,[44] who "knew what they were talking about."[45] There was close cooperation among those specialists from a range of party groups who "made their own agreement, which they then took to their groups," as one EP official re-members.[46]

The rapporteur, Mr. Leinen, was critical in forging this final compromise.[47] Mr. Leinen emphasized the role of European parties as building blocks of a federalist EU and as symbols of a politically integrated Europe.[48]

Hence, he considered the financing scheme as a first step toward genuine party organizations, a democratic infrastructure, and democratic political processes at the European level.[49] The party directive was thus an issue that was discussed in reference to the sovereignty-integration dimension,[50] and proponents and opponents of the proposal fell squarely into the pro- and anti-EU camps, respectively. Opposition against the proposal was based on resistance against anything that might constitute a building block of a transnational polity and transnational democratic processes.[51] MEPs taking this position were primarily from the anti-European right and emphasized that EU parties were artificially constructed bodies that should not be subsidized with public money.[52] Accordingly, two focal points dominated the process, both relating to the sovereignty-integration dimension: the *EU democracy* and *artificial constructs* focal points. These focal points are evident in the EP debate on the party statute during the first, and only, parliamentary reading. There are 70 references (per 10,000 input words) to the EU democracy focal point, while the artificial constructs focal point is referred to 31 times, as Table 5.4 shows.[53] Interestingly, the issue of legal personality was almost nonexistent during the plenary debates, as only four references were made to the fact that the directive does not, in fact, constitute a genuine party statute providing EU parties with a European legal personality.

As a result of this focus on the role of parties in facilitating European democracy, as well as the close cooperation between key actors across party lines who managed to find agreement on the details of the proposal, there was broad support for the directive. It was, in fact, the strategy of the rapporteur to be as inclusive as possible.[54] One key element ensuring a broad consensus was that potentially controversial aspects of the directive were deliberately removed from the agenda by the active participants in the deliberation process and by the rapporteur in particular. Specifically, it was argued that "the time was not yet ripe" for a genuine party statute

Table 5.4: Party statute, frequencies-of-use, content analysis

	# of input words	# of references to *EU democracy*	# of references to *artificial constructs*	# references to *legal personality*
1st reading	10,000	70	31	4
	(9,916)	(69)	(31)	(4)
	23 speakers	20 speakers	14 speakers	2 speakers

Note: Entries report number of references to various focal points in EP debates for every 10,000 input words. Actual number of input words and frequencies appear in parentheses.

which would require the specification of the legal status or a European-level legal personality of EU parties.[55] There was a distinct sense of uncertainty and insecurity about what it would mean if a European party would become active across member-state borders based on its European legal personality,[56] as well as concern about the coexistence of national and EU-level parties with regard to both European and domestic member state politics.[57] Hence, in order to avoid splitting up the existing coalition in favor of the financing scheme and postponing a decision,[58] it was decided in the Constitutional Affairs Committee to keep the issue off the table and to view the proposal of EU party financing as a first step toward a genuine European party statute.[59] Given the need for some legal status of EU parties, the final compromise stipulated that EU parties must have legal personality in the member state in which their seats are located, which essentially referred to Belgium.[60]

Therefore, the "real controversies" were effectively excluded from the final text, according to one EP official closely involved in the decision-making process,[61] allowing the party experts to convince their party colleagues of their positions.[62] As a result, the final agreement was not a genuine party statute, but merely a financing scheme addressing the immediately pressing issue of establishing an acceptable framework for the financing of EU parties.[63] Given the controversy surrounding the issue of EU parties, however, and the long-standing skepticism toward the very concept paired with national concerns about the impact of establishing transnational parties with any legal status, it has been described as a "miracle" that the directive came into existence at all.[64]

Voting patterns: the impact of the legislative process on voting outcomes

The decision-making process in the case of the EU party statute was dominated by two focal points that relate to the sovereignty-integration dimension, as both the issue of EU democracy and the claim that EU parties are artificially constructed entities lacking legitimacy relate to this ideological dimension. Accordingly, we should expect to find that MEPs voted based on their positions on the sovereignty-integration dimension, with pro-European MEPs voting in favor and EU-skeptics against. In contrast, the left-right divide should be insignificant in explaining voting patterns, since the deliberation process did not feature any focal points relating to the left-right dimension.

The dependent variable in this binomial logit regression analysis is the EP plenary vote in first reading, in which the party statute was adopted. This variable is dichotomous, where a value of zero equals a vote against the directive and a value of one means a vote in favor. The independent variables are, once again, the two ideology variables (left-right and sovereignty-integration) and the government status dichotomous variable. Additionally, I include a dichotomous variable that assumes a value of one if national party finance rules specify a ceiling on individual annual donations to political parties. I control for this factor because the most contentious issue providing for nationally based divisions in the EP concerned the legality of party donations and the question of limiting donations to particular levels.[65]

The results of the analysis show that, as predicted, pro-European MEPs voted in favor of the EU party statute, as the highly statistically significant, positive coefficient of the sovereignty-integration variable in Table 5.5 shows. Also as expected, the left-right variable does not achieve statistical significance. The table also indicates that MEPs from member states that specify ceilings on party donations were more likely to support the legislation (a result that makes sense given that the new legislation at the EU level also sets such limits), while government or opposition status at the national level does not account for positions toward the party statute. Finally, the

Table 5.5: Party statute, binomial logit regression estimates, first reading vote

	Floor vote, first reading
Left-right dimension	−.08
	(26)
Sovereignty-integration dimension	5.30***
	(63)
Government status	.58
	(35)
National ceiling on party donations	.75*
	(.31)
Constant	.84***
	(.23)
Number of cases	457
Log pseudo-likelihood	−150.99
Pseudo R^2	0.45

Note: Table entries are binomial logit estimates. Dependent variable: vote (Yes = 1, No = 0, Abstain = 0). Statistical significance is indicated as follows: p < .05*, p < .01**, p < .001***

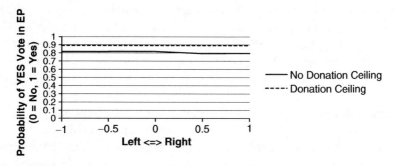

Figure 5.8 Party statute, mean predicted probability of Yes vote given left-right positions, first reading vote

regression model explains a substantial 45 percent of the variance in the voting patterns, as the pseudo-R^2 suggests.

Figures 5.8 through 5.10 display the predicted probabilities of voting in favor of the party statute.[66] The two graphs in Figure 5.8 confirm that the left-right divide was not predictive of voting patterns, as MEPs on the left were no more or less likely to support the party statute than MEPs on the right.

In contrast, Figure 5.9 illustrates the substantial impact of positions on the sovereignty-integration dimension in explaining vote choice. In fact, the probabilities of supporting the legislation as a function of pro-/anti-EU attitudes range from zero on the extreme EU-skeptic side of the spectrum to 100 percent at the pro-EU end.

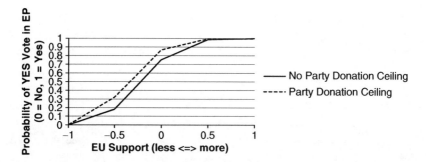

Figure 5.9 Party statute, mean predicted probability of Yes vote given levels of EU support, first reading vote

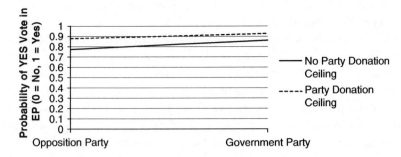

Figure 5.10 Party statute, mean predicted probability of Yes vote given government status, first reading vote

Finally, Figure 5.10 shows that government or opposition status in the national arena, and thus representation in the EU Council, barely affects the probability of MEPs voting in favor of the party statute.

In sum, the party statute was adopted by the EP on the basis of MEP positions on the sovereignty-integration dimension, which confirms our expectations. Pro-Europeans voted in favor of the legislation, while EU-skeptics opposed it. It was thus possible to predict voting patterns on the basis of the focal points dominating the deliberation of the legislative proposal.

Case 2: Conclusion

The EU party statute does not constitute a case in which there was a measurable shift in policy positions over time, as the legislative proposal was accepted in first reading and, for this reason, involved only one final roll-call vote. It does provide for a study in consistency of our key expectations, most importantly by confirming the hypothesis that it is possible to predict voting patterns on the EP floor on the basis of the focal points prevailing in the deliberation of the dossier. This was indeed the case with the party statute, where the discussion centered on the implications of the legislation for the development of EU democracy and the role of transnational political parties in this process. The discussion took place at a very general level, however, and was characterized by broad representations of the content and consequences of the particular policy issue under consideration, as the qualitative analysis illustrates. Accordingly, vote choice in the EP plenary was primarily based on MEP positions along the sovereignty-integration dimension, as the quantitative analysis shows, while there was neither a left-right nor a distinct national interest component influencing how MEPs voted on the floor.

The focus of the deliberations on the sovereignty-integration dimension provided the basis of a broad cross-party coalition supporting the legislation, as the majority of MEPs shares a pro-EU sentiment. As discussed earlier, one factor ensuring this broad consensus was that potentially controversial aspects of the directive at the urging of Mr. Leinen, most importantly the definition of a "legal personality" for EU parties, were deliberately kept off the agenda. As long as the time was perceived not to be "ripe" for the establishment of a genuine European-level legal personality, it was deemed preferable by the key actors to establish a pure party financing scheme presented as a first step toward a genuine European party statute. It was this minimal solution that secured the necessary support for the legislation.

Case 3: Proposals on fuel quality and emission standards for motor vehicles

In 1997, the EP began discussing three legislative proposals regarding emission standards for both personal and nonpersonal motor vehicles and the quality of petrol and diesel fuels. While technically three separate proposals, the EP treated them as one package of legislation aimed to reduce emissions and improve air quality. The legislation followed from and was introduced by the Commission on the basis of the "Auto-Oil Program," established in 1994, which aimed to develop scientific methods to establish emission standards for vehicles. The Auto-Oil Program involved an intense series of studies and negotiations between the Commission, auto manufacturers, and the oil industry focused on tougher standards for vehicle emissions and fuel quality. The idea was to use the expertise of these industries to establish the most cost-effective way to reduce the impact of pollution on air quality and human health (Commission of the European Communities 1996).

Two proposals concerned emission standards. The first, COD/1996/0164A, was supposed to tighten emission standards applicable to private cars and add new requirements, all in accordance with the results of the Auto-Oil Program. The initial Commission proposal provided for a two-stage reduction in exhaust emissions: A first reduction in various pollutants was to be applied from the year 2000 onward to certain types of vehicles and from 2001 onward to all new vehicles. In 2005, a second step was to be implemented on the basis of industrial feasibility and technological progress. Additionally, the proposal included provisions to improve emission test procedures, required petrol-driven cars to be equipped with an onboard diagnostic system, and provided new measures to enhance the testing of the conformity of the vehicles with durability requirements. The second proposal, COD/1996/0164B, targeted light commercial vehicles and also featured a two-stage approach. The first target dates ranged between the years 2000 and 2002 for different classes of nonpersonal vehicles and aimed to significantly reduce emissions of different pollutants against 1997 standards. A second regulatory stage was to be applied from 2005 onward, based on a new Commission proposal to be submitted to Parliament and Council in 1998.

The third element of the emissions package sought to improve the quality of fuel with a view to reducing emissions from automobiles (COD/1996/0163). It was to harmonize limit values for different parameters of lead-free petrol and diesel in the year 2000 and stipulated that afterward, only those fuels complying with the specifications of the directive would be authorized for sale in the member states. Furthermore, it provided for the development of a uniform system to monitor the quality of fuels distributed, as well as the gradual elimination of all leaded petrol by January 1, 2000. The initial proposal allowed for temporary exceptions from the limit values under specific circumstances, however, such as "serious socioeconomic problems" or a "sudden change in the supply of crude oil." Moreover, all new fuel specifications were to be reviewed in light of the Community air quality objectives and the economic viability of the measures in the near future.

Qualitative analysis: focal points and the legislative process

In its first reading reports on the emission standard proposals, the EP amended the Commission proposals to include a two-stage approach to the imposition of binding emission limits in 2000 and 2005, rather than indicative specifications for 2005, as favored by the Commission. The reports also called for tighter limits on exhaust emissions, the replacement of old vehicles or the retrofitting of antipollution devices, stricter emission control procedures, and the promotion of substitute fuels. Notably, the EP advocated the tool of tax incentives to encourage immediate compliance with stricter limits on pollutant emissions, which was one of the first times the use of such incentives was discussed as a genuine environmental instrument at the EU level. The ultimate goal was to regulate the reduction of

CO_2 emissions to effectively make cars with an average gasoline use of 5 liters per 100 kilometers mandatory by 2005 and cars with an average gasoline use of three liters per 100 kilometers mandatory by 2010.

Regarding the proposal on fuel quality, the EP also called for tighter mandatory minimum specifications than those proposed by the European Commission for petrol and diesel, as well as for the active use of tax incentives to facilitate the introduction of improved fuels. Parliament also introduced the possibility of derogation and a "phased-in approach," to enable member states facing serious economic difficulties to continue to authorize use of fuels not complying with the strict levels suggested by the EP until January 1, 2005.

The modified Commission proposal and the Council's common position accepted some of these requests, such as the use of tax incentives and measures to encourage faster progress toward replacing existing vehicles with low-emission vehicles. However, it rejected the EP's key demands for tighter limit values and the replacement of indicative with mandatory values for 2005, both with regard to emissions and fuel quality standards.

Parliament retabled most of the amendments adopted in first reading that were not incorporated in the common position in second reading, insisting on stricter limits and mandatory values, despite the insistence of Commission and Council that they could not accept these demands. Accordingly, the matter went into conciliation at the end of June 1998, where agreement was reached on all of the outstanding points. The key compromise lay in the Council delegation agreeing to compulsory limit values for 2005; in exchange, Parliament accepted the less stringent figures proposed by the Council for the specifications themselves, which were seen as a considerable improvement on the figures originally put forward by the Commission.[67] The compromise was widely viewed as a success for Parliament, as it achieved the adoption of a broader approach to the issues of emissions and fuel quality whereby benefits to health and the environment were taken into account when assessing the cost of measures to improve air quality.

Parliament adopted all three reports on September 15, 1998. It voted 454 to 3, with 7 abstentions, in favor of the proposal to reduce air pollution from passenger motor vehicles; 465 to 11, with 3 abstentions, in favor of the emissions proposal concerning light commercial vehicles; and 474 to 10, with 3 abstentions, in favor of the proposal on fuel quality.

The consideration of these three proposals by the EP began in late 1996 and early 1997, although the issues of fuel quality and emission standards had been on the table already for a number of years. Since the Commission proposal came out of the Auto-Oil Program—where Commission, automobile manufacturers, and the oil industry had shared ideas while excluding other stakeholders, such as social associations, nongovernmental organizations, and representatives of the EP—the Commission proposal was viewed with suspicion in the EP and perceived to be heavily biased in favor of the industry, at the expense of environmental standards.

Despite much controversy in the early stages of the proceedings and throughout the decision-making process,[68] the emissions package was adopted by the EP by overwhelming margins. The great majority of my respondents, when asked about this development, highlighted the role of the two rapporteurs in creating this result. These two individuals were Bernd Lange, a German member of the Socialist group, who was in charge of the legislation concerning emission standards (COD/1996/0164A and 0164B), and Heidi Hautala, a Finish Green, who was assigned to the fuel quality proposal (COD/1996/163).

The two rapporteurs had a very close working relationship, coordinated their efforts, and were "very serious, very committed"[69] to their objective of realizing an emissions proposal that was balanced and not as biased toward the industry, as the Commission proposal was viewed.[70] Their strategy revolved around three elements: to provide sound data challenging what was perceived to be exaggerated cost estimates of the industry and the Commission; to seek a broadly acceptable compromise across all party lines; and to get the right people involved in the effort. According to a number of respondents, finding a compromise began even before the first reading.[71] This effort "took a very, very long time," and involved a great number of technical meetings where the rapporteurs, EP officials, and representatives from the Council Presidency would "work and work and work."[72]

The emissions directives were very heavily lobbied, not just in the context of the Auto-Oil Program, but also during the parliamentary deliberation process. Both the oil and the car-manufacturing industries were pressing hard for the Commission proposal, which they saw as relatively moderate, and issued estimates underscoring the great costs they saw themselves facing if the EP proposals were accepted. To counter these suggestions, the rapporteurs sought to back up their argumentation with detailed economic calculations, according to an EP official.[73] Realizing that they may not get their proposals accepted otherwise, the rapporteurs had to provide "sound data to counteract"[74] the Commission proposal and were markedly successful, since the information was perceived as "great," in the words of one respondent, and "costs were [seen as] acceptable according to that."[75]

The efforts of the two rapporteurs were targeted at a broad, cross-party coalition in committee, and both rapporteurs took realistic positions and did not "ask for the earth in the end."[76] Mr. Lange, in particular, was perceived to be a very consensual rapporteur, who was cooperative and had a good working relationship with other actors across party lines.[77] While pushing in the direction of stricter standards, he always tried to bring on board the other political groups.[78] He was also perceived to be "extremely competent on the subject matter, which got him the reputation where he had good arguments, and in the end, people wouldn't question him."[79] He was trusted across party lines,[80] because he was, according to one member of the Environment Committee, "perfectly capable of speaking without any hypocrisy at a conference of industrialists or automobile manufacturers, but also at a conference of environmentalists—and making the same speech!"[81]

As a Finish member of the Greens, Ms. Hautala had to overcome some initial suspicion before being accepted a fairly unbiased broker by her conservative colleagues in committee.[82] In the end, however, both rapporteurs had proved their consensual credentials and were considered to be reliable and trustworthy, rather than partisan actors. They initiated numerous informational meetings and engaged in their own "discreet lobbying" so that in the end "people felt that they were not getting any nasty surprises."[83] They were "very astute" in getting the right people on board, according to one EP official, thus playing the political game while backing up their positions with the necessary data. Involving the right mix of participants was critical, as an EP official highlights: "We got the right people to be on the conciliation committee, the right people to sit in the final conciliation meetings from the EP side. You know, not too radical, people who could get it through, good negotiators."[84]

This perception is confirmed by another official, who remembers the group of participants as "well-informed, not extremist and, as such, reliable. So therefore, people would follow."[85] This very cooperative group included Ms. Hautala from the Greens, Mr. Lange and David Bowe (UK) from the PES, as well as Horst Schnellhardt and Karl-Heinz Florenz (Germany) from the EPP.[86] The arguments put forth by this group of actors revolved around the question of "cost-effectiveness" (the principle favored by the industry) and "best available technology" (the principle advocated on the EP side). Politically, the proponents of more stringent environmental standards emphasized issues such as the impact of air quality and climate change on public health, a discussion that, in later stages of the legislative process, also referred to the recently negotiated

Kyoto Protocol.[87] The themes emphasized by this group therefore created a *consumer protection* focal point.

While the proposals were discussed critically and controversially inside the committee, the consumer protection focal point so dominated the debate outside of the committee that one MEP maintains that the business and industry points of view and the "restrictions that [the legislation] would put in place" were not at all taken into account at the plenary level. There was a "lack of knowledge" concerning these implications of the legislation among regular parliamentarians, since "a lot of the reasoning arose from the committee and did not take account of different factors that we have across Europe."[88] The opponents of the proposal thus presented an alternative focal point by emphasizing *industry interests*, that is, the potential negative impact of the legislation on industries across the EU.

However, the content analyses of three debates in the EP plenary, held in April 1997, February 1998, and September 1998,[89] show that the industry interest focal point featured less prominently in the parliamentary deliberation process than the consumer protection focal point. Moreover, it was increasingly sidelined in the decision-making process, while the consumer protection issue continuously gained in prominence.[90] Table 5.6 shows that while there are only 133 references per 10,000 input words in the April 1997 debate, MEPs refer to the consumer protection issue 158 and 148 times per 10,000 input words in the second and third debates, respectively. At the same time, there are only 69 references per 10,000 input words to the industry interest focal point in the first debate, a number that drops to 52 in

Table 5.6: Fuel quality and emission standards directives, frequencies-of-use, content analysis

	# of input words	# of references to *consumer protection*	# of references to *industry interest*
1st reading	10,000	133	69
	(15,326)	(204)	(106)
	32 speakers	31 speakers	31 speakers
2nd reading	10,000	158	52
	(13,216)	(210)	(68)
	29 speakers	29 speakers	27 speakers
3rd reading	10,000	148	28
	(6,502)	(96)	(18)
	13 speakers	13 speakers	12 speakers

Note: Entries report number of references to various focal points in EP debates for every 10,000 input words. Actual number of input words and frequencies appear in parentheses.

the second debate. In the third debate, the number of references drops even more, to only 28 per 10,000 input words, indicating the decreasing importance of the industry interest issue.

In sum, the rapporteurs made sure that the process of decision-making in the EP was based on solid data and information disseminated across party groups by the right group of people, while their reputations as real environmental experts made a significant difference in creating a context for compromise, according to one EP official.[91] Furthermore, this effort took place in an atmosphere where the EP was only starting to use its new powers of legislation in the context of the codecision procedure, which provided the institution and its members with a new sense of assertiveness vis-à-vis Council and Commission. As a result, the emissions issue is remembered as one of the first cases "where the EP took a strong stance early in the codecision procedure,"[92] and it was described by Ken Collins (PES, UK), chairman of Environment Committee, as "a triumph for Parliament."[93]

Voting patterns: the impact of the legislative process on voting outcomes

Based on how these proposals proceeded through the legislative process, we should expect to find that in first reading the positions of MEPs on both ideological dimensions should be significant predictors of voting choice in the EP plenary. With the industry interest focal point in particular playing a prominent role in the discussion of the proposals at that point in time, we should expect to find two voting patterns. First, members of the political right should be less likely to support the proposals, since they ought to be more concerned with the perceived negative impact of the legislation on businesses. Second, Euroskeptics should be less inclined to support the legislation, as they are unlikely to support environmental regulation at the EU level.

In contrast, the decreasing emphasis on the industry interest focal point should reduce the impact of the left-right and pro-/anti-EU dimensions in third reading, especially in combination with the ideologically more neutral consumer protection focal point dominating the debate, which should undermine ideology-based divisions.

Due to collinearity issues between certain vote outcomes and the "type of capitalism" variables, however, statistical analyses are not straightforward with regard to the emissions proposals. Tables 5.7 and 5.8 show the frequencies of vote outcomes by "type of capitalism" for the first reading votes

Table 5.7: Fuel quality and emission standards directives, frequencies of vote outcomes by type of capitalism, including abstentions

		Liberal	Partial	Sectoral	National
COD/1996/0163	0 = No	2	34	2	n/a
	1 =Yes	53	75	155	42
	2 = Abstain	10	39	n/a	n/a
COD/1996/0164a	0 = No	3	29	4	n/a
	1 =Yes	52	99	149	40
	2 = Abstain	8	22	5	n/a

Table 5.8: Fuel quality and emission standards directives, frequencies of vote outcomes by type of capitalism, Abstentions = No

		Liberal	Partial	Sectoral	National
COD/1996/0163	0 = No	12	73	2	n/a
	1 = Yes	53	75	155	42
COD/1996/0164a	0 = No	11	51	9	n/a
	1 = Yes	52	99	149	40

of proposals 163 and 164a. Of concern for this analysis are the empty cells, for example in the sectoral and national coordinated market economy categories for the 163 proposal, which indicate perfect collinearity between the predictor variable and certain vote outcomes (i.e., the sectoral coordinated market economy variable predicts the absence of abstentions perfectly, and the national coordinated market economy variable predicts the absence of No votes and abstentions perfectly). Also methodologically problematic are the cases of almost perfect collinearity, where the cell value is very small, such as the two instances of No votes for the liberal and sectoral market economy categories; here, the two variables almost perfectly predict the occurrence of No votes.[94]

Consequently, I exclude the types of capitalism variables from these binomial logit regression analyses to focus only on the impact of the ideology variables. The dependent variable is dichotomous, where a value of zero equals a vote against and a value of one means a vote in favor. The independent variables are MEP scores on the left-right and sovereignty-integration dimensions.

The results of the simplified model must be viewed with caution and will serve here merely as illustrations of the likely impact and direction of the left-right and sovereignty-integration variables. Tables 5.9 and 5.10 show the results of the analyses for the first reading votes regarding proposals 163

Who Decides, and How?

Table 5.9: COD/1996/163, binomial logit regression estimates, first reading vote

	Floor vote, first reading
Left-right dimension	−3.24***
	(.50)
Sovereignty-integration dimension	.75**
	(.27)
Constant	1.98***
	(.24)
Number of cases	412
Log pseudo-likelihood	−159.43
Pseudo R^2	0.25

Note: Table entries are binomial logit estimates. Dependent variable: vote (Yes = 1, No = 0, Abstain = 0). Statistical significance is indicated as follows: $p < .05^*$, $p < .01^{**}$, $p < .001^{***}$

Table 5.10: COD/1996/164a, binomial logit regression estimates, first reading vote

	Floor vote, first reading
Left-right dimension	−3.27***
	(.65)
Sovereignty-integration dimension	2.11***
	(.37)
Constant	2.13***
	(.31)
Number of cases	411
Log pseudo-likelihood	−128.88
Pseudo R^2	0.32

Note: Table entries are binomial logit estimates. Dependent variable: vote (Yes = 1, No = 0, Abstain = 0). Statistical significance is indicated as follows: $p < .05^*$, $p < .01^{**}$, $p < .001^{***}$

and 164a. The results suggest that in first reading, the expected significances of the predictors and the directions of their relationships with the dependent variables find confirmation in the empirical data. As hypothesized, both ideology variables are statistically significant, in the expected direction, in the two votes. The left-right variable correlates negatively with the dependent variable, indicating that MEPs on the political right were more likely to oppose the legislative proposals; and the sovereignty-integration variable is positively related to the dependent variable, meaning that more pro-European MEPs were more likely to support the legislation.

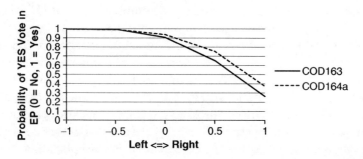

Figure 5.11 Fuel quality and emission standards directives, mean predicted probability of Yes vote given left-right positions, first reading votes, COD/1996/0163 and COD/1996/0164a

This vote pattern is also evident in the graphs presenting the predicted probability of votes in favor of the proposals. Figure 5.11 displays the predicted probability of a Yes vote given left-right positions, which decreases as we move toward the political right.[95]

Figure 5.12 shows that the probability of voting in favor increases with the pro-integration stance of MEPs.

In third reading, the EP adopted the joint proposal on the quality of petrol and diesel fuels (163) with 474 votes to 10 with 3 abstentions; the proposal to reduce air pollution from motor vehicles (164a) with 454 votes to 3 with 7 abstentions; and the proposal to reduce air pollution from light commercial vehicles (164b) with 465 votes to 11 with 3 abstentions. Due to this overwhelming majority in favor of the three legislative proposals, there is insufficient variance in the dependent variables to run meaningful statistical analyses, making a direct comparison with vote patterns in first

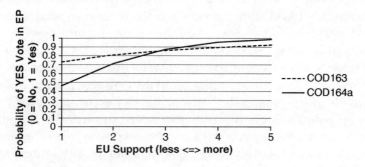

Figure 5.12 Fuel quality and emission standards directives, mean predicted probability of Yes vote given levels of EU support, first reading votes, COD/1996/0163 and COD/1996/0164a

reading impossible. Instead, I provide descriptive information about the MEPs who voted against the proposals or abstained.

Of the 15 MEPs who did not support the set of legislative proposals, 11 were French, 3 were Belgian, and 1 was Italian. Except for one member of the Union for Europe of the Nations, all were nonattached MEPs. All are far to the political right, with an average score of 0.60 on the left-right dimension, and all are pronounced Euroskeptics, with an average score of −0.78 on the sovereignty-integration dimension. Hence, aside from a very small group of nonattached, politically conservative, Euroskeptic MEPs, the rapporteurs actually managed to get the entire EP behind their positions in the final votes on the three proposals; the apparent left-right and pro-/anti-EU divisions observable in first reading disappeared in third reading as the consumer protection focal point became prevalent.

Case 3: Conclusion

The analysis of the emissions and fuel quality directives demonstrates the substantial impact individual MEPs can have on the positions of their nonexpert party colleagues and, ultimately, on legislative outcomes, since the EP's campaign for tighter emissions and fuel quality standards was successful despite significant opposition in both Council and Commission. A cohesive EP, however, which supported the more stringent guidelines with an overwhelming majority under the leadership of a group of legislative specialists from different party groups, ultimately succeeded in securing its most important objectives.

The role of the two rapporteurs in securing this outcome constitutes an important reason for Parliament's achievement, according to the majority of my respondents, who highlighted their expertise, abilities, and willingness to seek a broad compromise across party lines as their recipe for success. The compromise was established between party experts in the responsible Environment Committee, and this "right mix" of people constituted the basis for securing broad support for the committee position. On the basis of this "right mix," policy positions were aggregated across party groups, which accounts for the nearly unanimous decisions on the EP floor.

The proponents of the legislation advocated its merits by providing a consumer protection focal point that resonated with a large number of MEPs. This focal point affected voting behavior in first reading in the expected direction. Unfortunately, the data limitations for this set of proposals do not allow for as detailed an analysis as in other case studies. The consumer protection focal point, however, became increasingly dominant over time at the expense of a second focal point emphasizing the perceived negative impact of the legislation on the competitiveness of national industries. Accordingly, MEPs voted overwhelmingly in favor of the legislative proposals in third reading, while there had been substantial divisions earlier on.

Case 4: Liability for environmental damage

The purpose of the legislative proposal on "liability with regard to the prevention and remedying of environmental damage" (COD/2002/0021), introduced by the Commission in January 2002, was to create a regulatory framework that would establish an EU-wide system of liability for environmental damage. In the context of the proposed legislation, "environmental damage" included damage to wildlife and natural biodiversity protected at the EU and national levels, to the water courses regulated by the Water Framework Directive (2000/60/EC), as well as land contamination that causes serious harm to human health. The basis for the legislation was the "polluter-pays principle," according to which the operator who has caused the damage, or who is faced with an imminent threat of such damage occurring, should ultimately bear the cost associated with cleanup measures. Dating back almost a decade, when a Green Paper on Environmental Liability first introduced the principle in 1993, the polluter-pays principle was to provide the foundation for EU-level harmonization and regulatory control within the environmental field. The legislation was also building on a number of parliamentary resolutions on the matter and a White Paper on Environmental Liability published in 2000.[96]

At the time the legislation was introduced not all member states actually had legislation in place to address the issue of environmental liability. For example, this was the case in Portugal and Greece. Other member states' legislation did not adequately address the EU legislation's primary objective of "site cleanup" following pollution. The Commission proposal highlighted the need for this legislation by estimating that around 300,000 sites were already identified as contaminated or potentially contaminated across the EU, with cleanup costs estimated to total between EUR 55 and 106 billion. The lack of a harmonized framework at the EU level facilitated the exploitation of differences in national-level legislation and loopholes in the existing regulatory frameworks by economic actors, meaning that cleanup costs would come from public finances.

The objective of the liability legislation was to establish a framework that would either prevent or remedy environmental damage by forcing negligent operators to clean up polluted sites at their own expense or to reimburse public authorities who may have taken restorative measures. Taking account of the subsidiarity principle, the directive aimed to provide a minimum standard for restoring damaged sites, while leaving particular decisions regarding the measures to be taken by or on behalf of such operators to national authorities. The Commission proposal did, however, provide for the possibility that private actors or parties with a sufficient interest (such as environmental nongovernmental organizations) could request appropriate action by the competent authorities at the national level and challenge their subsequent action or inaction.

The critical controversies regarding the environmental liability directive concerned the question of the directive's scope, that is, what environmental damage and which occupational activities should be covered, and where they should apply;[97] the exemptions and defenses available to alleged polluters;[98] and the question of voluntary or compulsory insurance for industries.[99] In terms of scope, the directive included practices or activities involving heavy metals, dangerous chemicals, landfill sites, and incineration plants, but explicitly excluded other risky activities, such as oil transport and drilling operations. With regard to exemptions, the Commission proposal excluded "damage caused by an emission or event expressly authorized in a permit" (the "compliance with permit exception") and activities which are believed to be safe for the environment according to "the state of scientific and technical knowledge" when they occur (the "state-of-the-art exception"). Finally, the Commission proposal sought to "encourage" operators to invest in prevention by making insurance against environmental damage voluntary, rather than compulsory.

Qualitative analysis: focal points and the legislative process

Deliberation of the environmental liability directive in the EP was preceded by an unusually controversial conflict between the Environment and Legal Affairs Committees over which committee should be in charge of the proposal.[100] The dossier was first given to the Environment Committee, but this decision was challenged by the Legal Affairs Committee. While the Environment Committee emphasized that the liability scheme concerned legislation specific to the environment and was being reviewed by the Council of Environment Ministers, the Legal Affairs Committee argued that it should be responsible because the issue concerned third-party liability matters irrespective of the area of application (European Report 2002*a*). The conflict culminated in the extraordinary decision to have a plenary vote on the issue, rather than leave the decision to the Conference of Committee Chairmen, which normally resolves competency conflicts but could not find agreement regarding this particular dossier.[101] On July 3, 2002, the EP voted by 266 to 241 with 12 abstentions in favor of the Legal Affairs Committee. Toine Manders (European Liberal Democrat and Reform Party [ELDR], Netherlands) was chosen as the rapporteur. The Environment Committee would provide an opinion, with Mihail Papayannakis (GUE/NGL, Greece) as its rapporteur. Moreover, the Conference of Presidents decided to invoke Rule 47 of the EP's rules of procedure.[102] Rule 47 describes the "enhanced cooperation procedure," which applies when the Conference of Presidents decides that a legislative proposal falls almost equally within the competence of two committees, or when different parts of the issue under consideration fall under the competence of two committees. Under the procedure, the two committees set a common timetable and the rapporteur of the lead committee is supposed to seek agreement on a joint text with the rapporteur from the opinion-giving committee. Moreover, the amendments adopted in the opinion committee can be adopted by the lead committee without a vote.

Mr. Papayannakis was the first to table his report on the Commission proposal on behalf of the Environment Committee. In his report, he harshly criticized the proposal, starting with what he identified as inadequate definitions of key concepts such as biodiversity, land contamination, or soil and subsoil contamination. Also within the realm of definition, he highlighted that according to the Commission proposal, liability to restore "environmental damage" was triggered only above a degree of "seriousness," but that the proposal failed to define how the seriousness of damage was to be measured. In the opinion of the Environment Committee, measurement standards should include the extent and duration of the polluting impact, whether pollution is reversible or irreversible, and the sensitivity and rarity of the resources damaged.

The Environment Committee also wanted to extend the scope of the directive to include genetically modified organisms, cover damages associated with air pollution, and extend to all activities subject to Community environmental legislation, rather than the limited number of practices identified in the Commission proposal. It was also to include oil pollution and nuclear damage, which were excluded on the grounds that they are already covered by other international conventions.[103] The Environment Committee rejected the "compliance with permit" and the "state-of-the-art" exceptions specified in the Commission proposal, arguing that they undermined the effective implementation of the polluter-pays principle. Finally, the Environment Committee report demanded that insurance against environmental damage be mandatory, rather than voluntary, to ensure that costs associated with cleanup measures would not, ultimately, fall upon taxpayers (European Report 2003*b*).

Under Rule 47 of the Rules of Procedure, which defines the enhanced cooperation procedure, the lead committee can accept, without a vote, amendments from the opinion committee "where they concern matters which the chairman of the committee responsible considers . . . , after consulting the chairman of the committee asked for an opinion, to fall under the competence of the committee asked for an opinion, and which do not contradict other elements of the report." With regard to the environmental liability dossier, this meant in practice that most amendments proposed in the opinion report of the Environment Committee were not included in the first reading report tabled by the Legal Affairs Committee, since the report drafted by Mr. Manders aimed to strike a balance between the conflicting interests of industry and environmental concerns, and significantly weakened the proposal by reducing the total number of amendments from 303 to 12 (European Report 2003*c*). According to one respondent from the EPP, this was the result of the Environment Committee overstepping its competences by amending aspects of the report that fell within the jurisdiction of the Legal Affairs Committee.[104]

Another respondent close to Mr. Manders, however, explained that the enhanced cooperation procedure proved to be an exercise in "window-dressing" in the case of the environmental liability dossier because, in practice, it was the responsible rapporteur who decided what amendments "fall under the competence" of the opinion committee.[105] This meant that Mr. Manders decided "strategically" what amendments should be sent to the plenary.[106] Another respondent confirmed this reality by acknowledging that the decision is a political one in the end,[107] while an EPP member of the Legal Affairs Committee explained: "It is a huge advantage to be the main committee, and the rapporteur of the main committee, if he is arrogant enough, can bypass all the opinions. You have no legal obligation to take opinion amendments on board. You can practically say: Let's reject all the amendments of the Environment Committee, and no one can blame you."[108]

Members of the Environment Committee did blame Mr. Manders for his decision to include only one of every four amendments they introduced, however. In fact, the issue triggered an angry exchange of letters between the chairmen of the two committees.[109] It was not possible to seriously challenge the dominant policy coalition of EPP and Liberal MEPs in the Legal Affairs Committee, however, as everybody involved was well aware.[110] Accordingly, the Manders report was adopted by his committee in first reading by an 18 to 11 margin, against the votes of committee members from the left.

The Manders report centered on a series of "compromise" amendments aimed at bolstering the legislative majority necessary to pass the legislation. These amendments broadened the definition of the term "European biodiversity" to all protected species and sites where they live; extended the directive's scope to include nuclear and marine pollution (but only at the end of a transitional five-year period in the event that the relevant international agreements had not been ratified by the member states and/or the EU); sought to reduce the number of exemptions specified in the Commission proposal; and made financial security systems mandatory. Nevertheless, the report was perceived to be too lenient by more environmentally minded MEPs. Most importantly, the "compliance with permit" and the "state-of-the-art" exceptions remained part of the proposal, while scope and definitions concerning environmental damage were seen as unclear and arbitrary (European Report 2003c). Effectively, the Manders report was seen to exclude some of the greatest perceived threats to the environment, such as air pollution and genetically modified organisms, while providing exemptions that would allow operators to dodge the polluter-pays principle in practice. As a result, proponents of a stricter liability framework voted against the Manders report in committee and retabled in plenary amendments from the Papayannakis report.[111]

A number of the amendments seeking to strengthen the proposal were adopted in the EP plenary's first reading vote on May 14, 2003, if by very small margins.[112] The EP thus adopted amendments broadening the definition of the term "biodiversity" to cover habitats and species protected under European as well as national legislation and stipulated that those who are, or could be, responsible for potentially damaging activities should take preventive or restorative measures without governments requesting them to do so. Other amendments reduced drastically the number of exemptions permitting operators to avoid bearing the costs of environmental damage they have caused (by limiting these to cases of armed conflict and terrorist acts, exceptional and unavoidable natural phenomena, and to activities carried out within the framework of good agricultural and forestry practice). Finally, financial insurance systems for cases in which an operator cannot be held responsible would be mandatory, rather than voluntary, within 6 years after the directive entered into force (Spiteri 2003*a*, 2003*b*). The complete report, which significantly strengthened the directive from an environmental perspective in comparison to the report of the Legal Affairs Committee, was adopted by 310 in favor, 177 against with 23 abstentions. Accordingly, the plenary actually departed from the position of the lead committee,[113] which is quite unusual. Instead, it followed the line of the Environment Committee and thus adopted the more stringent proposal.[114]

Mr. Manders' liberal colleagues were particularly divided over the legislation in first reading. In fact, there were two voting lists in the Liberal Group suggesting how Liberal MEPs should vote in plenary. One was the vote suggestion of the rapporteur in the lead committee, Mr. Manders, the other one was the proposed positions of a senior Liberal member of the Environment Committee, Chris Davies. Liberal MEPs not familiar with the details of the dossier could then decide which one of their colleagues to follow when making their own vote choice.[115] Given the reputation of Mr. Davies as generally supportive of "green" legislation, more environmentally minded MEPs in the Liberal group followed Mr. Davies, while others decided to follow Mr. Manders' "industry-prone" approach. With a split voting list proposed by these two MEPs, "you know immediately whom to follow, irrespective of the topic that will be voted on," according to one Liberal respondent.[116]

The common position of the Council of Ministers was adopted on September 19, 2003, by qualified majority against the votes of Austria, Germany, and Ireland. The Council's common position accepted 26 of the EP's 48 amendments to the proposal, but leaned decisively toward the Commission proposal, rather than the more stringent EP position, with regard to the key issues. Most importantly, it provided for member states to include the "compliance with permit" and the "state-of-the-art" exemptions if they so chose, stipulated a voluntary rather than compulsory insurance regime, and excluded emissions and nuclear activities from the scope of the directive (European Report 2003*a*).

Unlike in first reading, the EP did not take a strong environmental stance in the second reading, where it followed the recommendation of Mr. Manders and adopted his report.[117] The proponents of the report were aided by the EP's decision-making rules, however, which stipulate the need for absolute majorities in second reading, that is, more than 50 percent of the total number of members. The Rules of Procedure thus made it less likely that the controversial amendments from first reading, in which a simple majority suffices, would be adopted in second reading.

While the Manders report in second reading proposed some measures that went beyond the Council's position (e.g. by including environmental damages linked to maritime navigation accidents in the directive's field of application), it did not provide for the stringent guidelines that many MEPs had hoped for. Most importantly, it accepted the Council's position of a voluntary, rather than mandatory, insurance scheme, while leaving open the future possibility of a compulsory system of financial guarantees by asking the Commission to evaluate the insurance situation 5 years after the legislation's entry into force. If proper instruments of financial guarantee were not adopted by then, the EP would ask the Commission to submit proposals for an obligatory insurance scheme, first for water and soil damage, and later for damage to biodiversity and natural habitats. With regard to the second question of controversy, the Legal Affairs Committee also accepted the "compliance with permit" and "state-of-the-art" defenses. The environmental liability legislation nevertheless went into conciliation, due to the small adjustments the EP made to the Council's common position.

The overall tone of the second reading report contradicted the more environmental line propagated by those in favor of a more stringent environmental framework for the liability legislation. In effect, it was an attempt by the political right, under the leadership of Mr. Manders, to outvote the opposition, rather than to seek a broadly acceptable compromise. This step was preceded by extensive negotiations across party and committee lines, which proved to be unsuccessful. The reasons for this failure to build consensus are unclear, as respondents provide different accounts for the circumstances under which negotiations broke down. Some indicate that the compromise proposals made by Mr. Manders were derived from negotiations across party and committee lines, even involving Mr. Papayannakis.[118] Others are more skeptical of Mr. Manders' motives and his abilities to forge a broad political compromise; one respondent describes Mr. Manders' handling of the dossier as "an example of how *not* to do legislation."[119] Despite early attempts to arrive at a compromise, it is quite evident that Mr. Manders eventually gave up on the idea of consensus-building and merely tried to push through his own agenda with the help of the EPP.[120] This was facilitated by the similarities between the positions taken by Council, Commission, and Mr. Manders.

Conciliation opened on January 27, 2004. The most important issue remained the question of voluntary versus obligatory insurance and when a voluntary system should be reevaluated. In this regard, the conciliation compromise of February 19, 2004, stipulated that the Commission would conduct an evaluation 6 years from the legislation's entry into force and would determine the need for a harmonized mandatory financial securities framework. It would also address the issue of a ceiling for liability and the exclusion of low-risk activities from the mandatory insurance scheme (European Report 2004). The EP accepted this compromise on 31 March. The legislation was to enter into force by the end of the year and national law would have to be introduced within 3 years. This outcome was significantly closer to the positions of the political right, while some of the less stringent requests of the Environment Committee were included in the legislation.[121] In the end, it was an outcome with which nobody was very content.[122]

One question that remains is whether this outcome would have been different had the Environment Committee been the lead committee. Respondents provide contradictory assessments of this possibility when asked directly. Some maintain that the outcome would very likely have been different,[123] while others acknowledge that this would at least have been a possibility.[124] A third group—notably all members of the EPP, whose positions regarding the issue were more or less realized in the final legislation—maintain that the outcome would have been the same, since it is the EP plenary that has the final say with regard to any committee report.[125]

In reality, much would support the conclusion that there was at least a good chance the outcome would have been different with Environmental Affairs in charge. There even seems to have been such an assumption in Parliament prior to the actual legislative process, since both committees competing for the lead lobbied hard, which is unlikely to have been just to gain prestige. In fact, the EPP chairman of the Legal Affairs committee, Giuseppe Gargani, went against the chairwoman of the Environment Committee, Caroline Jackson, who was a British Conservative and thus a colleague from his own party group but wanted to see her own committee handle the dossier. Especially the conservatives and liberals in the Legal Affairs Committee assumed that their policy agenda was more likely to succeed with their committee in the lead.[126] One EPP member explains: "We are stronger in Legal Affairs, because we have a strong alliance with the Liberals, but in Environmental Affairs, the Socialists are stronger because they have an alliance with the Greens and the smaller groups, and the Liberals in that committee are maybe more left-leaning."[127]

The Legal Affairs Committee had two critical advantages as the lead committee. First, it could, and did, suppress those amendments from the Environment Committee that it viewed as politically undesirable.[128] This authority was especially important in second reading when a simple majority suffices to adopt amendments in committee, but an absolute majority is needed in plenary. The Legal Affairs Committee thus had the *de facto* ability to decide what amendments had a good chance to stand or fall.[129] This, in addition to the possibility of setting the tone of the debate,[130] resulted in an increasing capacity for the Legal Affairs Committee to dominate the decision-making process after first reading.

Despite the evident disagreements over the content of the proposal, it was the initial conflict of competences that critically set the tone of the debate concerning the environmental liability legislation. As one EP official working closely with Mr. Manders explains, at first "nobody was interested" in this "technical, legally complex dossier that could only be understood by a few experts."[131] Over the course of the debate, however, the dossier was "made controversial" and "blown out of proportion. It was a hype!"[132] The dossier was very heavily lobbied[133] and, ultimately, there were a large number of people who were interested in the dossier.[134] Nonetheless, it was only the key players who actually understood the content and the potential implications of the dossier.[135] Many other actors

...jumped in at a very late stage not knowing what it is all about, and these people are very easy targets for sentiments...If you use sentiment, if you avoid the debate on substance, it is very easy to convince people and drag them into your camp...It was a disadvantage in finding a compromise that this dossier was so politicized.[136]

Three focal points dominated the debate concerning the environmental liability directive. The proponents of the legislation, including Mr. Manders, emphasized that the legislation would have to be realistic in striking a balance between environmental and industry concerns. This issue was summarized in references to the need for *workability*, or implementability, of the legislation. The proponents also provided a second focal point, which emphasized the desirability of the legislation from a pro-European point of view by emphasizing the need for *harmonization* of environmental regulation at the EU level. Finally, opponents of the legislation, primarily members of the Environment Committee, presented the dossier as a de facto *license to pollute*, due to its limited scope and important exceptions to the rules.

The content analyses of the EP debates on the environmental liability dossier show that the license to pollute focal point is most prominent during the first reading stage, when the conflict of competences between the Legal Affairs and Environment Committees was in full swing and the Environment Committee played a critical role in debate. At that time, this focal point is referenced 123 times per 10,000 input words. It remains important across the three reading stages, as Table 5.11 illustrates, since there was no broadly acceptable compromise agreement even at the end, but it is less visible with the decreasing role of the Environment Committee at the later stages of the decision-making process: the number of references drops to 74 in second and 35 in third reading.

The workability focal point also features prominently in all three reading stages. In contrast to the license to pollute focal point, however, it gains in prominence between the first and second readings, when it is referred to 77 and 96 times, respectively, per 10,000 input words. This is not surprising, since it constitutes the primary argument in the Legal Affairs Committee, which replaced the Environment Committee as the dominant actor over time. Ultimately, the workability issue replaces the license to pollute focal point as the dominant focus of the discussion. However, it is mentioned only 43 times in third reading, when the third focal point, centering on the subject of harmonization, becomes more prominent than in previous readings. While there are only 14 and 9 references to the harmonization focal point in first and second reading, it is referred to 23 times in third reading.[137]

Voting patterns: the impact of the legislative process on voting outcomes

As no roll-call vote was requested in the third reading stage of the legislative process, this quantitative analysis is limited to only one vote, namely the

Table 5.11: Liability for environmental damage directive, frequencies-of-use, content analysis

	# of input words	# of references to *workability*	# of references to *license to pollute*	# references to *harmonization*
1st reading	10,000 (14,619) 35 speakers	77 (112) 31 speakers	123 (180) 34 speakers	14 (21) 11 speakers
2nd reading	10,000 (9,574) 20 speakers	96 (92) 18 speakers	74 (71) 16 speakers	9 (9) 4 speakers
3rd reading	10,000 (3,968) 8 speakers	43 (17) 5 speakers	35 (14) 6 speakers	23 (9) 4 speakers

Note: Entries report number of references to various focal points in EP debates for every 10,000 input words. Actual number of input words and frequencies appear in parentheses.

vote on the first reading EP report. At that point in time, the Environment Committee still played a critical role under the enhanced cooperation procedure. Moreover, the conflict of competences between the Legal Affairs and Environment Committees had reached a second climax, following the initial EP vote putting the Legal Affairs Committee in charge of the legislation, as the Legal Affairs Committee had rejected the majority of amendments proposed in the Environment Committee opinion report. The Environment Committee reintroduced its amendments in the EP plenary, however; accordingly, the first reading report prescribed a strict liability framework that would not leave negligent operators much leeway in terms of scope and possible exemptions.

All three focal points identified in the aforementioned qualitative analysis were part of the deliberation process during the first reading stage. The workability and license to pollute focal points were presented as almost directly contradictory to one another, with the political right emphasizing the need for a balanced framework that would take both environmental and business interests into account and the political left arguing that the proposed framework directive watered down the "polluter-pays" principle beyond recognition. The directive was thus discussed in a left-right context and, accordingly, we would expect the analysis to show that MEP positions on the left-right are statistically significant predictors of vote choice. In particular, legislators from the political left should be more likely to support the stringent first reading proposal, while those on the right should oppose it.

At the same time, the harmonization focal point put an emphasis on the need for EU-level regulation facilitating the harmonization of environmental policy across the member states. Accordingly, we should expect MEP positions on the sovereignty-integration dimension to be statistically significant as well, with pro-Europeans more likely to support the legislation and EU-skeptics likely to oppose it.

The dependent variable in the binomial logit regression analysis is the EP plenary vote in first reading, where a value of zero equals a vote against the directive and a value of one means a vote in favor. The independent variables are the two ideology variables (left-right and sovereignty-integration), the government status dichotomous variable, and the set of dichotomous variables for "type of capitalism." The results confirm the expectations from above. As hypothesized, the coefficients of the two ideological variables are both statistically significant in the expected direction: leftists and pro-Europeans are more likely to support the legislation. This result is evident in Table 5.12, which presents the raw binomial logit estimates.

Figure 5.13 provides the predicted probability of a vote in favor of the liability legislation given MEP positions on the left-right dimension.[138] It shows that the probability of MEPs from the far left, center-left, and even the political center supporting the legislation was quite high in the first reading vote, with some variation between the four different types of capitalism. As we move further to the political right, however, the probability of a vote in favor of the legislation drops substantially.

Figure 5.14 displays the predicted probabilities of a Yes vote given positions on the sovereignty-integration dimension. The figure demonstrates that vote choice in first reading was also a function of positions on this dimension, with pro-Europeans much more likely to support the legislation than EU-skeptics.

Figure 5.15 demonstrates that government status at home increased the probability of an MEP supporting the proposal, meaning that MEPs whose national parties were represented in the Council were more likely to vote in favor. This trend is most pronounced for legislators from sectoral

Table 5.12: Liability for environmental damage directive, binomial logit regression estimates, first reading vote

	Floor vote, first reading
Left-right dimension	−5.29***
	(.55)
Sovereignty-integration dimension	4.11***
	(.80)
Government status	1.18***
	(.33)
Liberal market economy	1.17
	(.77)
Partial coordinated market economy	−.47
	(.49)
Sectoral coordinated market economy	−1.18*
	(.53)
Constant	1.07*
	(.47)
Number of cases	485
Log pseudo-likelihood	−131.78
Pseudo R^2	0.59

Note: Table entries are binomial logit estimates. Dependent variable: vote (Yes = 1, No = 0, Abstain = 0). "National Coordinated Market Economy" serves as the reference category. Statistical significance is indicated as follows: $p < .5^*$, $p < .01^{**}$, $p < .001^{***}$

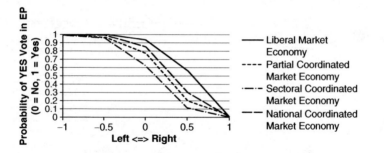

Figure 5.13 Liability for environmental damage directive, mean predicted probability of Yes vote given left-right positions, first reading vote

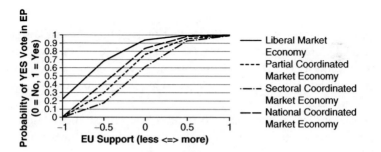

Figure 5.14 Liability for environmental damage directive, mean predicted probability of Yes vote given levels of EU support, first reading vote

coordinated market economies, who had the smallest initial inclination to support the legislation.

Finally, Figures 5.13 through 5.15 show that MEPs from liberal market economies were most likely to support the legislation, followed by MEPs from member states with national and partial coordinated market economies. Members from sectoral coordinated market economies, in contrast, were relatively less inclined to support the strict liability framework.

Case 4: Conclusion

This analysis of the environmental liability legislation highlights the importance of the key participants in the decision-making process and their ability to influence the policy positions of their nonexpert colleagues through the provision of focal points. It demonstrates, furthermore, that the level of controversy concerning particular pieces of legislation is difficult to forecast, as the initial conflict of competences between the Legal

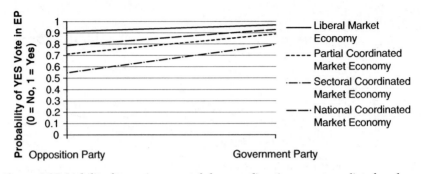

Figure 5.15 Liability for environmental damage directive, mean predicted probability of Yes vote given government status, first reading vote

Affairs and Environment Committees set the stage for an unusually controversial deliberation process. In other words, both the policy preferences of the great majority of MEPs and the intensity of the controversy surrounding the negotiation of the liability legislation are endogenous to the policymaking process.

The role of the Environment Committee was critical indeed and shows what can happen in a legislative process when two competing sets of specialists are involved in the deliberation of a dossier. The Environment and Legal Affairs Committees presented the legislation in two fundamentally different fashions, and the Environment Committee, despite losing its initial role as the lead committee, succeeded in shaping vote choice during the first reading plenary vote. The legislative rules limited its role in second reading, however, where the Legal Affairs Committee had more leeway in drafting a report along the lines of its political objectives. As a result, the final piece of legislation reflects the position of the Legal Affairs Committee more than that of the Environment Committee.

Unfortunately for this analysis, the final vote in third reading was not recorded, making an explicit comparison between the first and third reading votes on the EP floor impossible. The qualitative analysis suggests, however, that positions on the sovereignty-integration dimension became more potent predictors over time, at the expense of the salience of the left-right divide. This is for two reasons: First, with the decreasing involvement of the Environment Committee, the license to pollute focal point played a less important role in the deliberation process. This would likely entail a decrease in the perceived salience of the left-right dimension. Simultaneously, the prominence of the other two focal points increased. The growing emphasis on these focal points likely entailed an increase in the salience of the sovereignty-integration dimension. While the harmonization focal point emphasized the desirability of a framework for environmental legislation at the EU level and thus explicitly stressed a pro-EU element in the policy proposal, the workability focal point underlined that it may be better to have a suboptimal legislative framework than none at all. All this is speculative, but the evidence presented in previous case studies supports the likelihood of this scenario.

Case 5: The liberalization of port services in the EU

The purpose of the directive on "port services: market access and financing of maritime ports" (COD/2001/0047), often referred to as the "port package," was to establish a legal framework that would ensure fair access to the port services market across the EU. Port services refer to technical-nautical pilotage services, towage and berthing, all cargo-handling operations (including loading and unloading, stowage, transshipment, and other intra-terminal transport), and passenger services (including embarkation and disembarkation). The opening of the port services market was to occur while providing member states with the opportunity to create specific rules within this framework that would take into account the ports' geographic characteristics as well as local, regional, and national singularities. The legislation was thus supposed to combine the principle of subsidiarity with the recognition and enforcement of the EU's four freedoms (freedom of goods, persons, services, and capital) and existing EU competition rules.

At the time when the port services legislation was proposed by the Commission in early 2001, there was a great divergence of practice in the member states. While breaches of the existing regulations had been treated on a case-by-case basis in the past, the port package was to ensure a more systematic application of rules in the port sector to guarantee that all service providers would have a fair chance of entering the port services market. The overall goal was to avoid distortion of competition by improving and harmonizing national rules, regulations, and practices.

Qualitative analysis: focal points and the legislative process

The port services directive was one of the most controversial legislative proposals before the EP during its fifth term (1999–2004). The two most contested aspects of the proposal concerned the transparency of financial relations between member states and their ports and the range of services covered by the directive. The first was discussed in the context of "competition between harbors" (the financing of ports and port-related investments), while the second issue related to "competition within harbors" (the question of opening up access to services in individual ports). While the question of competition between ports was principally a source of interinstitutional disagreement between the EP on the one side and Council and Commission on the other, the question of services covered by the directive constituted a considerable source of controversy within the EP. Two types of port services took center-stage, namely "pilotage" (the guiding of vessels in and out of port) and "self-handling" (the situation where a port user provides its own port services personnel, rather than buying services from dockworkers in the port, e.g., by using its own land-based or seafaring crew and equipment for cargo-handling operations).

During the first parliamentary reading in November 2001 the EP amended the Commission proposal substantially. First, it included a provision requiring greater transparency with regard to public funding and the financial structures of European seaports. It also excluded pilotage from the directive and restricted self-handling to port users whose vessels fly the flag of an EU member state. This was to decrease the risk of social dumping, where specialized dockworkers would be replaced by under-qualified seafaring personnel from outside of the EU not covered by existing social, safety, training, and environmental regulations. By authorizing only ships flying EU member state flags, the EP sought to prevent the use of "flags of convenience" to minimize self-handling costs. The legislative resolution in first reading was accepted with 284 MEPs voting in favor, 230 against, with 31 abstentions.

Commission and Council did not accept the critical EP amendments concerning the transparency of financial relations and the scope of the directive, however, which the EP then reintroduced in second reading in March 2003. With regard to the question of self-handling, the EP sought to restrict authorization to seafaring crew members, rather than allowing the use of land-based personnel, and confirmed its insistence on permitting self-handling only for vessels flying the flag of an EU member state. It also insisted that self-handlers should be treated in the same way as other port service providers, meaning the same social protection standards and professional qualification requirements would apply. Once again, pilotage was to be completely excluded from the directive.

Following the EP's rejection of the Council's position, the port package went into conciliation at the end of September 2003. The conciliation agreement outlined that self-handling would be allowed only in cases where shipping companies use their own seafaring crew and their own equipment. The agreement also stipulated that a member state *may* require self-handling to be subject to prior authorization in accordance with criteria relating to employment and social protection standards, professional qualifications, and environmental considerations, and that national rules on training requirements, professional qualifications, employment, and social protection would not be affected directly by the legislation. With regard to pilotage, the compromise provided that this service should remain within the scope of the directive, but that the special importance of these services for the safety of maritime traffic would be emphasized. Moreover, the conciliation agreement specified that the responsible national authorities *may* recognize the "compulsory nature" of pilotage and set rules for the service deemed necessary for reasons of safety and of public service requirements, including limiting pilotage services to a single provider. Hence, the compromise agreement left the question of prior authorization for services to the discretion of the member states, thus confirming the position of Council and Commission on both the issues of self-handling and pilotage.

Concerning public funding and the financial structures of European seaports, the compromise extended the directive to include the establishment of "fair and transparent conditions of competition both in and between Community ports." To that end, every port and port service provider would be required to disclose its financial structures to the member states and the Commission. The Commission and the member states would use this information to evaluate the need for fair competition, and the Commission would draft a set of common guidelines on state funding for ports within 1 year of the directive's entry into force.

The EP's conciliation delegation had passed the conciliation compromise with a very narrow majority, but the EP plenary rejected the agreement on November 20, 2003, with 209 MEPs voting in favor, 229 against, and 16 abstentions.

While the question of financial relations and public funding of ports constituted an immediate source of conflict between EP, Commission, and Council, the controversy within Parliament did not materialize until after the first parliamentary reading. This first reading is remembered by a number of respondents involved in the deliberation of the proposal as having been relatively easy.[139] There was "some debate, but nobody was interested," according to one member of the responsible Committee on Regional Policy, Transport and Tourism; it was "a technical debate by those colleagues who have an interest in harbors or come from harbor areas."[140] Moreover, since the inclusion of measures to improve the transparency of public funding of ports into the scope of the directive was broadly favored across party lines,[141] the proposal passed smoothly through first reading.

Two developments, however, changed this dynamic during the process of deliberation in the later legislative stages. On the one hand, there was an external factor, namely increasing pressure from stakeholders concerned about the effects of the legislation on existing structures, in particular from port authorities, who wanted to keep control of their ports and port workers. In particular, the labor unions in the North Sea harbors in Germany, the Netherlands, and Belgium, representing the highly organized dockworkers, increasingly showed their opposition publicly; the climax was a number of strikes, as well as vocal and unruly demonstrations at the EP in Brussels and Strasbourg. Secondly, there was a change of mood within the EP, with the political left becoming more skeptical toward what was increasingly perceived to be one of many EU "liberalization initiatives."[142] This new focus on the merits of liberalization and privatization, placed in the broader context of globalization, constituted a significant change of focus from the first reading, where it played no role whatsoever.[143] Now, the political left maintained that the proposal was setting conditions for competition among service providers within harbors at the expense of highly qualified dockworkers and, as a result, of "safety standards and security norms."[144] Hence, *liberalization* and its negative implications for dockworkers and maritime safety became an increasingly prevalent focal point for the opponents of the directive.

The proponents of opening up European ports to competition, in contrast, maintained that ports were too expensive and a burden on the EU economy as a whole. In their view, the European economy could become more competitive by cutting excessive costs caused by rigid and protectionist structures. Operating ports could be more transparent, efficient, and less expensive. This would, according to proponents, benefit the overall aim of the Lisbon Agenda to make the EU the most competitive economy in the world by 2010. Therefore, the efficiency and *competitiveness of the EU economy* would improve if the port package were approved, which was the principal focal point for making the case in favor of the proposal.

This latter position was the one shared and promoted by the rapporteur responsible for the port services directive, Georg Jarzembowski. As a German Christian-Democrat, Mr. Jarzembowski was not perceived to be a pure economic liberal, but a socially oriented politician who in principle favors the involvement of social partners and trade unions in economic governance. With regard to liberalization issues, however, he was considered to be "the first to propose liberalization on transport issues."[145] As a result, the political left maintained that "when the rapporteur speaks of reducing the cost of port services he really means cutting wages, jobs and social protection."[146]

Mr. Jarzembowski enjoyed a reputation across party lines as one of the principal specialists on transportation issues. He was also known and respected as a skillful politician and tough negotiator with strong principles and objectives. While generally not perceived as dogmatic, even some of his party colleagues viewed him as headstrong at times and insistent on his own positions, which sometimes made it difficult to pursue an agenda of compromise across party lines.[147] Respondents generally characterized him not as the kind of rapporteur who instinctively seeks a compromise that is broadly acceptable across party lines, but one who sticks to his own positions when possible and is willing to take political gambles if he sees the odds to be in his favor. As some respondents indicated, however, Mr. Jarzembowski occasionally underestimated the extent of the opposition to his proposals,[148] and this was also the case with regard to the port services directive.[149] He evidently misjudged the majorities he could muster in the EP plenary, especially in the decisive third reading vote following the conciliation procedure between EP and Council.

While a time period of six weeks, with a possible two-week extension, is officially allocated to a conciliation between EP and Council, the process in the case of the port package took a single day until the issue was put to a vote in the conciliation committee. There was concern among the proponents of the proposal that a drawn-out negotiation process would undermine existing support for the directive and the "right side of the room was really pressing for an immediate solution," according to an EP official.[150] To this end, the rapporteur had pursued the strategy of finding a compromise with the Council of Ministers, which was not willing to give in to the demands of the left; once he realized that there was probably no possibility of "finding an agreement with the Socialists,"[151] he negotiated a compromise solution with the Council and tried to push it through in Parliament. Hence, much negotiation took place behind closed doors throughout the summer months preceding the conciliation procedure. While there had been no official exchange of text between Council and EP, just hours before the first conciliation meeting on September 29, 2003, a working document suddenly appeared "out of the blue," as one respondent remembers.[152]

Evidently, Mr. Jarzembowski speculated that he had the necessary majority in plenary to push this text through plenary with the votes of the Liberals, in particular, once it was accepted in the conciliation procedure. He was even willing to give up the support of a portion of his EPP colleagues, since he expected defectors from other party groups to make up for this loss.[153]

The most contested element in the conciliation text concerned the authorization procedure in the case of self-handling. The question was whether prior authorization by national authorities was to be voluntary, as the compromise agreement stipulated, or mandatory, as the critics of the proposal demanded. The conciliation committee voted in favor of the conciliation result to be forwarded to the EP plenary in a contested 8–7 vote. This outcome came as a surprise to the opponents of the directive in the committee, since the Socialist Vice President of the EP, Renzo Imbeni, unexpectedly voted in favor of the conciliation result. Mr. Imbeni justified this stance arguing that he wanted to leave the final vote to the EP plenary and not to bring the proposal down with his single vote.[154] To many of his party colleagues, however, this explanation was unacceptable; one Socialist remembers having been furious at the time.[155] Mr. Imbeni's Socialist colleagues suspected that he had cut a deal with the negotiators from the Parliament's right and the Council behind their backs.[156]

The outcome of the vote in the conciliation committee was thus extremely close and was due, in part, to some political maneuvering on the part of the rapporteur. As one respondent present in the conciliation meetings maintains,[157] a number of Flemish and Dutch EPP members who were to vote on the compromise agreement and would have rejected it were substituted, at the very last minute, by the rapporteur and group coordinator to ensure the approval of the compromise agreement. This type of maneuvering explains why in the case of the port services directive, the committee position in favor of the proposal did not translate into a positive vote in the EP plenary, where the proposal was defeated. Mr. Jarzembowski arranged for his position to pass through conciliation rapidly and took a gamble in plenary, where he believed he had the majority necessary for the proposal to pass, rather than continuing to negotiate a compromise text that might have satisfied some of his opponents. This compromise may well have been possible, however, especially with regard to the authorization procedure that could have been made "a little more waterproof."[158] While this is purely speculative, two respondents from opposite sides of the political spectrum did indicate in our conversations that they would have been willing to accept a compromise where the opening of the self-handling sector to competition was coupled with strict mandatory prior authorization. One economic liberal from the EPP side, though not satisfied even with the conciliation compromise "from a competitive perspective," indicated that he would have allowed "self-handling with or without the prior authorization,"[159] while a Socialist from a North-Sea country maintains that she would have supported a compromise providing for self-handling with prior authorization.[160] But according to the critics of the directive, the rigid positions of the key actors in committee on the conservative side made such an agreement impossible.[161]

The Socialists had two primary objectives in the second and third reading stages: to exclude both pilotage and self-handling from the scope of the directive.[162] In second reading, they felt that they were "almost there."[163] This sense made them fairly optimistic for the conciliation procedure and the third reading vote, but the rapporteur's strategy of pushing the compromise agreement, including a provision for the liberalization of self-handling, through the conciliation committee spoiled their efforts before genuine negotiations even started.[164] The fact that a Socialist Vice President was the one breaking the tie in favor of sending the compromise agreement to the plenary caused a particular stir among the Socialists dealing with the directive. The perception that a deal had been cut behind the Socialists' back between the rapporteur, the responsible Commissioner Loyola De Palacio, the Council negotiators, and Mr. Imbeni, intensified the opposition to the directive among the Socialist members handling the dossier on behalf of their party group.[165] The firm positions of Mr. Jarzembowski and Ms. de Palacio in particular angered the opponents of the directive, as they were perceived to be unresponsive to their arguments.[166]

As a result, the active participants from the political left began lobbying heavily to ensure a cohesive party line against the directive in the third reading vote,[167] an effort facilitated by the increasing outside pressure against the proposal by the dockworkers, a key constituency of the left.[168] One official from the Greens remembers that, in response, he mobilized his faction strongly: "We made sure that everybody takes part in the vote."[169] Similarly, a Socialist respondent described her efforts to bring the proposal down as follows:

I wrote to [the Socialist MEPs] saying "Be there! Don't lose this, this is a major fight." ... I worked like hell to get a position with everyone. ... Normally we try to handle the discussions in the committee working group because it is difficult on very technical issues to take positions in the big group. But on this ports thing, we had a very heavy discussion in the group and got the group's support to do it like this. It was absolutely a convincing effort.[170]

This reality is especially noteworthy because transport issues usually do not get much exposure in the PES group,[171] as deliberation and positioning is usually left to the experts.[172] Here, as in other groups, the policy experts had to make an active effort to establish a firm and cohesive line with regard to the port package.[173] Their activities were especially directed at those MEPs on the political left from the Southern EU member states, who thought that opening port services to competition would give their ports a competitive advantage over the highly structured ports in the Northern member states.[174] In the end, however, the lobbying campaign on the principle of antiliberalization paid off: "We won over most of our comrades from the Southern countries on the principle of liberalization," one Dutch Socialist remembers.[175]

This principle was communicated in a quite emotional fashion, however.[176] Even one opponent of the directive acknowledges that the antiliberalization drive was at least in part based on mistaken interpretations of the directive's consequences, which would have coupled liberalization with "very strong" elements of regulation. Instead, critical nuances were excluded from the discussion. As a result, a "vulgarized debate" ultimately turned an issue of "liberalization of services with regulation both at the European and the national level" into one of "complete liberalizations."[177] Discussion centered on a number of emotional key phrases like "social dumping" and featured frequent references to a metaphorical busload of Bulgarians, Chinese, Africans, Argentineans, Malaysians, or Filipinos "coming to self-handle ships, while the others would be fired from their very secure jobs."[178] As one member of the leftist GUE group explained: "I imagine it like this: some seaman from Burundi climbs in Piraeus [the harbor of Athens] on a crane and has to read the instruction manual in Greek, which he can't. So the whole thing is absurd!"[179]

Partially due to this simplified debate, one member of the transportation committee suspected that MEPs lacking the necessary expertise with regard to transport issues to genuinely evaluate the actual extent of the "liberalization" instituted by the port services directive opposed a policy proposal that they may have supported if they had the necessary background knowledge and considered the dossier more carefully.[180] Another respondent maintains, quite similarly, that despite the substantial degree of public attention to the issue and the high level of controversy in the EP, the majority of MEPs voting had no substantiated opinion regarding the port package.[181]

The shift in the discussion of the port package from the importance of EU competitiveness to concerns about the negative implications of "liberalization" is quite evident in the parliamentary debates in first reading (November 13, 2001), second reading (March 10, 2003), and third reading (November 18, 2003).[182] Table 5.13 shows that the first reading debate features 114 references per 10,000 input words to the EU competitiveness focal point, a number that declines steadily to 77 references in second and only 69 references in third reading. In contrast, the liberalization focal point is referenced 135 times in first, 283 times in second, and 292 times in third reading (all per 10,000 input words), showing its increasing dominance in the discussion concerning the port services directive.

Moreover, a second content analysis shows that the liberalization issue not only moved to the center of the debate, but was also discussed in a more emotional and severe fashion. For this analysis, I coded references to the liberalization issue by intensity. The most extreme references include such terms as "abuse," "cowboy ports," "crooks," "pirate workers," "ultra-liberal," "slavery," as well as references to the symbolic "busload" of Africans, Argentineans, or Malaysians. Table 5.14 shows that the use of such extreme terminology jumps from three incidents per 10,000 input words in first reading to 21 and 20, respectively, in the second and third reading stages.

Voting patterns: the impact of the legislative process on voting outcomes

It is hypothesized that we should be able to predict voting patterns in plenary on the basis of the dominant focal points. This quantitative

Table 5.13: Port services directive, frequencies-of-use, content analysis

	# of input words	# of references to *liberalization*	# of references to *EU competitiveness*
1st reading	10,000	135	114
	(7,397)	(100)	(84)
	21 speakers	18 speakers	19 speakers
2nd reading	10,000	283	77
	(10,755)	(304)	(83)
	28 speakers	28 speakers	25 speakers
3rd reading	10,000	292	69
	(13,708)	(400)	(94)
	34 speakers	34 speakers	31 speakers

Note: Entries report number of references to various focal points in EP debates for every 10,000 input words. Actual number of input words and frequencies appear in parentheses.

Table 5.14: Port services directive, frequencies-of-use, content analysis, extreme terminology

	# of input words	# of extreme terms
1st reading	10,000	3
	(7,397)	(2)
2nd reading	10,000	21
	(10,755)	(23)
3rd reading	10,000	20
	(13,708)	(28)

Note: Entries report number of references to various focal points in EP debates for every 10,000 input words. Actual number of input words and frequencies appear in parentheses.

analysis tests this proposition and serves to determine if prevailing focal points actually provided the basis for the formation of policy coalitions, that is, if they supplied a mutually acceptable equilibrium providing the basis for policy coalitions.

On the basis of the above-mentioned qualitative analysis, it is possible to formulate a series of specific hypotheses regarding the outcomes of the decision-making process in the case of the port package. We should expect to find that in first reading, MEPs vote based on their positions on the left-right divide as well as the sovereignty-integration dimension, since both the liberalization and the competitiveness focal points were important elements of parliamentary deliberation. Specifically, due to the emphasis on the competitiveness of the EU economy, pro-European MEPs should be more likely to support the proposal. Moreover, legislators from the political right should be more likely to support the proposal, since the question of liberalization factored into the discussion of the port package.

By the time of the third parliamentary reading stage, however, the focus of the debate had shifted substantially away from the question of EU competitiveness toward the liberalization issue and its perceived implications. As a result, the impact of MEP positions on the sovereignty-integration dimension should be less pronounced in third reading. Instead, the port package should be more of a left-right issue than it was in first reading, meaning that MEP positions on the left-right dimension should be more potent predictors of voting patterns. Specifically, the political left should be strongly opposed to the proposal, while the political right should be strongly in favor.

The dichotomous dependent variables in these binomial logit regression analyses are the votes in the first and third readings. The predictor variables are, once again, MEP NOMINATE scores on the two ideological dimensions, the government-opposition dichotomous variable, and dichotomous variables accounting for "type of capitalism." The results confirm the expectations from above. In first reading, as hypothesized, the coefficients of the two ideological variables are statistically significant in the expected direction, with pro-Europeans and legislators from the political right more likely to support the port package. Moreover, the pseudo-R^2 of 0.30 suggests that the regression model accounts for a respectable level of the variance in voting patterns. This result is evident in Table 5.15, which presents the raw binomial logit estimates.

To facilitate the interpretation of these results, predicted probabilities are presented in graphical form. Figure 5.16 displays the predicted probabilities of a vote in favor of the proposal along given left-right positions.[183]

This figure confirms that the probability of supporting the proposal in first reading increases the further to the right an MEP is located on the left-right dimension, for all four types of capitalism. The probability of voting in favor increases across the range of the left-right dimension by about 50 percent for MEPs from member states with liberal market economies, about 70 percent for MEPs from partial and coordinated market economies, and a little more than 60 percent for MEPs from member states with sectoral coordinated market economies.

Moreover, Figure 5.16 demonstrates that MEPs from liberal market economies are least likely to vote in favor of the port package, while legislators from sectoral coordinated market economies are most likely to support it. This trend is also evident in Figure 5.17, which presents the predicted probabilities of Yes votes along the sovereignty-integration dimension.

The figure demonstrates that the probability of supporting the proposal rises with increasing pro-EU attitudes of legislators. It also shows that the impact of positions on the sovereignty-integration dimension is quite substantial: The probabilities of voting in favor of the port package increase by about 60 percent across the range of the sovereignty-integration dimension for MEPs from liberal market economies, by about 80 percent for MEPs from partial and national coordinated market economies, and by almost 80 percent for MEPs from sectoral coordinated market economies.

Finally, Figure 5.18 shows that government status at the national level, which at the EU level means being represented in the Council of Ministers, entails a slightly decreased probability of supporting the port package in first reading; this is likely because at this stage of the legislative process, important conflicts between EP and Council were far from resolved.

Table 5.15: Port services directive, binomial logit regression estimates, first reading vote

	Floor vote, first reading
Left-right dimension	1.91***
	(.23)
Sovereignty-integration dimension	2.31***
	(.30)
Government status	−.43
	(.25)
Liberal market economy	−1.82***
	(.45)
Partial coordinated market economy	−.03
	(.36)
Sectoral coordinated market economy	1.00**
	(.38)
Constant	.14
	(.32)
Number of cases	536
Log pseudo-likelihood	−260.68
Pseudo R^2	0.30

Note: Table entries are binomial logit estimates. Dependent variable: vote (Yes = 1, No = 0, Abstain = 0). "National Coordinated Market Economy" serves as the reference category. Statistical significance is indicated as follows: $p < .05^*$, $p < .01^{**}$, $p < .001^{***}$

The impact of a shift in focal points between first and third reading is evident in the analysis of the third reading vote, the results of which are presented in Table 5.16. It shows that the coefficient of the left-right variable increases from 1.91 in first reading to 6.45 in third reading, while the coefficient of the sovereignty-integration variable not only decreases from 2.31 to 0.70, but actually becomes statistically insignificant.

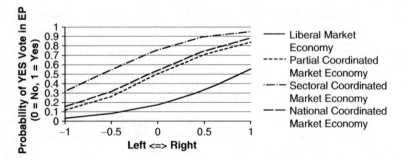

Figure 5.16 Port services directive, mean predicted probability of Yes vote given left-right positions, first reading vote

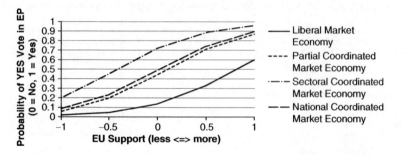

Figure 5.17 Port services directive, mean predicted probability of Yes vote given levels of EU support, first reading vote

This trend is also evident in the predicted probabilities for the left-right and sovereignty-integration dimensions in the EP's third reading vote. Figure 5.19 demonstrates that the probability of voting in favor of the directive increases dramatically across the left-right divide.

As hypothesized, the impact of positions on the left-right divide is much more pronounced in third than in first reading. The probability of voting in favor of the port package increases by 100 percent across the range of the left-right variable, meaning that MEPs on the far left end of the spectrum have a 100 percent probability of voting against the proposal, while those on the far right have a 100 percent probability of voting in favor. This applies for all four types of capitalism. In fact, even MEPs on the moderate left, with NOMINATE scores around −0.5, are almost certain to oppose the

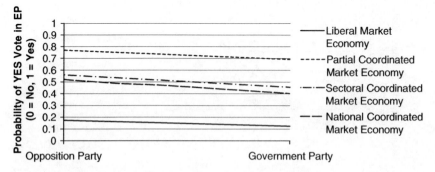

Figure 5.18 Port services directive, mean predicted probability of Yes vote given government status, first reading vote

171

Table 5.16: Port services directive, binomial logit regression estimates, third reading vote

	Floor vote, third reading
Left-right dimension	6.45***
	(.68)
Sovereignty-integration dimension	.70
	(.38)
Government status	.60
	(.35)
Liberal market economy	−1.63*
	(.69)
Partial coordinated market economy	−.40
	(.45)
Sectoral coordinated market economy	−1.45**
	(.46)
Constant	.24
	(.43)
Number of cases	422
Log pseudo-likelihood	−132.66
Pseudo R^2	0.54

Note: Table entries are binomial logit estimates. Dependent variable: vote (Yes = 1, No = 0, Abstain = 0). "National Coordinated Market Economy" serves as the reference category. Statistical significance is indicated as follows: p < .05*, p < .01**, p < .001***

port package in third reading, while MEPs on the center-right, with NOMI-NATE scores of 0.5, are almost certain to support it.

Meanwhile, the impact of positions on the sovereignty-integration dimension is moderate and much less than in first reading, as Figure 5.20 demonstrates. The probability of voting in favor of the port package

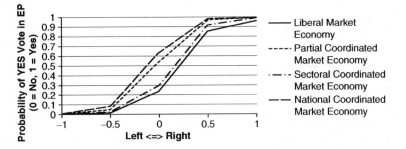

Figure 5.19 Port services directive, mean predicted probability of Yes vote given left-right positions, third reading vote

increases by only around 30 percent as we move from the anti-EU to the pro-EU side of the spectrum.

Figure 5.21 displays the predicted probabilities of voting in favor of the proposal as a function of national party government status. It shows that unlike in first reading, being in government at home slightly increases the probability of supporting the port package following the conciliation process between EP and Council in third reading, across the four "types of capitalism."

Finally, it is noteworthy that MEPs from member states with partial and sectoral coordinated market economies are less likely to support the port package in third reading than they were in first reading. While this result is not surprising for members from sectoral coordinated market economies, since the voluntary nature of the authorization procedures for self-handling stipulated in the conciliation compromise threatened existing structures in the North Sea ports in particular, this finding is less expected for members from partial coordinated market economies. It does confirm, however, that the political left was evidently successful in convincing their members from the Southern EU countries to oppose the port package in the final EP vote.

To summarize, the critical preference shift among legislators not directly involved in the deliberation of the port package was an increase in the perceived salience of the left-right divide between the first and third reading stages, at the expense of the salience of the sovereignty-integration dimension.

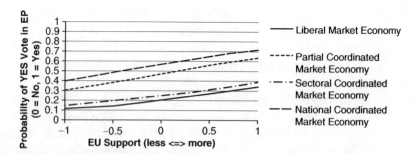

Figure 5.20 Port services directive, mean predicted probability of Yes vote given levels of EU support, third reading vote

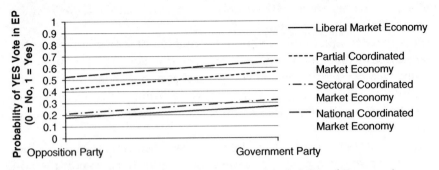

Figure 5.21 Port services directive, mean predicted probability of Yes vote given government status, third reading vote

Case 5: Conclusion

The analysis of the decision-making process in the case of the port services directive supports the expectations of the focal point model. First, it is evident that there was a distinct set of focal points emphasizing the perceived impact of the proposed legislation upon its implementation. As suggested by the focal point model, these focal points constituted broad representations of the content and consequences of the proposed legislation. As such, technical aspects of the proposal were largely absent from the discussion on the EP floor, where broad categorizations of what the legislation was "all about" dominated the deliberation. The focal points highlighted, on the one hand, the perceived positive impact of the port package on the competitiveness of the European economy by making port services less expensive and increasing the efficiency of the port sector across the EU, as well as within individual ports. This emphasis was fairly pronounced in first reading, but was sidelined by an increasing focus on a second aspect of the port services directive when the focal point emphasizing the perceived impact of "negative liberalization" on the job security of port workers and maritime safety gained prominence. Both focal points were provided by committee experts and picked up in the general discussion regarding the port package.

The quantitative analysis of EP votes in the first and third reading stages of the codecision procedure provides evidence for the proposition that a shift in focal points entails a shift in policy preferences, and thus affects political outcomes. Accordingly, it was possible to predict voting patterns on the basis of the prevailing focal points. While the positions of individual

MEPs on the sovereignty-integration ideological dimension were potent predictors of voting patterns when the competitiveness of the European economy was perceived to be at stake in first reading, these positions became less salient over time. Therefore, pro-European MEPs had a greater probability of voting in favor of the directive in first reading, while a pro-EU attitude had little effect in third reading.

Positions on the left-right divide constitute statistically significant predictors of voting behavior in both first and third reading stages, but the rising perception of the legislation as a left-right issue also substantially increased the impact of left-right positions on vote choice in third reading. This impact is so pronounced in third reading that even a moderate left-of-center MEP was almost certain to oppose the directive, while a moderate right-of-center MEP was equally assured to vote in favor.

The case of the port services directive also emphasizes how the political process and its participants play a significant role in affecting policy outcomes. That is, policy outcomes are not just an inevitable result of MEP's preexisting policy preferences. Particularly noteworthy is the fact that the perceived lack of willingness on the part of the rapporteur to cooperate and actively seek a compromise across party lines backfired in the end. Mr. Jarzembowski's strategy of trying to narrowly outvote the opponents of the proposal, rather than seek a compromise agreement that would be broadly acceptable, not only failed, but actually incensed the opponents of the directive. The perception that a deal had been struck between Commission, Council, the political right in the EP, and one Socialist EP Vice President created a special motivation for the active opposition to defeat the proposal completely. The fact that the rapporteur failed to get his own party on board while irritating the skeptics with supposedly furtive dealings ultimately brought the legislation down.

In sum, as long as the port package was viewed at least in part in terms of its European merit, as was the case in first reading, the policy coalition in favor of the legislation was in the majority. This changed over the course of the decision-making process and, in third reading, a leftist policy-coalition in combination with a small number of defectors from the EPP ultimately defeated the proposal.

Case 6: EU citizenship and the free movement of people

The purpose of the legislative proposal titled "Union citizenship: free movement and residence for citizens and their families within the member states' territory" (COD/2001/0111) was to enhance the rights of movement and residence of EU citizens across the EU member states. Based on the premise that the freedom of movement constitutes an integral part of the European integration process, the legislation was to create a common framework of legislation to harmonize the legal status of the EU citizen into a single set of rules.[184]

The underlying concept of the proposal was to enable EU citizens to move between member states on similar terms as citizens within each member state. Moving around across the EU for the purpose of changing residence or jobs was to become comparable to nationals moving around within their own member state. Accordingly, administrative and legal hurdles should be kept at a minimum.

The proposal was to form a single instrument streamlining the arrangements for exercising the freedom of movement within the EU while providing for legal clarity. In this effort, it was to fuse existing regulations and legislation into one coherent whole, thus replacing two existing regulations and nine directives. In this process, it was supposed to:

- streamline the arrangements for exercising freedom of movement;
- extend the right of residence without formalities to six months;
- grant the right of permanent residence after 4 years of residence in the host member state;
- make it easier for Union citizens' family members to exercise the right to move and reside freely, irrespective of nationality; and
- tighten the definitions of restrictions on the right of residence (European Commission 2001).

While the existing rules were based on different parts of the EC Treaty as their legal foundation and concerned particular categories of people (e.g., legislation applying specifically to students), the new, comprehensive directive was to pertain more broadly to all citizens of the EU and their families—regardless of nationality. In sum, the proposal was to substantially simplify the formalities for EU citizens and their families to exercise their rights of movement and residence across member states, cutting back barriers to the bare essentials.

Qualitative analysis: focal points and the legislative process

The directive on EU citizenship was about the free movement of people across the EU and the integration of existing legislation covering different aspects of the free movement of citizens. It was supposed to attach a practical value to the concept of EU citizenship by fusing different existing aspects of EU citizenship into a cohesive whole.[185] This fundamental purpose was hardly controversial in view of the general pro-European outlook in the EP,[186] since the great majority of MEPs agrees with and favors the principle of dual national and EU citizenships.[187]

Several aspect of the proposal exhibited initial potential for controversy, such as immigration and the coordination of social security systems, but it was difficult to anticipate that the key issue would turn out to be one of family definition and, specifically, the extension of citizenship rights to nontraditional and same-sex couples. In fact, the initial resistance to the proposal on the part of the EU member states centered on their reluctance to enhance the residence rights of family members who are not EU citizens, not the definition of what constitutes a family (European Report 2002b). While the relevance of the gay rights issue may have been obvious to some of those directly concerned with the issue, this relevance was not apparent to many legislators. Uninvolved members of Parliament only realized the significance of the issue once the process had started.[188]

Throughout the decision-making process, two opposing groups of members in the responsible Committee on Citizens' Freedoms and Rights, Justice and Home Affairs emphasized what they perceived to be the critical aspects of the EU citizenship directive. For the center-left, joined by Liberal committee members, the most important angle of the debate was that the extension of citizenship rights should not exclude those not covered by traditional definitions of what constitutes a family. To them, it was obvious that if citizens' rights are broadened, "you have to say to whom," as one MEP stressed in interview.[189] In effect, they provided a focal point emphasizing the question of *family definition*.

In response, the political right argued that the principle of subsidiarity bestowed the EU member states with the prerogative of defining marriage and that EU-level definitions should not be "imposed" upon the member states. Most importantly, these conservative committee members framed the issue in terms of the *practical value* of the legislation to the everyday life of EU citizens.

There is a general consensus among the respondents interviewed that without the family definition issue assuming such a prominent role, the directive would have been much less, or not at all, controversial. Even issues such as the circumstances allowing for the forceful expulsion of EU citizens and the time frame for achieving permanent residency,[190] which were of special importance to the Council throughout the codecision procedure and were initially considered to be crucial issues by EP insiders,[191] proved to be all but irrelevant in the deliberations of the EP.[192] The configuration of actors was crucial in pushing new issues to the forefront of the debate, however. The question of family definition in particular became so prominent in the debate because of the presence of a number of MEPs in the responsible committee for whom gay rights were of critical, if not primary, importance. Moreover, these members sat in the key groups of the EP and together formed a strong, intergroup lobby for the extension of the directive to same-sex couples. This group consisted of Michael Cashman and Joke Swiebel for the PES, Kathalijne Buitenweg and Jean Lambert for the Greens, and Sarah Ludford for the Liberals. These members represented a majority in the EP at the time that took a progressive approach with regard to value politics such as civil liberties, where the Liberals tended to back the political left in the Civil Liberties Committee.[193]

The delegates pushing the initiative constituted the key people of the parliamentary majority coalition in this particular policy area in the responsible committee and were able to muster a majority across party groups. This particular configuration of individuals was critical, according to one EP official, who maintains with regard to the gay rights issue that "if Cashman had been sitting with the UEN and Buitenweg had been unattached, it would not really have mattered." Instead, the debate was dominated by the "right mixture of people for making a difference in terms of policy outcomes."[194]

This group of people stood in sharp opposition to the rapporteur in the responsible committee, an Italian MEP from the EPP, whose handling of the dossier constitutes an important aspect of the deliberation and decision-making process. There was a strong perception on the part of the gay rights proponents that appointing Giacomo Santini as a Catholic, Italian conservative was not a sensible decision in the case of this particular dossier. Early on, however, it was not yet apparent that the family definition issue would be so high on the agenda, and one MEP suggests that Mr. Santini himself might have been unaware of what "he put his hands on."[195] Mr. Santini looked at the issue from a very narrow perspective; it may have never occurred to him that this issue might involve the question of family definition and same-sex couples. As the deliberation process unfolded, he began "to discover that EU citizenship involved all kinds of other questions."[196] Mr. Santini appeared hardly open for compromise on the family definition question in first reading, at least in the perception of his political opponents. This view is confirmed by the fact that Mr. Santini insisted in his explanatory statement to the first reading report that "'spouse' must necessarily mean a heterosexual spouse" and that he "considers it preferable to state this explicitly in the directive itself."[197] One Socialist MEP sums up this sentiment as follows:

[The issue] could have been less controversial if somebody else had written it, somebody else who might not have aroused the controversies that were there in the committee and was not going to stake them up. You can never prove that, but there were certain people who had given up taking reports on immigration, because they knew they were not going to get them through, because they know the way the committee was thinking. And I think Santini in some ways was a bit naïve in his approach, and ill advised in terms of what he could get through committee and what he couldn't.[198]

Mr. Santini indeed tried to push through his position in committee, without regard for the lack of majority support for it, and the discussion in first reading was poisonous. It even took on a combative personal tone aimed at Mr. Santini by some of the proponents of the family definition issue, who openly called him "Padre," in reference to his Catholicism and conservatism.[199]

Mr. Santini's position, which was shared by his EP party group colleagues, was that it was not up to Europe to define what constitutes a family, but that these types of definition should be the responsibility of the member states.[200] In this sense, he was the representative of his party group, rather than an agent of the committee or Parliament as a whole.[201] Initially, this position meant that Mr. Santini was unwilling to include any definition of family whatsoever. One result of Mr. Santini's perceived stubbornness was that there were actually separate coordinating meetings between the shadow rapporteurs of PES, Greens, ELDR, and GUE, which were kept purposely secret from the rapporteur himself.[202]

In first reading, Mr. Santini was outvoted both in committee (by a 23–16 margin, with one abstention, in favor of the report including the broad definitions of family) and in plenary (where 269 MEPs voted in favor, 225 voted against, and 46 abstained). Unhappy with this outcome, the rapporteur considered withdrawing his name from the procedure but decided to stay on, also in view of the second reading, where the gay rights proponents were unlikely to achieve the qualified majority necessary to force through their position against the opposition of the EPP.[203] Moreover, neither the Commission in its modified legislative proposal, nor the Council in its common position, accepted the amendments giving the right of residence to same-sex spouses and the registered or unmarried partners of EU citizens. Mr. Santini did realize, however, that he needed to be fairly neutral in second reading and to try not to upset anybody unnecessarily, and also that he might need to make some concessions on the family definition issue.[204] Even some of his political opponents acknowledge that he moved away from his initial stance of representing his party group toward the wider job of legislating for the Parliament as a whole.[205]

In second reading, Mr. Santini advocated a compromise package, which stipulated that the definition of "family member" also includes the registered partner if the legislation of the host member state treats registered partnership as equivalent to marriage. In other words, same-sex partnerships would be recognized across the borders of member states whose national status quo recognized these types of partnerships. The rapporteur supported this compromise despite his personal beliefs and his stance in first reading that all definitions should be left to the member states. Moreover, Article 3 of the second reading report was made to state that member states should "facilitate entry and residence" for "the partner with whom the Union citizen has a durable relationship, duly attested," and that the burden of proof when denying entry or residence lay with the member state. This article was left purposely vague to allow for an ultimate interpretation by the European Court of Justice.[206] Moreover, the compromise could be regarded as a first step toward the full recognition of the citizenship rights of same-sex couples in that it automatically expanded its scope once national authorities passed regulations inclusive of these partnerships.

This compromise hardly satisfied anybody, despite the fact that the proposal was a major step forward in terms of citizenship and the free movement of people across the Union.[207] Its practical implications with regard to the conciliation of existing legislation were quite substantial, and it promised to make life easier for citizens moving across the EU, since the movement of people was no longer bound to the professional status of a person but simply to his or her status as an EU *citizen*. In fact, the compromise could be interpreted as a broad reinterpretation of what constitutes a "foreigner" in the EU member states.

Yet, the prominent role of the family definition issue throughout the process did not lead many members of Parliament to perceive the compromise package as a particularly satisfying outcome. This perception was exacerbated by the distinct sense of victory of the center-left after the first parliamentary reading and the hope to achieve the same result in second reading. Given the mechanics of the codecision procedure this was unlikely, however, since the proponents of a broad family definition needed a qualified majority of 314 votes in second reading for their amendment to stand. In order to succeed, they actually would have had to win over some members from the EPP, which appeared to stand solidly behind their rapporteur. Also important was the prospect of imminent enlargement and, specifically, the accession of Poland to the EU.[208] The center-left suspected that Poland would under no circumstances agree to a compromise deal in the Council that included any concession to same-sex couples, such as the watered-down compromise package. Moreover, the compromise with the Council was negotiated with the then-Italian Council Presidency, which had identified the issue as one of its key priorities and was very keen to push through the directive. The Italian was followed by the Irish Presidency, however, and there was a realization that the Irish had "no intention of touching this with a very, very long pole," according to one respondent.[209]

Hence, there was a growing sense of time pressure in the cross-party coalition pushing for a broad family definition, and also a recognition that an agreement might not be possible under the terms spelled out in first reading. For this reason, the group coordinators of PES and Liberals, Anna Terron and Sarah Ludford, decided that it was preferable to achieve a compromise result, even if it did not go as far as had been hoped. They decided to promote the improved proposal, rather than go into conciliation and take the risk of letting the entire procedure lapse, and were able to convince their party groups of the merit of this decision. The selling point was that it was better to have some result than no result. Therefore, the emphasis put on the two focal points from the previous reading stage began to shift, with the family definition issue becoming less salient for some critical committee members who had previously supported the extension of citizens' rights to nontraditional partnerships. At the same time, the question of facilitating mobility through the dismantling of existing barriers and the fusion of existing legislation into one coherent whole increased in importance.

The findings of the content analyses of EP debates in first and second reading, presented in Table 5.17, confirm that the family definition question dominates the discussion in the first reading debate, with the practical value issue of secondary, yet noteworthy, importance: MEPs refer to the family definition issue 95 times per 10,000 input words in the first reading debate, while the practical value issue yields only 73 references. In second reading, this pattern is reversed: The question of family definition is raised only 52 times per 10,000 input words, while the practical value issue is referred to 87 times. We can thus see that the total number of references to the family definition question drops from 95 to 52, while

Table 5.17: European Union citizenship directive, frequencies-of-use, content analysis

	# of input words	# of references to *family definition*	# of references to *practical value*
1st reading	10,000	95	73
	(7,401)	(70)	(54)
		17 speakers	15 speakers
2nd reading	10,000	52	87
	(3,452)	(18)	(30)
		8 speakers	7 speakers

Note: Entries report number of references to various focal points in EP debates for every 10,000 input words. Actual number of input words and frequencies appear in parentheses.

the number of references to the practical value issue increases from 73 to 87.[210]

In the end, providing legislation for the free movement of citizens across the EU had priority. Hence, the responsible committee passed the compromise agreement by a broad 23–4 margin; the plenary followed suit by rejecting all amendments to the Council's common position, thus adopting the proposal in second reading excluding the broad definition of what constitutes a family.

Voting patterns: the impact of the legislative process on voting outcomes

We hypothesized that we should be able to predict voting patterns in plenary on the basis of the prevailing focal points. This section quantitatively tests this proposition. Overall, the analysis will determine if the prevalent focal points actually provided the basis for the formation of policy coalition, that is, if they supplied a mutually acceptable equilibrium around which policy coalitions revolved.

On the basis of the qualitative analysis, it is possible to formulate a series of hypotheses concerning the expected outcome of the decision-making process in the case of the EU citizenship directive. Since the family definition issue dominated the deliberation process during the first reading stage and relates to the left-right divide, we should expect to find that MEPs voted based on their positions on the left-right dimension. Specifically, MEPs from the political left should vote in favor and MEPs from the political right against the proposal including the broad definition of what constitutes a family. The practical value question was not absent from the debate in first reading, however, and relates to the sovereignty-integration dimension. Therefore, positions on the sovereignty-integration dimension should also matter in explaining vote choice, but to a lesser degree. Specifically, we should expect that pro-European MEPs voted in favor of the directive.

Unfortunately, because the EU citizenship dossier was adopted in second reading, there is no final vote on the legislative resolution. The critical amendment extending citizens' rights to nontraditional partnerships and families, however, was decided by roll-call vote in second reading. This amendment (Amendment 4) was the most controversial aspect of the legislative proposal throughout the decision-making process. In fact, its inclusion in the first reading draft determined the major dividing line in the EP. Therefore, we can compare the positions MEPs assumed toward the legislative resolution in first reading with their positions toward the family definition amendment in second reading. The vote on Amendment 4 is thus used as a proxy for the nonexistent roll-call vote on the final legislative resolution in second reading.

Since the focus of the debate shifted away from the family definition issue toward the practical implications of the Citizenship dossier, we should expect to find that MEP's positions on the left-right dimension are irrelevant as predictors of voting patterns in second reading. Positions on the sovereignty-integration dimension, in contrast, should become the critical explanatory variable. Since pro-Europeans should now be inclined to reject the family definition amendment, we should expect to find that a more pro-European position entails a greater probability of voting against the amendment.

The dependent variables in this analyses are the individual votes on the legislative report in first reading and on Amendment 4 in second reading. These variables are dichotomous. A value of zero equals a vote against directive and a value of one means a vote in favor. The independent variables are the MEP NOMINATE scores on the left-right and sovereignty-integration dimensions, a dichotomous variable based on the national government or opposition status of particular national party delegations, and a dichotomous variable with a value of one for MEPs from member states where national legislation allows same-sex marriages. This variable assumes a value of zero for all member states except Denmark and the Netherlands.

The results of the analysis are presented in Table 5.18. The regression model explains a substantial part of the variance, with a pseudo-R^2 of 0.55. As predicted, MEPs from the political left voted in favor of the legislative report including the broad family definition in first reading, while MEPs from the political right strongly opposed it, as the negative coefficient of the left-right variable demonstrates. The positive sign of the sovereignty-integration variable confirms the expectation that MEPs with more pro-EU attitudes are more likely to support the legislation. Finally, the negative coefficient of the government status variable demonstrates that MEPs from parties that are in opposition in their national political arenas have a greater probability of voting in favor of the legislation in first reading, which makes sense given that the Council, where government MEPs are represented, opposed the broad family definition.

Figure 5.22 illustrates the impact of the left-right predictor. The predicted probability of MEPs voting in favor of the proposal declines the more they are positioned toward the political right.[211] This decline is very substantial, as MEPs on the far left had a 100 percent probability of voting in favor of the directive and MEPs on the far right had a 100 percent probability of voting against. Not surprisingly, MEPs from countries that allow same-sex marriages are more inclined to support the proposal.

Figure 5.23 provides the predicted probabilities of voting in favor of the legislation as a function of positions on the sovereignty-integration dimension. Moving from the EU-skeptics on the left of the x-axis toward the

Table 5.18: European Union citizenship directive, binomial logit regression estimates, first reading vote

	Floor vote, first reading
Left-right dimension	−4.72***
	(.40)
Sovereignty-integration dimension	2.93***
	(.42)
Government status	−1.69***
	(.42)
National same-sex marriage legislation	1.88*
	(.74)
Constant	.33
	(.18)
Number of cases	514
Log pseudo-likelihood	−159.84
Pseudo R^2	0.55

Note: Table entries are binomial logit estimates. Dependent variable: vote (Yes = 1, No = 0, Abstain = 0). Statistical significance is indicated as follows: p < .05*, p < .01**, p < .001***

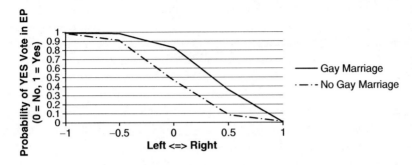

Figure 5.22 European Union citizenship directive, mean predicted probability of Yes vote given left-right positions, first reading vote

Europhiles on the right increases the probability of a Yes vote by close to 100 percent. Once again, this trend is consistent for all MEPs, but more pronounced among MEPs from member states with national legislation allowing same-sex marriage.

Finally, Figure 5.24 demonstrates that MEPs from parties that are in opposition in their national political arenas have a greater probability of voting in favor of the legislation in first reading. This would be expected, since the EP took a position in favor of a broad definition of what constitutes a family in first reading, which the Council opposed. Also not surprisingly, MEPs from both government and opposition parties in countries that allow same-sex marriage are more likely to support the legislation.

Table 5.19 displays the results of the binomial logit regression result of the second reading vote on Amendment 4. The negative coefficient of the

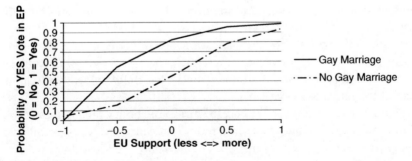

Figure 5.23 European Union citizenship directive, mean predicted probability of Yes vote given levels of EU support, first reading vote

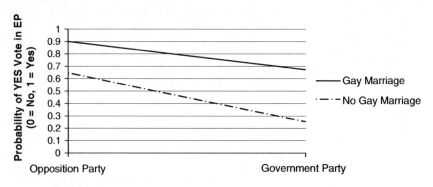

Figure 5.24 European Union citizenship directive, mean predicted probability of Yes vote given government status, first reading vote

left-right variable shows that MEPs from the political right remained strongly opposed to the broad definition of what constitutes a family. Similarly, government status at home still results in a smaller probability of voting in favor of the same-sex family definition amendment, which was opposed by the Council. Unlike in first reading, however, a more pro-European attitude now entails a smaller probability of supporting the amendment: the coefficient of the sovereignty-integration variable now features a negative sign. Finally, unlike in first reading, MEPs from countries that allow same-sex marriages actually have a smaller probability to vote in favor of the amendment. This is likely because their status quo was not affected by the compromise agreement.

Figure 5.25 displays the predicted probabilities of votes in favor of the amendment in second reading. It shows that left-right positions were not irrelevant in explaining positions toward the family definition amendment in second reading, but that only the very far left voted in favor. The probability of supporting the amendment already drops substantially when moving from the far-left to the center-left. MEPs to the right of the center-left were certain to vote against the amendment. In fact, the probability of voting in favor of the amendment decreases by 100 percent between NOMINATE scores of -1 and 0 on the left-right divide, that is, along half of the range of the variable.

Figure 5.26 illustrates the expected shift in the policy preferences of pro-European MEPs. While pro-EU attitudes entailed a greater probability of supporting the proposal in first reading *including* the broad family definition, this pattern is now reversed, as the downward slopes indicate.

Table 5.19: European Union citizenship directive, binomial logit regression estimates, second reading vote, Amendment 4

	Floor vote, second reading, Am. 4
Left-right dimension	−8.48***
	(1.28)
Sovereignty-integration dimension	−2.62***
	(.36)
Government status	−1.46*
	(.68)
National same-sex marriage legislation	−1.37**
	(.47)
Constant	−3.38***
	(.47)
Number of cases	476
Log pseudo-likelihood	−59.10
Pseudo R^2	0.72

Note: Table entries are binomial logit estimates. Dependent variable: vote (Yes = 1, No = 0, Abstain = 0). Statistical significance is indicated as follows: $p < .05^*$, $p < .01^{**}$, $p < .001^{***}$

Finally, Figure 5.27 shows the minimal impact of government or opposition status in the second reading vote. For opposition as well as government parties, the probability of voting in favor of Amendment 4 was small or even insubstantial.

In sum, the critical change between the first and second reading stages was a shift in the positions of the political center and the center-left. While the political right consistently opposed a broad family definition and the far left consistently promoted it, centrist and center-left MEPs were

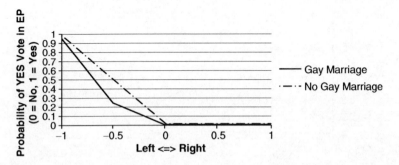

Figure 5.25 European Union citizenship directive, mean predicted probability of Yes vote given left-right positions, second reading vote, Amendment 4

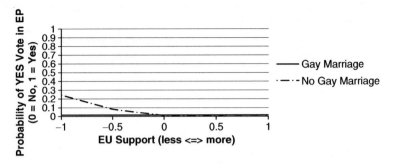

Figure 5.26 European Union citizenship directive, mean predicted probability of Yes vote given levels of EU support, second reading vote, Amendment 4

ultimately willing to accept legislation that no longer included what had been one of their key demands. Specifically, the analysis suggests that the policy preferences of MEPs shifted as the sovereignty-integration dimension became more salient during the second reading stage. Figures 5.28 and 5.29 display and confirm the voting patterns in more detail: while pro-EU legislators, especially from the political center and the center-left, were very likely to support the radical EU citizenship proposal in first reading, they were very unlikely to support the broad definition of what constitutes a family in second reading. These MEPs evidently followed their political leaders in the responsible committee when choosing to support a diluted legislative proposal over the alternative of letting the entire procedure lapse. The shift in focal points thus entailed a critical change in voting patterns. As a result, the only MEPs in favor of the radical definition of what

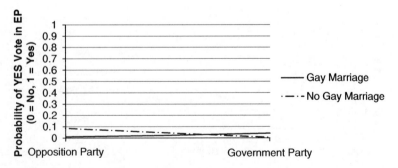

Figure 5.27 European Union citizenship directive, mean predicted probability of Yes vote given government status, second reading vote, Amendment 4

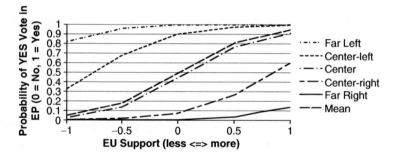

Figure 5.28 European Union citizenship directive, mean predicted probability of Yes vote given levels of EU support (by ideology), first reading

constitutes a family in second reading were those on the far left, as well as Euroskeptic left-of-center MEPs.

Case 6: Conclusion

The case of the EU citizenship directive provides solid evidence in favor of the focal point model. It shows that policy preferences shift even when outcome preferences remain stable and that, in the case of the EU citizenship directive, policy preference shifts were the result of a change in the way critical actors on the political center and the center-left viewed and presented the proposal to their colleagues. While they initially assumed positions toward the proposal based on their outcome preferences on the left-right divide, they decided during the second reading stage that realizing

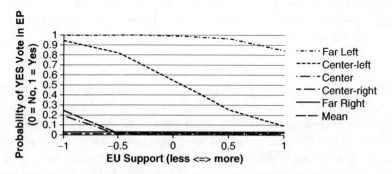

Figure 5.29 European Union citizenship directive, mean predicted probability of Yes vote given levels of EU support (by ideology), second reading vote, Amendment 4

a proposal establishing a comprehensive notion of EU citizenship broadly beneficial to a majority of EU citizens took precedence over the definitional issues propagated in first reading.

The transmission mechanism for these positions from committee to plenary is also noteworthy in view of the general findings in Chapter 3. While Socialists, Liberals, Greens, and members of the GUE faction voted solidly in favor of the report including the amendment establishing a broad family definition in first reading, only Greens and GUE MEPs stuck to this position in the committee vote on the compromise report in second reading. Following their committee representatives throughout the procedure, 84 percent of all Socialists and Liberals voted in favor of the proposal in the first reading plenary vote (with 15% abstaining and only 1% voting against), while in second reading, 97 percent voted against Amendment 4 and only 3 percent in favor. This suggests that party positions are indeed endogenous to the policy-making process: When committee members shift their own policy preferences and the focus of the debate through the provision of focal points, they affect the policy positions of those MEPs who perceive to share a common set of outcome preferences with them, namely their party colleagues in plenary. We can thus predict voting patterns on the basis of the prevailing focal points.

The first reading stage of the legislative process featured a dominant left-right focal point, which provided the basis for a policy coalition of Socialists, Greens, Liberals, and the far left. The family definition focal point provided a basis for this policy coalition because it appealed to the outcome preferences of MEPs on the left-right divide. In second reading, the focal point and, thus, the general direction of the debate shifted away from the left-right conceptualization of the citizenship issue toward a pro-/anti-EU view. As a result, MEPs in plenary, following their committee representatives, perceived their positions on the sovereignty-integration dimension as more salient to the decision at hand and a new policy coalition of pro-Europeans consisting of political right, center, and center-left pushed the proposal through against the votes of the far left.

The qualitative analysis confirms our expectations about the characteristics of focal points and how they are disseminated among MEPs not directly involved in the dossier. It demonstrates that deliberations were dominated not by technical details of the proposal, but by broad representations of what the legislative proposal was all about, since the prevalent focal points emphasized the question of "citizenship for whom" (the family definition question) and the actual implications of the legislation (the practical value issue). These focal points emphasized the perceived consequences of the proposal, rather than its technical details, and targeted the outcome preferences of the EP's nonexperts: The family definition issue was a clear left-right issue, while the practical value of the legislation to EU citizens was an issue relating broadly to the question of EU integration. The focal points were provided and propagated by the members of the responsible committee, and the configuration of the key players was critical in shaping the decision-making process. These actors did not simply provide voting instructions, however; in fact, even the powerful group coordinators had to "sell" the compromise package to their party groups. This was especially noticeable on the political left, where support for the broad definition of what constitutes a family was deep-rooted. As a result, party positions toward the proposal were not predetermined, but actually shifted during the deliberation process.

Conclusion

These case studies illustrate how invested nonexperts make decisions under conditions of uncertainty about the likely implications of their policy choices. Like all MEPs who lack the necessary information and expertise to define their own policy preferences, invested nonexperts rely on external input that ties specific policy proposals to their outcome preferences. Yet, while some legislators may be indifferent toward a particular piece of legislation and content to follow their expert colleagues on the basis of perceived preference coherence alone, invested nonexperts do not only seek cues as to what policy positions they ought to take; they also want to know *why* they should adopt these positions. In other words, they want to know how a policy proposal relates to their most preferred outcomes and thus demand a justification for their policy choice. This justification is provided by their expert colleagues in the responsible committee in the form of focal points, or simplified images about the expected consequences of a piece of legislation upon its implementation.

The case studies in this chapter demonstrate that focal points affect how invested nonexperts interpret the content and implications of different legislative proposals, which allows them to translate their outcome preferences into policy preferences. This, in turn, determines the positions they adopt with regard to each legislative proposal, the configuration of policy coalitions and, ultimately, legislative outcomes. As expected, the quantitative analyses of plenary votes show that it is possible, upon identifying the focal points provided by policy experts in the responsible committee, to predict which dimension of contestation structures voting patterns on the EP floor. In other words, we can explain how the ideal points of individual legislators on the two primary dimension of the EP's ideological space are "translated" into policy preferences and policy positions.

Each case study features a set of distinct focal points emphasizing the perceived impact of the proposed legislation upon its implementation. These determine what dimensions of political contestation MEPs perceive to be most salient with regard to the issue at hand. As we would expect, the focal points are broad representations of the content and consequences of the proposed legislation, while technical details are largely absent from the discussion outside of the responsible committee. This is because the purpose of focal points is to minimize uncertainty about how a particular policy proposal relates to the outcome preferences of invested nonexperts, which means that focal points simplify complex pieces of legislation by highlighting which aspects should be considered to be of particular importance.

Perceived preference coherence plays a key role in the focal point model because invested nonexperts are not receptive to just any focal point, but only to focal points provided by those expert colleagues in the responsible committee with whom they perceive to share a common set of outcome preferences. Hence, perceived preference coherence with the providers of focal points assures invested nonexperts that their most preferred outcomes are likely approximated, which enables them to make the "right" policy decision. Focal points also facilitate decision-making at the aggregate level, however. This is because invested experts supply focal points strategically to influence legislative outcomes, which enables the generally small handful of experts who are actively deliberating and negotiating a legislative proposal to steer the compromise that has been formulated at the committee level through the remainder of the legislative process. This is realized in two ways: First, policy outcomes are the result of a structured process in which invested experts *create* opportunities for policy choice through the provision of focal points. These focal points determine what outcome preference—or which dimension of political contestation—their invested nonexpert colleagues perceive to be relevant and salient concerning the issue at hand. This transforms a situation with multiple policy solutions (or outcome equilibria) into one where some outcomes are more likely than others. This process is based on persuasion, however, which points to the dynamic nature of EP politics. As the case studies demonstrate, we have to look beyond party discipline if we want to understand how cohesive party positions come about.

Second, invested experts can keep potential controversies off the table when a proposal is transferred from committee to plenary, thus preventing what are often complex compromises negotiated within parties, across parties, and even across EU institutions from unraveling on the EP floor. This is critical for the efficient resolution of policy processes in which no party group alone has a majority and policy coalitions have to be built anew for each legislative proposal (Hix, Kreppel, and Noury 2003). It ensures that the party rank and file do not undermine the deals that have been struck between the small number of invested experts from the different party groups in the EP and representatives from the Commission and Council of Ministers—often following significant initial levels of controversy. As Kreppel (2006: 250) emphasizes: "Although amendments, even controversial ones, can be and are initiated on the floor of the full plenary, this generally occurs as the result of a failure to reach consensus within the committee (between the core political actors) or as a show of protest by the more extreme political actors on the left and right of the political spectrum."

Controversy can arise from within the EP, but it can also be augmented by events on the outside, such as attempts by government or party leaders in the member state capitals to influence the behavior of "their" MEPs, the lobbying activities of interest groups or, as in the case of the port services directive, demonstrations outside of the EP buildings in Brussels and Strasbourg. Most importantly, such events may raise awareness of potential controversies among MEPs not directly involved in the negotiation of a particular policy proposal, thus turning them from indifferent into invested nonexperts. This makes it more difficult for invested experts to steer the legislative process. However, the case studies suggest that outside actors influence decision-making processes and outcomes in the EP only to the extent that their arguments and policy positions are picked up by invested experts inside the chamber. It seems, for example, that competing focal points are not directly introduced from the outside, but ultimately have to be advocated by invested experts to be successful. This may have played a role in the case of the port services directive, where active lobbying efforts helped shape the debate inside the EP. In the case of the proposals on fuel quality and emission standards, in contrast, lobbying on the part of the car and oil industries was similarly pronounced but failed to impact the policy outcome, with the key difference being that the invested experts inside the chamber did not adopt positions advocated on the outside.[212]

For all these reasons, in the words of one respondent, "it certainly matters who is in charge of a report: who are the rapporteur, shadows, coordinators?"[213] The way the rapporteur handles her report is of particular importance, as it can make a great difference if she is looking to capture the middle ground and draft a report that is broadly acceptable across party group lines, or if she attempts to promote her national or individual position.[214] The rapporteur has the ability to decisively shape subsequent stages of the decision-making process through her initial report and her behavior throughout.[215] This is partially a substantive issue, but also relates to the "tone of language" of the rapporteur; if "just the style of presentation is highly confrontational," according to one MEP, it affects the process of deliberation.[216] The reputation of the rapporteur also plays an important role. If she has the reputation of seeking cooperation and compromise, this will positively affect how she and her report are received in committee as well as in the plenary.[217] This willingness and ability to compromise and go beyond national, partisan, or personal convictions is, in fact, what respondents identified as a primary factor of what makes a strong rapporteur, together with expertise and contacts across party lines.[218] One illustrative example for the importance of reputation was provided by a parliamentary official, who describes the reputation of Bernd Lange, the rapporteur of two of the proposals on fuel quality and emission standards, as follows:

If you were to do a study of all the reports done by Mr. Lange, you would find that 99 times out of 100, his proposals are adopted unanimously. In the past five years, the time I spent here, anything that he ever did, he was just blindly followed.... Everybody thought that he was not going to pull a fast one. Even the EPP went along with him on lots of stuff, on nearly everything.[219]

It is important to emphasize, however, that the ability of the small number of active participants in the pre-floor decision-making process to influence legislative outcomes is constrained by a key characteristic of focal points, namely that they must appeal to the exogenous outcome preferences of invested nonexperts if they are to influence policy outcomes. Focal points are not created out of thin air, as Chapter 4 emphasizes, but must reflect and target stable ideological predispositions in an effort to sway policy preferences one way or another. This limits the potential for agency loss in the delegation of decision-making power from the chamber to the EP's standing committees, which helps balance two desirable but inherently contradictory features of any form of representative government: efficient policymaking and the representativeness of policy outcomes. The PPC dynamic provides for efficient legislative policy choice while yielding political outcomes that do not deviate too far from the preferences of the members of the institution as a whole.

Throughout, the case studies reveal a level of importance of persuasion in EP decision-making that defies the notion of predetermined policy preferences and policy positions; this reconfirms a key finding from Chapter 3, which emphasizes their endogeneity. Policy preferences can and do shift even when outcome preferences remain stable. If invested experts modify their own positions and the focus of the debate, or when new actors enter the stage and gain prominence, policy preferences and outcomes shift accordingly. As a result, the level of controversy concerning particular pieces of legislation is difficult to forecast, because deliberation and decision-making processes depend to a substantial extent on the configuration and interactions of key actors. In the case of the EU citizenship proposal, for example, the presentation of the issue in terms of family definition and nontraditional partnerships created a level of contention that was unexpected even to other MEPs.

While the case studies share a great number of characteristics—such as the endogeneity of policy positions, the importance of particular actors and their configuration in shaping policy preferences and outcomes, and the possibility of predicting voting patterns on the basis of the dominant focal points—each legislative proposal also features particularities that shed additional light on the nature of deliberation and policy-making in the EP. The analysis of the EU citizenship proposal, for example, demonstrates that a seemingly noncontroversial issue becomes highly contested when certain aspects of it are highlighted by a key group of committee specialists. In contrast, the party statute analysis shows how controversy is stifled when contentious issues, such as the legal personality of EU-level political parties, are deliberatively kept off the agenda. The fuel quality and emissions case illustrates that legislation can pass with an overwhelming margin when critical actors steer it successfully through both the committee and plenary stages, even if there appears to be an "objective interest" not to support legislation that evidently hurts key industries. The port package, in contrast, features a rapporteur that was perceived as uncooperative and thus faced an uphill battle that he ultimately lost. A similar lesson can be drawn from the environmental liability proposal, which also demonstrates the importance of which committee handles the legislation and shows that two distinct sets of specialists in separate committees may provide competing focal points. If this is the case, a high level of controversy ensues. Finally, the analysis of the takeover directive demonstrates that focal points not only affect the salience of the two ideology dimensions when decisions are made on the EP floor, but that they may even influence the direction in which the dimensions matter.

These nuances are quite instructive and provide for intriguing insights into EP politics that would go unnoticed in an analysis that focuses on legislative outcomes alone. Hence, the mixed methods approach employed here to analyze policy processes *and* outcomes based on a deductively derived theoretical model broadens our understanding of EP politics beyond the static theories advanced in previous studies.

Appendix: Coding details for content analyses

Case 1: The EU takeover directive

Focal point 1: single market

Community dimension, harmoniz- (and relevant endings), internal market, single market, subsidiarity, harmonization directive, framework directive, "vessel of the European Union"

Focal point 2: workers' rights

Consultation; inform and consult; "mergers go wrong"; employ- (and relevant endings); job- (and relevant endings); restructur- (and relevant endings); social; stakeholder; trade unions; trade unionists; works councils; unemploy- (and relevant endings); worker- (and relevant endings); workforce

Focal point 3: level playing-field

Article 9, defens- (and relevant endings), Electricité de France, EdF, hostile action, level playing-field, neutral- (and relevant endings), poison pills, unfairness

Case 2: The statute and financing of EU-level political parties

Focal point 1: EU democracy

Accountability, clarity, constitutionalization, integration, legitimacy, unification, democr- (and relevant endings), transparen- (and relevant endings), European ideal, European objectives

Focal point 2: EU parties as artificial constructs

Artificial, banquets, beanfeasts, corruption, opaque, secret, totalitarian, discriminat- (and relevant endings), tax- (and relevant endings), pile of cash, so-called European political parties, Warsaw Pact

Alternative (hypothetical) issue presentation: legal personality

Actual European statute, legal personality, legal persons

Case 3: Proposals on fuel quality and emission standards for motor vehicles

Focal point 1: consumer protection

Acid, alternative, asthma- (and relevant endings), cancer- (and relevant endings), carcinogenic, cardiovascular, children, clean- (and relevant endings), crop- (and relevant endings), death- (and relevant endings), die prematurely, disease, ecolog- (and relevant endings), energy, environment- (and relevant endings), eutrophication, greenhouse effect, harm, health- (and relevant endings), human, illness- (and relevant endings), innovati- (and relevant endings), Kyoto, lung complaints, mortality, pollut- (and relevant endings), quality, Rio, safety, sustainable, technical development, technical feasibility, technically feasible, toxic, WHO, World Health Organization

Focal point 2: industry interest

American- (and relevant endings), closures, competit- (and relevant endings), cost- (and relevant endings), economic- (and relevant endings), egalitarianism, employment, flexibility, Japanese, jobs, Korean, labor market, manufacturers, small and medium-sized businesses, monopoly, north- (and relevant endings), shareholder value, SMEs, social, solidarity, south- (and relevant endings), unemployment, the United States, U.S. legislation, world markets

Case 4: Liability for environmental damage

Focal point 1: workability

Achievable, business, companies, competition, distortions, efficient, gain, implementable, impractical, incalculable, moderate, patchwork, pragmatic, profit, proportional, realistic, reasonable, sensible, unworkable, well-balanced, America- (and relevant endings), cost- (and relevant endings), econom- (and relevant endings), industr-, (and relevant endings), practical- (and relevant endings), relocat- (and relevant endings), workab- (and relevant endings), direct proportion, in proportion, scientific knowledge, small- and medium-sized small businesses, small companies, United States

Focal point 2: license to pollute

Agricult-, AZF, Aznalcoyar, biodiversity, dangerous, dumping, ecosystem, environment, environmentally-friendly, Erika, fauna, flora, forest, genetically-modified organism (GMO), health, biological diversity, ecolog- (and relevant endings), environmental objectives, environmental protection, environmental responsibilities, Exxon Valdez, genetic- (and relevant endings), green fundamentalists, habitat- (and relevant endings), human lives, license to pollute, loopholes, maritime disaster, Natura 2000, nuclear accidents, oil, pesticides, precautionary, Prestige, Priolo, public funds, public health, public purse, radiation, radioactive, Seveso, species, sustainab- (and relevant endings), tax- (and relevant endings), Tricolor, vague

Focal point 3: harmonization

Lisbon, harmonis- (and relevant endings), European model, internal market, level playing-field, viability of Europe, people of Europe, uniform European framework, European standards, the whole of the EU, European society, citizens of the EU, European citizens, European principle, European model

Case 5: The liberalization of port services in the EU

Focal point 1: liberalization

Abuse, accidents, African, anti-social, Argentineans, cheap, collective agreements, collective bargaining, collisions, competent pilots, competent port workers, cowboy ports, crooks, cutting, dangerous, detriment, developing countries, developing world, developing-world, disasters, dockers, ecological, economizing, employ- (and relevant endings), environment- (and relevant endings), Erika, exploit- (and relevant endings), Filipinos, flags (of convenience), globali- (and relevant endings), health, illegal contractors, illegal support, inexperienced, insecurity, job- (and relevant endings), jungle, Karin Cat, labour, liberal, liberalis- (and relevant endings), Malays- (and relevant endings), paid, pay, pernicious, Philippinos, pirate, poor, poorly organized, ports of convenience, Prestige, privatization, qualifi- (and relevant endings), quality, race for profit, ruthless, safety, salar- (and relevant endings), security, slavery, social, solidarity, strik- (and relevant endings), subsidiarity, taxpayers, trade union, train- (and relevant endings), Tricolor, unemploy- (and relevant endings), unionist, unions, unsafe, unskilled, untrained, wage, well-trained, workers, working condition, working conditions, working environments, ultra-Liberal

Focal point 2: EU competitiveness

Business, cheaper services, compete, competition, competitive, economy, effective- (and relevant endings), efficien- (and relevant endings, e.g., bureaucracy), entrepreneur- (and relevant endings, e.g., bureaucracy), Euro-sclerosis, financial, growth, harmonization, internal market, investment, level playing-field, leveling, Lisbon, modern, modernize, monopol- (and relevant endings, e.g., bureaucracy), open up, opening up, openness, regulation, single market

Extreme terminology

Abuse, accidents, African, Argentineans, collisions, cowboy ports, crooks, developing countries, developing world, developing-world, disasters, Erika, exploit- (and relevant endings), Filipinos, illegal contractors, illegal support, Karin Cat, Malays- (and relevant endings), pernicious, Philippinos, pirate, Prestige, race for profit, ruthless, slavery, Tricolor, ultra-Liberal

Case 6: EU citizenship and the free movement of people

Focal point 1: practical value (of legislation)

Administrative, barriers, burden, bureaucr- (and relevant endings, e.g., bureaucracy), clari- (and relevant endings, e.g., clarify), combines, common market, competitive, content to EU citizenship, core of EC law, employment, enlargement, European identity, facilitat- (and relevant endings, e.g., facilitate), family member, free market for people, historic, hurdles, labor force, Lisbon, milestone, mobility, obstacles, one legal instrument, red tape, multiplicity of regulation, replace, restrictions, simplif- (and relevant endings, e.g., simplify), single act, single legal instrument, single text, step forward, streamline

Focal point 2: family definition

Civil liberties, cohabit, definition of "family," discrimination, equal rights, equal treatment family, gender, heterosexual, homosexual, immigration, marriage, mutual recognition, mutually recognized, nondiscriminatory, same-sex, sex, sexual, social rights, two men, two women, unmarried

Notes

1. In selecting these cases, I limited the pool of possible choices to dossiers that were decided under the codecision procedure, where the EP is an equal partner of the national governments of the EU member states, during the 1999–2004 legislative term. I selected fairly high-profile issues based on the same logic as in Chapter 3, because it is in these instances that MEPs are most likely to form their own positions, independent of their committee experts. Hence, if I find that even here what happens in committee largely determines what happens on the floor, then we can have some confidence that these patterns are no different when it comes to less important issues. I excluded cases where the controversy was of a technical or definitional nature, rather than content-driven, as the focal point model is concerned with deliberation, persuasion, and contestation on substantive issues. Among the remaining legislative proposals, I sought to assure variance in critical case characteristics, such as issue area, committee jurisdiction, party membership of the rapporteur, number of parliamentary readings, and level of initial controversy.
2. Respondent #35.
3. Respondent #38.
4. Respondents #25, 59.

5. Respondent #16.
6. Respondents #16, 59.
7. For these analyses, I first identify a series of keywords in each set of debates, which I code consistent with the dominant focal points identified in the preceding qualitative analysis. I then use the content analysis program TEXTPACK to provide frequency-of-use details for each category.
8. The possible outcome categories for EP roll-call votes are votes in favor of the legislation, votes against, or abstentions. Some cases suffer from within-group multicollinearity with regard to the abstention category, however, as there is usually only a small number of abstentions for each vote. Hence, the analyses in this chapter treat abstentions as *de facto* votes against the proposed legislation (since under absolute majority rule, abstaining has the same effect as voting against) and use binomial logit analysis instead of multinomial logit. However, when possible, multinomial logit analyses were performed to ensure the robustness of the findings. The results of the multinomial logit analyses mirrored those of the binomial logic analyses and did not provide for substantively noteworthy differences. Hence, for the sake of consistency of presentation across all six case studies, only the results of the binomial logit analyses are presented and discussed.
9. This set of variables falls into four categories: liberal market economy (Ireland and the United Kingdom); partial or family-oriented coordinated market economy (France, Italy, Spain, Greece, and Portugal); sectoral coordinated market economy (Germany, Austria, and Benelux countries); national coordinated market economy (Scandinavian countries) (Kitschelt et al. [1999], Rhodes and Van Apeldoorn [1997]).
10. For more complete information and discussion of the directive's history and content, see Berglöf and Burkart (2003).
11. EP Legislative Observatory.
12. Respondent #12.
13. Debate of the EP, June 25, 1997.
14. Subsidiarity is the principle whereby the Union does not take action (except in the areas which fall within its exclusive competence) unless it is more effective than action taken at national, regional, or local levels.
15. Respondent #27.
16. Debates of the EP, December 12, 2000 and July 3, 2001.
17. Respondents #65, 74.
18. Respondent #50.
19. Respondents #50, 65.
20. Coding details can be found in the appendix.
21. Respondent #60.
22. Respondents #27, 60, 65.
23. Respondents #27, 60, 65, 74.
24. Respondent #65.

25. Respondent #13.
26. Respondent #57.
27. Respondent #24.
28. Theodorus J. J. Bouwman (Greens/EFA, Netherlands), debate of the EP, July 3, 2001.
29. Respondent #74.
30. The vote in the second reading was not a roll-call vote and is thus not considered here.
31. To calculate the probabilities presented in the following figures, the remaining variables were held constant at their means.
32. Having a legal personality allows a group of persons to act as if it were an individual for purposes such as lawsuits, property ownership, and contracts. This allows for easy conduct of business by having ownership, lawsuits, and agreements under the name of the legal entity instead of the several names of the people making up the entity. Here, a European-level legal personality would have entailed, for example, that European parties could hire their own staff, signs their own contracts, and be tax and criminally liable.
33. The Court of Auditors checks EU revenue and expenditures for legality and regularity and ensures that financial management is sound.
34. Respondents #23, 40, 67.
35. Respondents #14, 23.
36. Respondents #3, 14, 40, 67.
37. Respondents #23, 37, 40, 41, 63, 67.
38. Respondents #40, 41.
39. Respondents #5, 41, 67. The idea was to avoid providing funds to parties that were overtly antidemocratic.
40. Respondents #40, 67.
41. Respondent #40.
42. Respondent #3.
43. Respondent #67.
44. Respondent #67.
45. Respondent #3.
46. Respondent #67.
47. Respondents #3, 14.
48. Respondents #3, 40, 67.
49. Respondent #40.
50. Respondents #37, 40, 41, 63.
51. Respondent #14.
52. Respondent #5.
53. Coding details can be found in the appendix.
54. Respondents #40, 67.
55. Respondents #23, 40, 67.
56. Respondent #40.

57. Respondent #41.
58. Respondents #3, 67.
59. Respondents #3, 23, 41, 63, 67.
60. Respondents #40, 41.
61. Respondents #63, 67.
62. Respondents #14, 67.
63. Respondents #3, 40, 41, 67.
64. Respondents #3, 40, 67.
65. EU member states with a ceiling on how much an individual donor can contribute to a political party per year are: Belgium, France, Greece, Ireland, Italy, Portugal, and Spain. All other member states do not have a ceiling in place.
66. To calculate the probabilities presented in the following figures, the remaining variables were held constant at their means.
67. The EP agreed to the Council's suggestions with the exception of Amendment 27 in the fuel quality directive, where limit values were left unchanged by the Council.
68. Respondents #18, 22, 51.
69. Respondent #51.
70. Respondents #18, 51.
71. Respondents #18, 62.
72. Respondent #51.
73. Respondent #18.
74. Respondent #18.
75. Respondent #4.
76. Respondent #51.
77. Respondents #9, 42, 47, 51, 77.
78. Respondents #62, 77.
79. Respondent #42.
80. Respondent #47.
81. Respondent #77.
82. Respondents #18, 51.
83. Respondent #51.
84. Respondent #18.
85. Respondent #51.
86. Respondents #4, 22.
87. Respondents #4, 42, 62.
88. Respondent #16.
89. These debates considered the three proposals jointly, with the result that they do not correspond directly to the first, second, and third parliamentary readings. Specifically, the first debate concerned the EP's report in the first readings of the directives on emissions from private motor vehicles (COD/1996/0164A) as well as the fuel quality proposal (COD/1996/163). The second debate took place at the second reading stage for those two proposals, but also concerned the

first reading EP report of the proposal on emissions from nonpersonal motor vehicles (COD/1996/164B). Finally, the third debate followed the conciliation procedures for all three proposals.

90. Coding details can be found in the appendix.

91. Respondent #62.

92. Respondent #42.

93. As quoted in the Legislative Observatory, available at http://europarl.europa.eu.

94. In situations where an independent variable almost perfectly predicts the occurrence of a certain outcome, STATA reports neither the standard error of that variable nor the chi-squared statistics for the whole model, making the substantive interpretation of the model impossible.

95. To calculate the probabilities presented in the following figures, the second independent variable was held constant at its means.

96. *Green Papers* are documents drafted by the European Commission that are intended to stimulate debate and launch a process of consultation at the European level on a particular topic. These consultations may then lead to the publication of a *White Paper*, which are Commission documents containing proposals for Community action in a specific area.

97. Respondents #6, 35.

98. Respondents #6, 35, 71, 72.

99. Respondents #6, 29, 34, 35, 71, 34.

100. Respondents #29, 35, 71, 72.

101. Respondents #29, 35.

102. Respondents #29, 49, 71, 72.

103. This question raised some distinct national concerns and positions. Many Spanish members, for example, favored a strict liability framework that included both preventive and remediary measures following the recent 'Prestige' oil spill caused when an oil tanker sank in 2002 off the Galician coast. Thousands of kilometers of Spanish and French coastline were polluted and the local fishing industry was devastated. The Prestige spill was the largest environmental disaster in Spanish history. Similarly, for MEPs from Austria and Ireland the question of including or excluding nuclear technologies in the scope of the directive was of special interest because neither country uses nuclear energy for industrial purposes (Respondents #35, 2, and 6).

104. Respondent #49.

105. Respondent #71. Internal communication between the chairman of the Legal Affairs Committee, Guiseppe Gargani, and the chairwoman of the Environment Committee, Caroline Jackson, also indicates that the Environment Committee did not feel properly consulted with regard to the timetable for considering the legislation, which according to Rule 47 of the Rules of Procedure ought to be jointly drawn up by the two committees (Jackson letter to Gargani, January 31, 2003).

106. Respondent #71.

107. Respondent #72.
108. Respondent #35.
109. Respondent #71.
110. Respondents #2, 6, 35, 71, 72.
111. Respondents #29, 72.
112. See the Legislative Observatory, available at http://europarl.europa.eu, for details.
113. Respondents #6, 72.
114. Respondent #72.
115. Respondents #9, 71.
116. Respondent #9.
117. See the Legislative Observatory, available at http://europarl.europa.eu, for details. See also European Report (2003*d*).
118. Respondents #6, 35, 71, 72.
119. Respondent #9.
120. Respondents #71, 72.
121. Respondent #35.
122. Respondent #29.
123. Respondents #2, 6, 29, 71.
124. Respondents #35, 72.
125. Respondents #30, 34, 49.
126. Respondents #2, 35.
127. Respondent #35.
128. Respondent #71.
129. Respondent #29.
130. Respondent #2.
131. Respondent #71.
132. Respondent #71.
133. Respondents #6, 71.
134. Respondents #34, 35, 49, 71.
135. Respondents #6, 72.
136. Respondent #71.
137. Coding details can be found in the appendix.
138. To calculate the probabilities presented in the following figures, the remaining variables were held constant at their means.
139. Respondents #1, 19, 25, 70, 78.
140. Respondent #78; also Respondent #19.
141. Respondents #1, 32, 55.
142. Respondent #78.
143. Respondent #78.
144. Respondent #78.
145. Respondent #78.
146. Arlette Laguiller (GUE/NGL, France), as cited in European Report (2003*e*).

147. Respondents #25, 70.
148. Respondent #55.
149. Respondents #19, 32, 44, 70.
150. Respondent #28.
151. Respondent #32.
152. Respondent #28.
153. Respondent #32.
154. Respondent #28.
155. Respondent #43.
156. Respondent #43.
157. Respondent #28.
158. Respondent #28.
159. Respondent #76.
160. Respondent #75.
161. Respondent #43.
162. Respondents #19, 43, 78.
163. Respondent #43; also Respondent #1.
164. Respondent #28.
165. Respondents #43, 78.
166. Respondents #43, 70.
167. Respondents #1, 43, 70.
168. Respondents #44, 55, 78.
169. Respondent #1.
170. Respondent #43.
171. Respondents #19, 43.
172. Respondent #19.
173. Respondents #1, 19, 25, 43, 70, 75.
174. Respondents #31, 43, 70, 75, 78.
175. Respondent #75. This effort was quite successful. While the political left (i.e., those with NOMINATE scores smaller than 0) had been quite divided in first reading (120 in favor, 147 against, and 22 abstentions; right: 164 in favor, 83 against, and 9 abstentions), it was much more cohesive in third reading (19 for, 199 against, and 4 abstentions; right: 168 in favor, 19 against, and 12 abstentions). In the PES, 52 MEPs had voted against the proposal in first reading and 107 in favor, while in third reading, 128 voted against, 10 in favor, and 3 abstained).
176. Respondent #78.
177. Respondent #25.
178. Respondent #78.
179. Respondent #44.
180. Respondent #25.
181. Respondent #1.
182. Coding details can be found in the appendix.

183. To calculate the probabilities presented in the following figures, the remaining variables were held constant at their means.

184. EU citizenship is based in principle on four Treaty articles. Article 14 enshrines the 'four freedoms' for the movement of goods, persons, services, and capital. Article 17 confers EU citizenship to all nationals of a member state. Article 18 grants EU citizens the "right to move and reside freely within the territory of the member states," while Article 39 bans employment and payment discrimination on grounds of member state nationality. It also allows member state workers to travel and work freely across the EU and to reside in all member states for job purposes.

185. Respondent #59.

186. Respondent #66.

187. Respondent #11.

188. Respondent #59.

189. Respondent #7.

190. The question of expulsion refers to the circumstances under which EU citizens can be expelled from the territory of a host member state if they have resided there for many years, in particular when they were born and have resided there throughout their lives. The final compromise allowed such expulsion only where there are imperative grounds of public security, while the right of permanent residence applied to all Union citizens and their family members who have resided in the host member state during a continuous period of 5 years without becoming subject to an expulsion measure.

191. Respondent #8.

192. Respondent #11.

193. Respondents #7, 59.

194. Respondent #59; also Respondent #66.

195. Respondent #38.

196. Respondent #21.

197. Explanatory Statement to the First Reading "Report on the proposal for a EP and Council directive on the right of citizens of the Union and their family members to move and reside freely within the territory of the member states" (COD/2001/0111); available at http://europarl.europa.eu.

198. Respondent #21.

199. Respondent #8.

200. Respondents #11, 64.

201. Respondent #21.

202. Respondent #7.

203. Respondent #8.

204. Respondent #8.

205. Respondent #38.

206. Respondent #8.

207. Respondents #8, 59.

208. Respondents #7, 8, 38.
209. Respondent #59.
210. Coding details can be found in the appendix.
211. To calculate the probabilities presented in the following figures, the remaining variables were held constant at their means.
212. Respondents #4, 18, 42, 77.
213. Respondent #77; also Respondents #28, 29, 33, 51, 78.
214. Respondents #4, 7, 18, 21, 38, 56.
215. Respondents #14, 30, 34, 35, 37, 38, 48.
216. Respondent #38.
217. Respondents #9, 17, 33, 38, 42, 47, 51.
218. Respondents #4, 9, 17, 18, 25, 33, 42, 47, 70.
219. Respondent #9.

Chapter 6

Conclusion: Delegation, Efficiency, and Representation

The central research question of this book has been how individual Members of the European Parliament (MEPs) make decisions on the wide range of policy proposals they routinely handle. In answering this question, we have not only learned how legislators make policy choices, but also how individual-level positions are aggregated and about the roles of parties and committees in this process. This provides for new, valuable insights into policy-making in the European Parliament (EP) and forces us to carefully reconsider fundamental aspects of what we thought we knew about politics in the European Union's only directly-elected institution.

The conclusions we draw about politics in the EP are based not just on analyses of the political *outcomes* we observe at the aggregate level but also on the *process* of individual-level policy choice. The mixed methods approach required for this endeavor allows us to challenge key aspects of the received wisdom on EP politics. These analyses show that EP decision-making is founded on a division of labor (Skjæveland 2001) and an exchange of information between expert and nonexpert legislators based on perceived preference coherence (PPC). Perceived preference coherence may not explain every single policy choice made in the EP, but I maintain that the decision-making dynamic I describe constitutes the "normal" way MEPs make policy choices. Perceived preference coherence explains who decides, and how, most of the time.

Legislative decision-making is often treated as an example of committee voting, where a small number of voters has full information and well-defined preferences regarding the policy alternatives on the table (Hinich and Munger 1997). In reality, however, legislators are often quite uninformed about the policies they enact, not because they are too lazy or do not care, but because of very real external constraints on their ability to collect information on the great number of policy proposals with which they are routinely confronted. Legislators cannot be experts on all issues and they are limited in their ability to make fully informed choices when deliberating and passing new laws. For this reason, it is problematic to conceptualize policy preferences as exogenous inputs into legislative decision-making processes for most legislators. While their outcome preferences (such as ideological predispositions and constituency concerns) serve as the basis for decisions they make in supporting or opposing particular policies, these outcome preferences can be at odds with each other. Policy-makers may consider different policy outcomes as desirable, especially when they lack the expertise and resources to build genuine cause-and-effect knowledge concerning specific legislative proposals. Hence, the translation of outcome preferences into policy preferences and actual policy choice is a complicated process involving complex decisions under conditions of competing interests, substantive uncertainty, and asymmetric information. It is, therefore, important to make a strict analytic distinction between outcome and policy preferences, to expound the problems associated with the translation of the former into the latter, and to consider the interaction between structure, actors, and processes in the translation process.

Given these realities, policy choice in legislative politics more closely resembles a mass elections model, where voters are assumed to possess only a limited amount of information on the choices they face. Perceived preference coherence serves as a decision-making "shortcut" that helps legislators make informed choices about complicated policy alternatives under these conditions. Indifferent MEPs, who do not attach much salience to a given policy proposal, rely directly on perceived preference coherence when making decisions on the EP floor. They simply adopt the positions of those invested experts in the responsible EP committee with whom they perceive to share a common set of outcome preferences. In contrast, invested nonexperts seek to find out how a policy position relates to their outcome preferences and, therefore, they depend on the focal points provided by invested legislative experts. Yet, perceived preference coherence critically comes into play again because invested nonexperts follow the focal points of the invested experts whose outcome preferences they perceive to most closely match their own.

In the absence of complete information about the link between their own outcome preferences and the policy positions of their expert colleagues, however, nonexpert legislators have to rely on *perceived outcome preference coherence*, rather than *actual policy preference coherence*, when making policy choices on the EP floor. This means that MEPs must rely on a proxy for shared outcome preferences when making decisions. This proxy is common party affiliation. Therefore, the first important way in which parties "matter" in the EP is by serving as umbrellas for groups of legislators with shared outcome preferences.

Common party affiliation means membership in the same EP party group for those MEPs who are not represented by one or more members of their own national party delegation in the responsible committee. In this case, they are most likely to follow their EP party group expert colleagues when voting on the floor. If they are, however, represented in committee by one (or more) of their own, they are most likely to follow these national party colleagues. This means that there is a second important way in which parties matter in EP politics, as the endogenous party positions formulated in the responsible committee are the result of coordination among members of the same party group. This coordination is necessary if perceived preference coherence among national party colleagues is to be aggregated into cohesive EP party groups positions. Common party group affiliation helps structure policy choice in the pre-floor stage of the legislative process, with the goal of establishing broadly inclusive party positions that are acceptable to as many representatives of national party delegations as possible. If this objective is realized in the deliberation and negotiations between the relatively small number of active participants from the same party group, the probability that the party will present a united front when voting on the EP floor is almost assured. A common position among party group colleagues in committee thus improves the odds that EP party groups, national party delegations, and individual members see their most preferred outcomes realized, as within-party aggregation creates a more powerful and influential voting bloc.

Policy positions created in committee are aggregated to the committee working group, the party working group, and ultimately the party plenary. This happens either directly, when indifferent nonexperts adopt these positions as they cast their votes on the EP floor, or indirectly, when invested nonexperts follow a prevailing focal point provided by a united committee working group. If, on the other hand, MEPs from the same party group are unable to arrive at a common position in committee and, in particular, if there is disagreement between representatives from different national party delegations, party group cohesion breaks down. This is not the result of national parties being the more powerful principal who can more credibly threaten to sanction disloyal MEPs (Hix 2002; Hix, Noury, and Roland 2007), however, with the "order" to deviate from the EP party group line being issued by the party leaderships in the national capitals or coming more directly from the national party delegation leadership in the EP. Rather, it is a function of policy experts from a particular national party delegation disagreeing with the substantive policy stance negotiated within the committee working group. As Chapter 3 demonstrates, however, common positions between members of the same party in the responsible committee are the norm during the pre-floor policy-making process, and party cohesion the result.

Accordingly, the "party effect" in EP politics is not based on party discipline: The mechanism by which MEPs make decisions and EP party groups become cohesive is perceived preference coherence. This suggests that party politics in the EP is not quite as "normal" as previous research suggests, if by "normal" we mean a dynamic where party leaderships dominate the law-making process through their capacity to reward party loyalists or to sanction those who do not conform to the official party position. Yet, the party effect we observe in the EP is not based on shared preferences either; it is neither *just* preferences nor *just* a party effect can account for the high levels of unity we observe. This by itself is no striking observation, since few commentators would actually maintain that it is truly one or the other. However, the PPC model suggests that the two do not have independent effects that can simply be added up to account for party cohesion. Instead, this book conceptualizes and shows their effects to be mutually contingent, which means that viewing parties and preferences as analytically separate and competing explanations for party cohesion effectively undermines our efforts to explain it. Yet, without a mixed methods approach it would be quite difficult—if not impossible—to tease out the nuanced relationship between parties and preferences and their effects in legislative politics. After all, their effects, as hypothesized in the extant literature, are observationally equivalent with regard to policy outcomes. It is only by combining quantitative and qualitative methods and data to look at both political processes and outcomes that we can discover and explain their mutually contingent roles in legislative decision-making.

It would thus be useful to consider the applicability of the PPC model in other legislative contexts as well. Decision-making on the basis of perceived preference coherence is more likely in some institutional contexts than others, however. For example, one should expect to see fewer decisions made on the basis of perceived preference coherence in legislatures that are not policy-making or at least strongly policy-influencing, since legislators are expected to rubber-stamp decisions made at the executive level rather than to form policy preferences and positions of their own. Similarly, legislators who are elected in single-member electoral districts may rely less on perceived preference coherence than legislators elected from national party lists, as they are forced to consider the impact of a given policy proposal on the specific constituency to which they are accountable.[1] Finally, the ability of individual legislators to form independent policy preferences and positions is a function of the informational resources available to them. For example, legislators with a large staff may not have to rely on perceived preference coherence when making decisions on issues outside of their realms of expertise. However, as Hall (1996) demonstrates for the U.S. Congress, even legislators in a relatively resource-rich policy-making legislature who are elected in single-member districts cannot be equally active and involved in every policy proposal before them, which suggests that there is room for the PPC dynamic even in those institutional settings.

The PPC model proposes that party cohesion would be quite substantial in the EP even in the absence of party control. While party discipline may not be entirely absent from EP politics, it is neither a *necessary* nor a *sufficient* condition for party group cohesion. EP party groups are not cohesive because exogenously imposed party positions are enforced from above through hierarchical party structures. Instead, party politics in the EP is principally based on deliberative interactions among party policy experts in the responsible committees and, subsequently, on the exchange of information between expert and nonexpert legislators. The party effect in EP politics is based on persuasion and coordination, rather than coercion, and the policy deliberation and negotiation process in committee is pursued in such a way as to *create* a party effect.

Hence, committees play a major role in EP politics as both repositories of policy expertise and as the primary arenas of legislative deliberation and negotiation. Policy-making powers are distributed horizontally across different committees rather than rooted in the vertical hierarchy of EP party organizations; policy positions are created and policy decisions principally made in committee. The official "party lines" of EP party groups are not established by the party leadership and imposed on the rank and file, but rather they are endogenously formulated in an active deliberation process among expert members of the relevant EP committee. Those party members in the responsible committee who actively participate in the deliberation and negotiation of a particular piece of legislation serve as the *de facto* leadership of their party groups, which means that intra-party politics in the EP are more decentralized than in many other legislatures. Once a common position has been found within the committee working group, it is very unlikely to be altered in the party plenary or by the formal party leadership. Key to this normal decision-making process is the exchange of information between expert and nonexpert legislators, and this book investigates how information is distributed, disseminated, and received in the decision-making process.

This means that I not only conclude that EP committees are informational (Krehbiel 1993), but I also show *how* they are informational. To indifferent nonexperts, they are informational through the PPC dynamic. To invested experts, they are informational through focal points, which serve as the mechanism of information exchange between policy experts and invested nonexperts. They enable invested nonexperts to relate a particular policy proposal to their most preferred outcome, and thus to translate their outcome preferences into policy preferences, by shifting attention toward particular aspects of a legislative proposal. This shapes the prevailing interpretations of the content and consequences of a given piece of legislation, thus making certain policy outcomes more likely than others, as Chapter 5 illustrates.

This dynamic adds a distinctly strategic dimension to the aggregation of policy positions from the responsible committee to the EP plenary, which raises the possibility that the positions that come out of committee may be far removed from those of the EP's median legislator. This danger is mitigated in three ways, however. First, the provision of focal points is constrained by the normative and political context within which the focal point provider operates. That is, for focal points to be effective in shaping policy choices, they must reflect already existing outcome preferences; they have to appeal to the other legislators' *exogenous* sets of norms and values. The provision of focal points is thus constrained by the existing ideological space. They cannot be "free-floating." Second, the EP's committees are informational, and thus constitute broadly representative microcosms of the chamber as a whole (McElroy 2006), which decreases the risk that the policy positions formulated in committee deviate far from the preferences of the parent chamber. Third, the policy positions of the EP party groups may be formulated by their informational agents in the responsible committee, but ultimately they are the result of an aggregation process that features a series of "information filters" that serve as checks against agency loss. As described in Chapter 3, they must pass through and be ratified by the committee working group, the party working group, and the party plenary before they are accepted as the formal party group line. At each of those stages, objections against the positions advocated by the committee experts can be voiced and brought to the attention of the group, which means that invested experts have to be careful not to overstep their mandate. As a result, it is quite possible for the experts to *shape* a policy outcome, but it would be difficult for them to force through a policy decision that was in manifest opposition to the collective interests of the party or Parliament. In other words, safeguards in the decision-making process alleviate the danger that the agents' positions deviate too far from the outcome preferences of their principals.

It would, for these reasons, be inappropriate to conclude from the findings of this book that decision-making in the EP revolves around a small number of actors with the ability to bias policy choices in their favor, while the majority of the people's representatives are effectively excluded from the policy-making process. Moreover, the delegation and decision-making system on the basis of perceived preference coherence has a number of distinct advantages. The first is greater efficiency through a specialized committee system that provides important "economies of operation" (Mattson and Strøm 2004: 93). Committees possess the information, skills, resources, and, perhaps most importantly, the time that the legislature collectively lacks. Focusing only on issues within their jurisdictions, committees craft legislation more efficiently than the parent chamber could as a whole, especially in an interinstitutional process where the final agreement has to be reached together with the Council of Ministers. This increases legislative productivity and, given the involvement of genuine policy experts in the committee stage, the quality of legislation. The focus on committee experts ensures that only those who have a true appreciation of the intricacies of often highly technical pieces of legislation are involved in forging party positions and compromise agreements across party lines. Instead of second-, third-, or fourth-best solutions, often accompanied by unintended and unanticipated consequences, policy experts are able to make "good" policy.

Furthermore, policy positions are not predetermined, but are created endogenously in the policy-making process. This strengthens the cooperative element in EP decision-making and disperses power both within the legislature and within the EP party groups. The reality that those legislators active in the deliberations and negotiations of a particular legislative proposal are the *de facto* party leaders may well be a welcome and beneficial diffusion of influence in a legislature that is characterized by a greater degree of heterogeneity than most, and the result may be policy outcomes that promote and defend the interests of the largest number of people possible more effectively than those based on party lines imposed exogenously by the party leadership. After all, invested experts have to build support for the policy positions they advocate on the basis of persuasion, rather than coercion, as the case studies in Chapter 5 demonstrate. In other words, just like the creation of common party group positions in committee is based on a dynamic coordination process between expert legislators, the aggregation of policy preferences and positions from committee to plenary is a more dynamic political process than the rather static party control and shared preferences models would suggest.

Ultimately, the delegation and decision-making system on the basis of perceived preference coherence provides an efficient way for various political actors to overcome important structural weaknesses when making decisions on complex issues, while nonetheless realizing broadly representative policy outcomes. EP politics is thus both dynamic and efficient. Individual legislators can make informed decisions that approximate their most preferred outcomes on issues outside of their realms of expertise, while actively making legislation in those policy areas where they are specialists. The expert representatives of national party delegations in committee can help shape the policy positions of their party groups, while coordination across national parties in committee ensures cohesive EP party groups and thus maximizes policy influence on the EP floor. Finally, EP party groups form cohesive blocs of legislators that engage in competitive politics with each other, despite their inability to control their rank and file through sanctions and rewards. This means that EP parties are capable of fulfilling the important roles that make political parties an indispensable part of democratic governance (Ranney 1975; Katz 1987; Aldrich 1995; Müller and Strøm 1999; Polsby and Schickler 2002). Even without access to traditional methods of control over their members, and despite great levels of internal heterogeneity, legislative parties in the EP can act internally cohesive and externally competitive in carrying out their policy commitments to Europe's citizens.

Note

1. The statistical analyses in Chapter 3 do not find evidence for this effect in the case of the EP, but this does not preclude the possibility in other legislatures.

Bibliography

Aldrich, J. (1995), *Why Parties? The Origin and Transformation of Political Parties in America*, Chicago: University Of Chicago Press.

——and Rohde, D. (1997–8), 'The Transition to Republican Rule in the House: Implications for Theories of Congressional Politics', *Political Science Quarterly*, 112(4): 541–67.

————(1998), 'Measuring Conditional Party Government', Paper presented at the 1998 Annual Meeting of the Midwest Political Science Association, Chicago.

————(2000), 'The Consequences of Party Organization in the House: The Role of the Majority and Minority Parties in Conditional Party Government', in J. Bond and R. Fleisher (eds), *Polarized Politics: Congress and the President in a Partisan Era*, Washington, DC: Congressional Quarterly Press, pp. 31–72.

————(2001), 'The Logic of Conditional Party Government: Revisiting the Electoral Connection', in L. Dodd and B. Oppenheimer (eds), *Congress Reconsidered*, Washington, DC: Congressional Quarterly Press, pp. 269–92.

Andeweg, R. and Thomassen, J. (2008), 'Pathways to Party Unity: Sanctions, Loyalty, Homogeneity, and Division of Labor in the Dutch Parliament', Paper presented at the 2008 Annual Meeting of the American Political Science Association, Boston.

Arrow, K. (1963), *Social Choice and Individual Values*, New Haven, CT: Yale University Press.

Attinà, F. (1990), 'The Voting Behaviour of the European Parliament Members and the Problem of Europarties', *European Journal of Political Research*, 18(2): 557–79.

Austen-Smith, D. and Riker, W. (1987), 'Asymmetric Information and the Coherence of Legislation', *American Political Science Review*, 81(3): 897–918.

Baumgartner, F., Jones, B. and MacLeod, M. (2000), 'The Evolution of Legislative Jurisdiction', *The Journal of Politics*, 62(2): 321–49.

Beach, D. (2005), *The Dynamics of European Integration: Why and When EU Institutions Matter*, Houndmills: Palgrave Macmillan.

Benedetto, G. (2005), 'Rapporteurs as Legislative Entrepreneurs: The Dynamics of the Codecision Procedure in Europe's Parliament', *Journal of European Public Policy*, 12(1): 67–88.

——(2007), 'Consensus and Legislative Politics in the European Parliament', Paper presented at the 2007 Conference of the European Consortium for Political Research, Pisa.

217

Bennedsen, M. and Nielsen, K. (2004), 'The Impact of a Break-Through Rule on European Firms', *European Journal of Law and Economics*, 17(3): 259–83.

Berglöf, E. and Burkart, M. (2003), 'European Takeover Regulation', *Economic Policy*, 36(1): 173–213.

Black, D. (1958), *The Theory of Committees and Elections*, New York: Cambridge University Press.

Blondel, J., Sinnott, R. and Svensson, P. (1998), *People and Parliament in the European Union*, Oxford: Clarendon Press.

Bowler, S. (2002), 'Parties in Legislature: Two Competing Explanations', in R. Dalton and M. Wattenberg (eds), *Parties without Partisans*, Oxford: Oxford University Press, pp. 157–79.

——and Farrell, D. (1995), 'The Organizing of the European Parliament: Committees, Specialization and Co-ordination', *British Journal of Political Science*, 25(2): 219–43.

Brzinski, J. (1995), 'Political Group Cohesion in the European Parliament, 1989–1994', in C. Rhodes and S. Mazey (eds), *Union, Vol. 3: Building a European Polity?*, Boulder: Lynne Rienner, pp. 135–58.

Carrubba, C., Gabel, M., Murrah, L., Clough, R., Montgomery, E. and Schambach, R. (2006), 'Off the Record: Unrecorded Legislative Votes, Selection Bias, and Roll-Call Vote Analysis', *British Journal of Political Science*, 36(4): 691–704.

Clegg, N. (2004), 'Hans and the cookie jar', *The Guardian*, 8 April 2004.

Collins, K., Burns, C. and Warleigh, A. (1998), 'Policy Entrepreneurs: The Role of European Parliament Committees in the Making of EU Policy', *Statute Law Review*, 19(1): 1–11.

Commission of the European Communities (1996), 'The European Auto Oil Programme', *Directorate Generals for Industry, Energy and Environment, Civil Protection and Nuclear Safety* (XI/361/96).

Cooper, J. (1977), 'Congress in Organizational Perspective', in L. Dodd and B. Oppenheimer (eds), *Congress Reconsidered*, Washington, DC: Congressional Quarterly Press.

Corbett, R., Jacobs, F. and Shackleton, M. (2007), *The European Parliament*, 7th edn, London: John Harper Publishing.

Cox, G. (2000), 'On the Effects of Legislative Rules', *Legislative Studies Quarterly*, 25 (2): 169–92.

——and McCubbins, M. (1993), *Legislative Leviathan: Party Government in the House*, Berkeley: University of California Press.

————(2005), *Setting the Agenda. Responsible Party Government in the U.S. House of Representatives*, Cambridge: Cambridge University Press.

Dalton, R. and Wattenberg, M. (2002), 'Unthinkable Democracy: Political Change in Advanced Industrial Democracies', in R. Dalton and M. Wattenberg (eds), *Parties without Partisans*, Oxford: Oxford University Press, pp. 3–18.

Diermeier, D. and Feddersen, T. (1998), 'Cohesion in Legislatures and the Vote of Confidence Procedure', *American Political Science Review*, 92(3): 611–21.

Downs, A. (1957), *An Economic Theory of Democracy*, New York: Harper & Row.

Eldersveld, S. (1964), *Political Parties: A Behavioral Analysis*, Skokie, IL: Rand McNally.

European Commission (2001), 'Commission wishes to enhance Union citizens' right of movement and residence', *RAPID Press Release*, May 23, 2001.

——(2003), 'Commission proposes rules on statute and financing of European political parties', *RAPID Press Release*, February 19, 2003.

European People's Party (2005), Press Release, May 25, 2005.

——(2008), Press Release, February 20, 2008.

European Report (2002*a*), 'Environment: Legal Affairs Committee to manage liability dossier', July 6, 2002.

——(2002*b*), 'Free Movement: Member states wary of plan to boost EU citizens' residence rights,' February 23, 2002.

——(2003*a*), 'Environment Council: Ministers take first steps towards EU Liability system', June 18, 2003.

——(2003*b*), 'Environment: Eurochambers and Parliament critical of Environmental Liability Directive', January 23, 2003.

——(2003*c*), 'Environment: Liability proposal watered down in European Parliament', May 3, 2003.

——(2003*d*), 'Environment: Parliament resists efforts to tighten up liability directive', December 20, 2003.

——(2003*e*), 'Shipping: Parliament excludes pilotage from liberalisation of port services', March 12, 2003.

——(2004), 'Environment: Conciliation agreement clinched on liability directive', February 21, 2004.

Faas, T. (2003), 'To Defect or Not to Defect? National, Institutional and Party Group Pressures on MEPs and Their Consequences for Party Group Cohesion in the European Parliament', *European Journal of Political Research*, 42(6): 841–66.

Farrell, D. and Scully, R. (2007), *Representing Europe's Citizens? Electoral Institutions and the Failure of Parliamentary Representation*, Oxford: Oxford University Press.

Farrell, H. and Héritier, A. (2003*a*), 'The Invisible Transformation of Co-decision Procedure: Problems of Democratic Legitimacy', *Swedish Institute for European Policy Studies*, Report 2003/7, Stockholm.

——(2003*b*), 'Formal and Informal Institutions Under Codecision: Continuous Constitution-Building in Europe', *Governance*, 16(4): 577–600.

——(2004), 'Interorganizational Negotiation and Intraorganizational Power in Shared Decision Making: Early Agreements under Codecision and Their Impact on the European Parliament and Council', *Comparative Political Studies*, 37(10): 1184–212.

Gabel, M. and Hix, S. (2007), 'From Preferences to Behaviour: Comparing MEPs' Survey Responses and Roll-Call Voting Behavior', Paper Presented at Tenth Biennial Conference of the European Union Studies Association, Montreal.

Garrett, G. and Weingast, B. (1993), 'Ideas, Interests, and Institutions: Constructing the European Community's Internal Market', in J. Goldstein and R. Keohane (eds), *Ideas and Foreign Policy Beliefs, Institutions, and Political Change*, Ithaca: Cornell University Press, pp. 173–206.

Gilligan, T. and Krehbiel, K. (1987), 'Collective Decision-Making and Standing Committees: An Informational Rationale for Restrictive Amendment Procedures', *Journal of Law, Economics, and Organization*, 3(2): 287–335.

————(1989), 'Asymmetric Information and Legislative Rules with a Heterogeneous Committee', *American Journal of Political Science*, 33: 459–90.

————(1990), 'Organization of Informative Committees by a Rational Legislature', *American Journal of Political Science*, 34(2): 531–64.

Häge, F. and Kaeding, M. (2007), 'Reconsidering the European Parliament's Legislative Influence: Formal vs. Informal Procedures', *European Integration*, 29(3): 341–61.

Hall, R. (1996), *Participation in Congress*, New Haven: Yale University Press.

Han, J. (2007), 'Analysing Roll Calls of the European Parliament: A Bayesian Application', *European Union Politics*, 8(4): 479–507.

Hausemer, P. (2006), 'Participation and Political Competition in Committee Report Allocation: Under What Conditions do MEPs Represent Their Constituents?', *European Union Politics*, 7(4): 505–30.

Hinich, M. and Munger, M. (1994), *Ideology and the Theory of Political Choice*, Ann Arbor: University of Michigan Press.

————(1997), *Analytical Politics*, New York: Cambridge University Press.

Hix, S. (1999*b*), 'Dimensions and Alignments in European Union Politics: Cognitive Constraints and Partisan Responses', *European Journal of Political Research*, 35 (1): 69–106.

——(2001), 'Legislative Behavior and Party Competition in the European Parliament: An Application of Nominate to the EU', *Journal of Common Market Studies*, 39(4): 663–88.

——(2002), 'Parliamentary Behavior with Two Principals Preferences: Parties, and Voting in the European Parliament', *American Journal of Political Science*, 46(3): 688–98.

——(2004), 'Electoral Institutions and Legislative Behavior: Explaining Voting Defection in the European Parliament', *World Politics*, 56(1): 194–223.

——and Lord, C. (1997), *Political Parties in the European Union*, New York: St. Martin's Press.

——Kreppel, A. and Noury, A. (2003), 'The Party System in the European Parliament: Collusive or Competitive?', *Journal of Common Market Studies*, 41(2): 309–31.

——Noury, A. and Roland, G. (2005), 'Power to the Parties: Cohesion and Competition in the European Parliament, 1979–2001', *British Journal of Political Science*, 35(2): 209–34.

————(2007), *Democratic Politics in the European Parliament*, New York: Cambridge University Press.

Hooghe, L. and Marks, G. (1999), 'The Making of a Polity: The Struggle over European Integration', in H. Kitschelt, P. Lange, G. Marks, J. Stephens (eds), *Continuity and Change in Contemporary Capitalism*, New York: Cambridge University Press, pp. 70–97.

——(2001), *Multi-level Governance and European Integration*, Boulder: Rowman & Littlefield.

——and Wilson, C. (2002), 'Does Left/Right Structure Party Positions on European Integration?', *Comparative Political Studies*, 35(8): 965–89.

Hotelling, H. (1929), 'Stability in Competition', *Economic Journal*, 39: 41–57.

Hoyland, B. (2006), 'Allocation of Codecision Reports in the 5th European Parliament', *European Union Politics*, 7(1): 30–50.

Huber, J. (1996), 'The Vote of Confidence in Parliamentary Democracies', *American Political Science Review*, 90(2): 269–82.

Judge, D. and Earnshaw, D. (2003), *The European Parliament*, New York: Palgrave MacMillan.

Kaeding, M. (2004), 'Rapporteurship Allocation in the European Parliament: Information of Distribution?', *European Union Politics*, 5(3): 353–78.

——(2005), 'The World of Committee Reports', *Journal of Legislative Studies*, 11(1): 82–104.

Kasack, C. (2004), 'The Legislative Impact of the European Parliament under the Revised Co-Decision Procedure: Environmental, Public Health and Consumer Protection Policies', *European Union Politics*, 5(2): 241–60.

Katz, R. (ed) (1987), *Party Governments: European & American Experiences*, Berlin: de Gruyter.

King, G., Tomz, M. and Wittenberg, J. (2000), 'Making the Most of Statistical Analyses: Improving Interpretation and Presentation', *American Journal of Political Science*, 44(2): 341–55.

Kingdon, J. (1981), *Congressmen's Voting Decisions*, 2nd edn, New York: Harper & Row.

Kitschelt, H., Lange, P., Marks, G. and Stephens, J. (eds) (1999), *Continuity and Change in Contemporary Capitalism*, New York: Cambridge University Press.

König, T., Lindberg, B., Lechner, S. and Pohlmeier, W. (2007), 'Bicameral Conflict Resolution in the European Union: An Empirical Analysis of Conciliation Committee Bargains', *British Journal of Political Science*, 37(2): 281–312.

Krehbiel, K. (1991), *Information and Legislative Organization*, Ann Arbor: Michigan University Press.

——(1993), 'Where's the Party?', *British Journal of Political Science*, 23(2): 235–66.

Kreppel, A. (2002), *The European Parliament and Supranational Party System*, Cambridge: Cambridge University Press.

——(2006), 'Understanding the European Parliament from a Federalist Perspective: The Legislatures of the United States and European Union Compared', in A. Menon and M. A. Schain (eds), *Comparative Federalism: The European Union and the United States in Comparative Perspective*, Oxford: Oxford University Press, pp. 245–71.

Kreppel, A. and Gungor, G. (2006), 'The Institutional Integration of an Expanded EU, or, How "New" European Actors Fit into "Old" European Institutions', *Reihe Politikwissenschaft*, Wien: Institut für Höhere Studien.

Kreps, D. and Wilson, R. (1982), 'Sequential Equilibria', *Econometrica*, 50(4): 863–94.

Lord, C. (1998), 'Party Groups, EP Committees and Consensus Democracy', in D. Bell and C. Lord (eds), *Transnational Parties in the European Union*, Brookfield, VT: Ashgate, pp. 204–17.

Mamadouh, V. and Raunio, T. (2002), 'Allocating Reports in the European Parliament: How Parties Influence Committee Work', *European Parliament Research Group Working Paper* 7.

——————(2003), 'The Committee System: Powers, Appointments, and Report Allocation', *Journal of Common Market Studies*, 41(2): 333–51.

Marks, G. and Wilson, C. (2000), 'The Past in the Present: A Cleavage Theory of Party Positions on European Integration', *British Journal of Political Science*, 30(3): 433–59.

Matthews, D. and Stimson, J. (1975), *Yeas and Nays: Normal Decision-Making in the U.S. House of Representatives*, New York: Wiley.

Mattson, I. and Strøm, K. (1995), 'Parliamentary Committees', in H. Döring (ed), *Parliaments and Majority Rule in Western Europe*, Frankfurt: Campus Verlag, pp. 249–307.

——————(2004), 'Committee Effects on Legislation', in H. Döring and M. Hallerberg (eds), *Patterns of Parliamentary Behaviour*, Aldershot: Ashgate, pp. 91–112.

McElroy, G. (2002), 'Committees and Party Cohesion in the European Parliament', *European Parliament Research Group Working Paper* 8.

——(2003), *In Pursuit of Party Discipline: Committees and Cohesion in the European Parliament*, Ph.D. diss. University of Rochester.

——(2006), 'Committee Representation in the European Parliament', *European Union Politics*, 7(1): 5–29.

——(2007), 'Legislative Politics as Normal? Voting Behavior and Beyond in the European Parliament', *European Union Politics*, 8(3): 433–48.

——and Benoit, K. (2007), 'Party Groups and Policy Positions in the European Parliament', *Party Politics*, 13(1): 5–28.

Mehta, J., Starmer, C. and Sugden, R. (1994), 'Focal Points in Pure Coordination Games: An Experimental Investigation', *Theory and Decision*, 36(2): 163–85.

Minder, R. (2004), 'MEPs fraud claims probed', *Financial Times*, March 14, 2004.

Müller, W. and Strøm, K. (1999), *Policy, Office, or Votes? How Political Parties in Western Europe Make Hard Choices*, (eds), Cambridge: Cambridge University Press.

Neuhold, C. (2001), 'The 'Legislative Backbone' or Keeping the Institution Upright? The Role of European Parliament Committees in the EU Policy-Making Process', *European Integration Online Papers*, 5(10).

Norpoth, H. (1976), 'Explaining Party Cohesion in Congress: The Case of Shared Policy Attitudes', *American Political Science Review*, 70(4): 1156–71.

Noury, A. (2002), 'Ideology, Nationality, and Euro-Parliamentarians', *European Union Politics*, 3(1): 33–58.

Ozbudun, E. (1970), *Party Cohesion in Western Democracies: A Causal Analysis*, Beverly Hills: Sage.

Peterson, J. and Bomberg, E. (1999), *Decision-Making in the European Union*, London: McMillan.

Polsby, N. and Schickler, E. (2002), 'Landmarks in the Study of Congress since 1945', *Annual Review of Political Science*, 5: 333–367.

Ranney, A. (1975), *Curing the Mischiefs of Faction*, Berkeley: University of California Press.

Rasmussen, A. and Shackleton, M. (2005), 'The Scope for Action of European Parliament Negotiators in the Legislative Process: Lessons of the Past and for the Future', Paper presented at the 9th Biennial EUSA Meeting, Austin, TX.

Raunio, T. (1996), *Party Group Behaviour in the European Parliament*, Tampere: University of Tampere Press.

——(1997), *The European Perspective: Transnational Party Groups in the 1989–1994 European Parliament*. Aldershot: Ashgate.

——(2000), 'Losing Independence or Finally Gaining Recognition? Contacts Between MEPs and National Parties', *Party Politics*, 6(2): 211–23.

Reif, K. and Schmitt, H. (1980), 'Nine Second-Order National Elections: A Conceptual Framework for the Analysis of European Election Results', *European Journal of Political Research*, 8(1): 3–44.

Rhodes, M. and Van Apeldoorn, B. (1997), 'Capitalism versus Capitalism in Western Europe', in M. Rhodes, P. Heywood, and V. Wright (eds), *Developments in West European Politics*, New York: St. Martin's Press, pp. 171–89.

Riker, W. (1986), *The Art of Manipulation*, New Haven: Yale University Press.

——(1990), 'Heresthetics and Rhetoric in the Spatial Model', in J. Enelow and M. Hinich (eds), *Advances in the Spatial Theory of Voting*, New York: Cambridge University Press, pp. 46–65.

Ringe, N. (2005), 'Policy Preference Formation in Legislative Politics: Structures, Actors, and Focal Points', *American Journal of Political Science*, 49(4): 731–45.

Rittberger, B. (2007), *Building Europe's Parliament: Democratic Representation Beyond the Nation State*, New York: Oxford University Press.

Sabatier, P. and Whiteman, D. (1985), 'Legislative Decision Making And Substantive Policy Information: Models of Information Flow', *Legislative Studies Quarterly*, X(3): 395–421.

Schelling, T. (1960), *The Strategy of Conflict*, London: Oxford University Press.

Schneider, G., Steunenberg, B. and Widgrén, M. (2006), 'Evidence with Insight: What Models Contribute to EU Research', in R. Thomson, F. Stokman, C. Achen and T. König (eds), *The European Union Decides*, Cambridge: Cambridge University Press, pp. 299–316.

Scott, D. (2001), *The Salience of Integration: The Strategic Behavior of National Political Parties in the European Union*, Ph.D. diss. UNC Chapel Hill.

Scully, R. (2000), 'Democracy, Legitimacy and the European Parliament', in M. Green Cowles and M. Smith (eds.), *The State of the European Union*, Vol. 5, Oxford: Oxford University Press, pp. 228–45.

Selck, T. (2006), 'The Effects of Issue Salience on Political Decision-Making', *Constitutional Political Economy*, 17(1): 5–13.

Selck, T. and Steunenberg, B. (2004), 'Between Power and Luck: The European Parliament in the EU Legislative Process', *European Union Politics*, 5(1): 25–46.

Shackleton, M. (2005), 'Parliamentary Government or Division of Powers: Is the Destination Still Unknown?', in N. Jabko and C. Parsons (eds), *The State of the European Union*, Vol. 7, New York: Oxford University Press, pp. 123–43.

——and Raunio, T. (2003), 'Co-Decision Since Amsterdam', *Journal of European Public Policy*, 10(2): 171–87.

Shepsle, K. (1979), 'Institutional Arrangements and Equilibrium in Multidimensional Voting Models', *American Journal of Political Science*, 23(1): 27–59.

——and Weingast, B. (1981), 'Structure-Induced Equilibrium and Legislative Choice', *Public Choice*, 37(3): 503–19.

Skjæveland, A. (2001), 'Party Cohesion in the Danish Parliament', *Journal of Legislative Studies*, 7(2): 35–56.

Sorauf, F. (1964), *Political Parties in the American System*, Boston: Little Brown.

Spiteri, S. (2003a), 'Environment: MEPs vote on "polluter pays" rules', *EUObserver.com*, May 14, 2003.

——(2003b), '"Polluter pays" law one step closer', *EUObserver.com*, May 15, 2003.

Thomassen, J., Noury, A. and Voeten, E. (2004), 'Political Competition in the European Parliament', in G. Marks and M. Steenbergen (eds), *European Integration and Political Conflict*, New York: Cambridge University Press, pp. 141–64.

Thomson, R., Stokman, F., Achen, C. and König, T. (2006), *The European Union Decides*, Cambridge: Cambridge University Press.

Tsebelis, G., Jensen, C., Kalandrakis, A. and Kreppel, A. (2001), 'Legislative Procedures in the European Union', *British Journal of Political Science*, 31(4): 573–99.

van der Brug, W. and van der Eijk, C. (2007), *European Elections and Domestic Politics*, Notre Dame: Notre Dame University Press.

Wall, J. and Lynn, A. (1993), 'Mediation: A Current Overview', *Journal of Conflict Resolution*, 37(1): 160–94.

Weingast, B. and Marshall, W. (1988), 'The Industrial Organization of Congress', *Journal of Political Economy*, 96(1): 132–63.

Westlake, M. (1994), *A Modern Guide to the European Parliament*, London: Pinter.

Whitaker, R. (2001), 'Party Control in a Committee-based Legislature? The Case of the EP', *Journal of Legislative Studies*, 7(4): 63–88.

——(2005), 'National Parties in the European Parliament: An Influence in the Committee System?', *European Union Politics*, 6(1): 5–28.

Whiteman, D. (1995), *Communication in Congress: Members, Staff, and the Search for Information*, Lawrence, KS: University of Kansas Press.

Williams, M. (1995), 'The European Parliament: Political Groups, Minority Rights and the Rationalisations of Parliamentary Organisation. A Research Note', in H. Döring (ed), *Parliaments and Majority Rule in Western Europe*, New York: St. Martin's, pp. 391–405.

Yoshinaka, A., McElroy, G. and Bowler, S. (2006), *Rapporteurs in the European Parliament*, Paper presented at the 2006 Annual Meeting of the Midwest Political Science Association, Chicago.

Zwier, R. (1979), 'The Search for Information: Specialists and Nonspecialists in the U.S. House of Representatives', *Legislative Studies Quarterly*, IV(1): 31–42.

Index